THE METAMORPHOSES
OF DON JUAN'S WOMEN
EARLY PARITY TO LATE MODERN PATHOLOGY

The Metamorphoses of Don Juan's Women
Early Parity to Late Modern Pathology

Ann Davies

Spanish Studies
Volume 28

The Edwin Mellen Press
Lewiston•Queenston•Lampeter

Library of Congress Cataloging-in-Publication Data

Davies, Ann, 1961-
 The metamorphoses of Don Juan's women : early parity to late modern pathology / Ann Davies.
  p. cm. -- (Spanish studies ; v. 28)
 Includes bibliographical references and index.
 ISBN 0-7734-6343-7
 1. Literature, Modern--History and criticism. 2. Don Juan (Legendary character) in
literature. 3. Masculinity in literature. 4. Sex role in literature. 5. Identity (Philosophical
concept) in literature. I. Title. II. Spanish studies (Lewiston, N.Y.) ; v. 28.

PN57.D7D28 2005
809'.93351--dc22

2004057898

This is volume 28 in the continuing series
Spanish Studies
Volume 28 ISBN 0-7734-6343-7
SpS Series ISBN 0-88946-734-X

A CIP catalog record for this book is available from the British Library

The Edwin Mellen Press
Box 450
Lewiston, New York
USA 14092-0450

The Edwin Mellen Press
Box 67
Queenston, Ontario
CANADA L0S 1L0

The Edwin Mellen Press, Ltd.
Lampeter, Ceredigion, Wales
UNITED KINGDOM SA48 8LT

Printed in the United States of America

To my mother and father

Acknowledgements

My thanks to Barry Ife at King's College London, Peter Evans at Queen Mary, University of London and Mike Thompson at the University of Durham; also colleagues at the University of Newcastle, particularly Phil Powrie and Chris Perriam; and long-suffering family and friends without whose encouragement this book would not have been possible.

A version of some material in this book has previously appeared in the *Bulletin of Hispanic Studies* Vol. LXXVI/3 (1999), and *European Studies* Vol. 17 (2001), and I am grateful for permission to reproduce it here. I would also like to thank Suhrkamp Publishers for permission to cite from Max Frisch's *Don Juan oder die Liebe zur Geometrie* and Baerenreiter for permission to cite from Mozart and da Ponte's *Don Giovanni*. All reasonable efforts have been made to trace other copyright holders.

Table of contents

Acknowledgements   ix
Preface by B. W. Ife   xi

1. Introduction   1
Heterosexual relations as a vehicle of change   9
Sex and gender as historical phenomena   15
Don Juan: discourse or myth?   19
The question of selectivity   30

2. The search for identity   35
The earlier works   41
The later plays   55

3. The early plays   77
Noblewomen   87
Peasant women   94
'Hysterical' women   100

4. The Romantic era   123
Kierkegaard and Hoffmann: nineteenth-century attitudes   123
Zorrilla and doña Inés   134

5. The twentieth-century plays   151
Shaw   152
Frisch   170

6. The male characters   187
Figures of authority: kings and fathers   192
The servant   196
The Octavio figure   207
Fear and hatred of women   216

7. Punishment   227
The need for punishment   230
Affirmation of the community and suppression of the individual   235
Zorrilla's pantheon   241
Twentieth-century notions of punishment   245

8. Conclusion and coda:
a reappraisal of Tirso de Molina   257
Coda: Tirso de Molina and the characterization of women   268

viii

Bibliography   275
Index   285

Preface

There is not one don Juan, but several. There are literally hundreds of works of Western literature inspired by this emblem of defiant depravity. Yet when scholars come to write about him, they try to reduce this extraordinary variety to a single archetype. Somehow or other, the many variations on the don Juan character must be made to conform to the mythical template of the libertine. Perhaps this is a measure of the dominance achieved by the protagonists of Mozart or Molière —often thought to form an artistic summit among all the works available. Or perhaps it is due to the shadow cast by Tirso's 'original'. Yet this reductive approach neglects the fact that each new reincarnation adds something new to the template. Later writers may not have been able entirely to escape from the constraints of don Juan's received status as libertine, but there is something telling in the fact that they have all made the attempt.

This book, then, takes as its starting point not one don Juan, but many. It argues that the meaning of the don Juan phenomenon lies just as much in the differences between the various don Juans as in their contribution to a modern myth. It considers not so much what don Juan is, but what don Juan becomes —his shift from the carefree libertine to the angst-ridden philosopher. Later authors —in this book the focus is on Kierkegaard and Hoffman, Zorrilla, Shaw and Frisch— clearly felt a need to break away from the earlier models of Tirso, Mozart and Molière: the question is why. Ann Davies responds to this challenge by positing that the changes in the don Juan figure reveal an increasing anxiety over masculine identity.

In this struggle over don Juan's identity as a male individual, the women play a crucial role. A particularly pernicious habit of those who write about don Juan is their habit of taking don Juan at his own estimation: as a man whom, ultimately, no woman can resist. Such critics seem to share in the wishful thinking of many don Juans. This book refuses to take don Juan's word for it that all women are secretly desperate to be seduced, and that their protests of wronged virtue act merely as a respectable cover for their reprehensible sexual desire. It does argue, though, that the women are the key to understanding don Juan's own identity, so that it is time we looked past don Juan at the women themselves.

Thus the focus of the study lies with individual female characters as much as with don Juan. It reveals that, far from simply wielding malicious power over them, don Juan depends on these women for his very identity. And the profound shifts in don Juan literature manifest themselves clearly in the different portrayals of don Juan's relationships with his women. Never do the women merely reflect his identity back, but rather, they shape it —and this moulding of his identity becomes, by the twentieth century, pathological manipulation. This will come as no surprise to anyone familiar with recent critiques of Victorian literature and art from a feminist perspective (Elaine Showalter and Bram Dijkstra come to mind), but don Juan's participation in the nineteenth-century fear of women as pathological creatures has gone hitherto unremarked. Here the author redresses the balance.

Of course, it is nothing new to write don Juan's history. But history implies change as well as continuity. This book does not supersede previous histories of don Juan, but reminds us that history is not the mere passing of time, during which the don Juan works pile up one on top of another. History is an active ingredient in the lives and relationships of men and women, and Ann Davies's attempt to emphasize that fact is a vital and necessary reminder. And perhaps it is as history that don Juan has most to say to us nowadays. Don Juan as myth does not seem quite so relevant in an age when Western sexual morals have undergone radical change and the punitive force of religion is not what it was when the statue first arrived on stage to drag don Juan to Hell. To read don Juan as history, however, is to recover some of the figure's vitality, and recuperate his meaning as not so much eternal as perennial.

B.W. Ife
Cervantes Professor of Spanish
King's College London

Chapter 1: Introduction

This study is an attempt to examine the literary figure of don Juan from a historical point of view. It is also a tentative approach to tracing historical change in gender relations, as found in different literary works devoted to don Juan. As society and social ideas alter over time, so this in turn affects our perception of gender relations and their sexual expression. While one single literary character, even one as significant and as developed as don Juan is, cannot by itself adequately represent large-scale changes in social history, it can nevertheless indicate to us certain notions of gender relations and possible reasons for the ways in which they change. Don Juan has often been considered as an eternal, mythical figure – a phenomenon that I will discuss below – but it is more than time to consider him as a historical, changing entity, and to learn from these changes and developments.

This study proposes, in brief, that the relations developed between don Juan and women reveal a growing sense of crisis in masculine identity. The idea that don Juan's history might attest to a crisis in masculinity may at first seem unlikely, since don Juan has as a figure become synonymous with rampant male sexuality, to the extent that his habit of treating women as objects for serial sex strongly indicates a rearguard force of misogyny. However, I am going to argue that the notion of masculine crisis is indeed to be found within don Juan works. I am not alone in surmising that don Juan's masculine identity might be problematic: others have suggested this before. Otto Rank's study of don Juan,[1] for instance, considers the psychological problems that have led don Juan to his career of

---

[1] Otto Rank, *The Don Juan Legend*, trans. by David G. Winter, (Princeton: Princeton University Press, 1975).

fornication, while Gregorio Marañon's polemic proposed that no mature man, confident in his sexuality, would act in the way don Juan does.[2]

The figure of don Juan acts as an example of what Michel Foucault calls discourse on sexuality. Foucault argues that from the seventeenth century onwards - the era, in fact, when don Juan first appeared - sex became a common subject of discourse, 'the nearly infinite task of telling - telling oneself and another, as often as possible, everything that might concern the interplay of innumerable pleasures, sensations, and thoughts which, through the body and the soul, had some affinity with sex'.[3] And Foucault particularly notes:

> ...what distinguishes these last three centuries is the variety, the
> wide dispersion of devices that were invented for speaking about
> [sex], for listening, recording, transcribing, and redistributing what
> is said about it: around sex, a whole network of varying, specific,
> and coercive transpositions into discourse.[4]

I believe that don Juan acts as one such device for talking about sexual matters: the figure provides us with a discourse about sexuality. However, sexuality does not exist in a vacuum, but occurs in a specific social context; and discourses of sex affect and are affected by the societies in which they take place, as Foucault's studies on sexuality have shown. More particularly, sexual relationships affect and are affected by other, social relations between different individuals - especially gender relations. The concept of gender relations in terms of the don Juan phenomenon situates itself primarily in sexuality and sexual relations, but these are affected by the social context in which they occur. Gender relations include both the sexual and the social, which impact upon each other. Don Juan

---

[2] Quoted in James Mandrell, *Don Juan and the Point of Honor: Seduction, Patriarchal Society, and Literary Tradition* (University Park: Pennsylvania State University Press, 1992), pp.237-242.
[3] Michel Foucault, *The History of Sexuality: an Introduction,* trans. by Robert Hurley (Harmondsworth: Penguin, 1990), p.20.

thus becomes not only a discourse of sex but also one of relations between men and women.

It is this discourse, these shifting relations and negotiations that don Juan carries out with others (and particularly women) over time that will provide the focus of this study. The principal emphasis will be the female characters of don Juan literature, and the way in which don Juan relates to them. I will argue that, as we approach and enter the twentieth century, attitudes towards women in don Juan plays become more hostile and that this shift in attitudes parallels changes in ideas about the male individual. In other words, the growing sense of crisis that I believe to be found within don Juan's literary history, manifests itself specifically in heterosexual relations between men and women.

A quick review of don Juan's literary history readily suggests that this symbol of unleashed male sexuality has given writers the opportunity to argue over issues to do with sex, and thus to provide a discourse wherein notions about male and female sexuality have been proposed, expanded and refuted. Far from being a timeless entity untouched by historical changes in thought and in literature, don Juan reveals himself to be subject to changes in ideas. His discourse is very much a modern one: scholars have searched for sources of the don Juan story that date from before the seventeenth century, but without any conclusive evidence. While certain features of the tale have their forerunners, such as the deathly dinner guest (a skull or statue), and while men of dubious sexual intentions exist in earlier Spanish drama, no one has yet identified a clear ancestor to don Juan. Don Juan thus emerges, as far as we can tell, during the epoch that Foucault pinpointed as the beginning of a proliferation of sexual discourses.

---

[4] Foucault, p.34

4

We can for now keep to the conventional understanding that don Juan's discourse began with Tirso de Molina, author of *El burlador de Sevilla*.[5] His play, dating from some time in the early seventeenth century,[6] has provided the basis from which all other versions were to draw their framework of characters and plot, either directly or indirectly through the work of others. Although future authors were to place their own interpretation on events and characters, they rarely departed from them completely; and we encounter time and again doña Ana, don Octavio and the statue as well as don Juan and his servant (who assumes a variety of names). Some scholars dismiss Tirso's work as of little worth compared to the later works of Molière and Mozart, believing the original to be merely a piece of heavy-handed didacticism.[7] Clearly such disparagement is misplaced, since *El burlador* laid the foundations for later interpretations of the theme. Its significance in the history of don Juan cannot be overestimated. In a coda to this work, I will return to the question of Tirso's role as creator of the don Juan figure.

---

[5] For the sake of convenience I assume Tirso to be the author of *El burlador*, while being aware that his authorship is open to doubt. Tirso's claim to the play has recently been the subject of much onslaught by Alfredo Rodríguez López Vázquez – see, for instance, the introduction to his edition of *El burlador* (Madrid: Cátedra, 1994). Luis Vázquez replies for the defence in '*El burlador de Sevilla*: claramente de Tirso, y no de Claramonte (breve anotación crítica)', *Bulletin of the Comediantes* 47 (1995), 183-190; as does James A. Parr, 'On the Authorship, Text, and Transmission of *El burlador de Sevilla y convidado de piedra*', in *Tirso de Molina: His Originality Then and Now* ed. by Henry W. Sullivan and Raúl A. Galoppe, Ottawa Hispanic Studies 20 (Ottawa: Dovehouse, 1996), 206-220.

[6] The exact date of the play is also a matter for conjecture. Daniel Rogers and Gwynne Edwards both argue that the play could have been written any time between 1616 and 1625. A printed version was published in 1630. See Rogers, *Tirso de Molina: 'El burlador de Sevilla'*, Critical Guides to Spanish Texts 19 (London: Grant and Cutler, 1977), 16-17; and Tirso de Molina, *The Trickster of Seville and the Stone Guest (El burlador de Sevilla y el convidado de piedra)*, ed. by Gwynne Edwards (Warminster: Aris and Phillips, 1986), p.xx.

[7] See Beryl Schlossmann, 'Disappearing Acts: Style, Seduction, and Performance in *Dom Juan*', *MLN* 106 (1991), 1030-1047; p.1033; Peter Conrad, 'The Libertine's Progress', in *The Don Giovanni Book: Myths of Seduction and Betrayal*, ed. by Jonathan Miller (London: Faber, 1990), 81-92; p.82.

Don Juan quickly found his way into Italian theatre, and particularly the *commedia dell'arte*, where the theme became entangled in stock comedy and pantomime. The don Juan plays of this era were usually farces, and characters and plot usually fell victim to the demands of slapstick humour, though they nevertheless maintained the rudiments of plot and *dramatis personae*. From Italy the story passed to France where noted dramatists took up the theme: from this era comes Molière's *Dom Juan* of 1665, and significant versions were also written by Dorimon, Villiers and Corneille (the latter an 'improvement' of Molière's original piece). These versions often gave new interpretations to the protagonist's personality, introducing new levels of villainy and blasphemy. Versions that appeared on the English or German stage took don Juan's villainous nature further. The depravity of don John in Shadwell's *The Libertine* (1675) is an example: here the protagonist, in the company of his equally evil friends, commits rape and murder on a scale that rapidly becomes incredible.

Other don Juan plays continued to appear throughout the seventeenth and eighteenth centuries, but the theme reached a turning point in 1787 when Mozart and his librettist Lorenzo da Ponte used it as a basis for their opera *Don Giovanni* - by far the best known interpretation of the story. Da Ponte drew not only on Molière's play but also a later work by Carlos Goldoni as well as an opera by Giovanni Bertati. But while *Don Giovanni* is an important don Juan work in its own right, its influence on future dramatists and authors was to prove considerable. Until this point don Juan plays remained on the whole works with a clear moral message of the need for repentance. But once *Don Giovanni* became popular, many writers reinterpreted the story as a tale of Romanticism. Foremost amongst these was the writer E. T. A. Hoffmann. His tale - *Don Juan: eine fabelhafte Begebenheit die sich mit einem reisenden Enthusiasten zugetragen* (1813) - was to help establish a new role for don Juan as a Romantic idealist who sought the ideal woman, and who was destined to be disappointed in his search. J.

W. Smeed traces the influence of Hoffmann's interpretation on a generation of writers in the nineteenth century, pointing out that the impact of Hoffmann was to elevate don Juan to the status of a true hero.[8] Previous works, including that of Mozart and da Ponte, treated the protagonist as villainous; but Hoffmann understood don Juan as more truly heroic. Don Juan's rebellion, according to Hoffmann, transcended a career of mere womanizing to challenge the powers of Hell itself. Smeed takes care to point out that Hoffmann's interpretation cannot be derived from Mozart's opera in any straightforward way. Another writer who drew heavily on *Don Giovanni*, though for different purposes, was Søren Kierkegaard, who devoted a part of his work *Either/Or* (1843) to a discussion of love, marriage and sex in Mozartian opera. He concluded that don Giovanni, the embodiment of seduction, proved the perfect vehicle to reflect Mozart's music; and that, in turn, music is the best way to portray seduction. Smeed also observes that some authors countered Romantic interpretations with more sceptical treatments of don Juan's seductive career, thus demonstrating that the Romantic interpretation of the story had not obliterated more negative perceptions of the character.[9]

Also in the nineteenth century, Byron wrote his poem *Don Juan*. The poem, however, does not feature the usual plot and cast of characters: Byron gave the name of don Juan to an attractive young Spaniard who undergoes a series of unrelated adventures around the world. This character has nothing in common with his namesakes in Tirso, Molière and Mozart beyond the name and an ability to charm women - unconsciously, in the case of the poem. The place of Byron in the don Juan canon is debatable.[10] But we can, perhaps, detect at this point that

---

[8] J. W. Smeed, 1990. *Don Juan: Variations on a Theme* (London: Routledge, 1990), chs. 2 and 4.
[9] Smeed, ch.5.
[10] Moyra Haslett argues that Byron's don Juan, contrary to previous critical opinion, very much belongs to the don Juan canon since contemporary readers of the poem interpreted it in the light of their own awareness of don Juan's literary and theatrical tradition. Her argument is, however, problematic. Quite apart from the fact that we do not ourselves have to accept the valuation of

don Juan's name was beginning to become detached from his character, to be applied to any personable young man with a tendency to love affairs. An awareness grew of don Juan's womanizing that did not depend on a knowledge of the traditional story. Don Juan became a synonym for any seducer, and his name could be given to any man that had a way with women. Some writers would in the future concentrate on this archetype, treating don Juan as a modern *pícaro*, in preference to rewriting the old plot and characters.

Tirso's original play had by this time given rise to many works dedicated to the don Juan theme within Europe, but his home land of Spain had not kept pace with the development of the genre. In Spain, only Antonio de Zamora produced a version of any significance - *No hay deuda que no se pague y convidado de piedra* - in 1744. But in the nineteenth century the traditional figure became confused with a historical Spanish libertine who repented, to create the character don Juan de Maraña (or Mañara, as it is sometimes written). In this version, don Juan repents of his sins after witnessing his own funeral - a traditional tale that goes back to before Tirso's day. This new character would be seized on by Mérimée and Dumas *père*, as well as by Spanish writers. The new note of repentance would also recur in Zorrilla's *refundición* of Tirso's original play - *Don Juan Tenorio*, in which don Juan finds salvation through the love of a good woman. This version is better known to Spaniards today than *El burlador*, and is performed annually. Zorrilla's play seemed to herald a renaissance in Spanish interpretations of don Juan. Other Spanish versions included: Unamuno's *El hermano Juan*, Valle-Inclán's *Las galas del difunto* and *Sonatas*, Azorín's *Don Juan*, Pérez de Ayala's *Tigre Juan* and Torrente Ballester's *Don Juan*. Ortega y

---

Byron's contemporaries, her argument merely illustrates the problem that *any* supposed don Juan work is read in the light of other don Juan works, as I point out on p.28. Byron's poem has itself become a source for later treatments of the don Juan figure, most recently in the 1995 film *Don Juan de Marco*. We should not underestimate the importance of the poem, but I would still claim that it depicts an archetypal womanizer rather than a don Juan directly derived from Tirso's story. See Haslett, *Byron's* Don Juan *and the Don Juan Legend* (Oxford: Clarendon Press, 1997).

Gasset discussed don Juan in his writings: while the influence of the don Juan figure was discernible in Pérez Galdós's *Doña Perfecta* and Alas's *La Regenta*.

As he approached and entered the twentieth century, and as part of the reaction against Romantic interpretations, don Juan turned philosophical. This seems as much a logical development arising from his role as a Romantic hero as a reaction against it, since his quest for the ideal woman might naturally lead on to quests for other ideals. Perhaps the most philosophical don Juan is George Bernard Shaw's in *Man and Superman* (1903). Shaw invented a character who has higher (rather Nietzschean) goals to aim for than the pursuit of women. The Swiss playwright Max Frisch later drew on such ideas for *Don Juan oder die Liebe zur Geometrie* (1953, revised 1961). Here don Juan prefers mathematical principles to female relationships. By the time of the twentieth century a well-developed sense of don Juan as a stock literary figure had also come into being. Don Juan became the focus for essay treatment by Albert Camus (in *The Myth of Sisyphus*); Foucault discussed the figure in passing in his *History of Sexuality*; and attempts were made at psychoanalysis of don Juan's character, most notably by Otto Rank and Julia Kristeva.[11] A body of critical literature on the don Juan phenomenon has simultaneously developed.

This brief historical overview should demonstrate that there is not one sole interpretation of the don Juan figure, for don Juan has been redrawn by hundreds of authors. Smeed cites a figure of over 600 works devoted to the character, though he does not give his source for that number.[12] Some interpretations conflict with others. The clearest example is that of the Romantic works when contrasted with earlier or with modern interpretations; comparison of individual works would reveal finer nuances of distinction between different don Juans.

---

[11] Rank, *The Don Juan Legend;* Julia Kristeva, *Histoires d'amour* ([n.p.]: Denoël, 1983).
[12] Smeed, p.182.

Nevertheless, the cursory historical outline of don Juan that I have given above readily indicates that ideas about the character have shifted over time, and that twentieth-century authors saw him rather differently from Tirso and the *commedia dell'arte*. But if don Juan as a character has been subject to shifts in perception, the quality he is supposed to embody, male sexuality, has been subject to similar shifts.

Heterosexual relations as a vehicle of change

Don Juan, popularly understood, personifies some of the worst traits of male heterosexuality, including lack of responsibility for his own actions and an exploitation of the double standard that has granted men sexual licence while denying the same to women.[13] The new critiques of heterosexuality and patriarchy that have resulted from the inclusion of lesbian and gay perspectives in debate on this area, have been extremely valuable, allowing us to question more radically assumptions about heterosexuality as given, and thus traditional gender roles as unchangeable. The emphasis on the construction of female, gay and lesbian identities challenges the common presumption of masculinity as the norm that has propped up patriarchal society. [14] This development has, of course, influenced our ability to see sexuality as a historical phenomenon open to change. Research into and discussion of human sexuality has increasingly moved away from the presumption of heterosexuality as the norm, to see other forms of sexual expression as valid and, in consequence, to see sexuality in terms of socially negotiated preferences rather than as natural (or unnatural) tendencies. This

---

[13] Gerald Wade argues that don Juan's aggressive sexuality in fact masks concerns with homosexuality and bisexuality. Wade thus provides another example of a critic who has seen something problematic in the notion of don Juan as a symbol of male sexuality. (Gerald E. Wade, 'The Character of Don Juan of *El burlador de Sevilla*: a Psychoanalytical Study', *Bulletin of the Comediantes* 31/1 (1979), 33-42).

[14] See, for instance, Jeffrey Weeks, *Against Nature: Essays on History, Sexuality and Identity* (London: Rivers Oram Press, 1991), and Judith Butler, *Gender Trouble: Feminism and the Subversion of Identity* (New York: Routledge, 1990).

challenge to more traditional patriarchal mores is valuable and necessary; but it carries the danger of taking patriarchy at its own estimation, and assuming too easily that male heterosexual identity is unproblematic. Such theories thus tend to emphasize the idea that female identity derives from the male norm and ignore the possibility that I wish to explore here - that the male individual attempts to derive his identity from women and that, as the notion of his individuality changes, so do his relations with women.[15] This, I will argue, is the case of don Juan.

The emphasis given to homosexuality and lesbianism does not mean that heterosexual expression ceases to be important. On the contrary, as Anthony Giddens argues in his study *The Transformation of Intimacy*, relations between men and women are undergoing a transformation of which the outcome is hard to predict.[16] Changes in intimate relations have had a profound impact on both women and men, and the consequences can be disturbing:

> There is little doubt that new emotional antagonisms are opening up between the sexes. The sources of both male and female rage bite even more deeply than either of the foregoing accounts suggests. The phallus is only the penis: what a numbing and disconcerting discovery this is for both sexes! The claims to power of maleness depend upon a dangling piece of flesh that has now lost its distinctive connection to reproduction. This is a new castration indeed; women can now see men, at least on a cognitive level, as just as much a functionless appendage as the male sexual organ itself.[17]

---

[15] Anthony Giddens, whose ideas I will draw on, is an exception: he traces the ways in which male identity has become problematized as a result of greater autonomy for women.

[16] Anthony Giddens, *The Transformation of Intimacy* (Cambridge: Polity Press, 1992), 153-6.

[17] Giddens, *Transformation*, p.153.

It is not just that a sense of male sexuality is being undermined, but that this undermining gives rise to hostility and rage: Giddens frequently touches on the potential for physical violence in these changes to sexual relations. The above passage reinforces the concept of masculinity as an entity in crisis: it emphasizes an equation of masculinity with redundancy and a loss of power. The symbolic value of the penis, the ultimate marker of masculinity, has gone, and with it men's ability to identify themselves as male (and thus as powerful). Giddens focuses on today's society, but as he himself suggests, these changes go back a long way – certainly as far back as the nineteenth century and maybe beyond. R. W. Connell has also taken up the idea of violence as an indicator of what he calls 'crisis tendencies [...]in the modern gender order'.[18] Connell stresses a *tendency* to crisis as opposed to a crisis pure and simple, usefully reminding us that not all men are equally threatened (some men suffer more than others), but he also goes on to say that these crisis tendencies 'in power relations threaten hegemonic masculinity directly'.[19] These tendencies to crisis may not affect all men in the same way and to the same extent; but the sense of malaise, I would argue, is more pervasive, so that we can talk of a crisis in masculinity even though men do not all materially suffer to the same extent.

The sexual historian Jeffrey Weeks also suggests to us a tension in gender relations that may additionally reflect itself in don Juan's sexual defiance:

> Sexuality is a fertile source of moral panic, arousing intimate questions about personal identity, and touching on crucial social boundaries. The erotic acts as a crossover point for a number of tensions whose origins are elsewhere: of class, gender, and racial location, of intergenerational conflict, moral acceptability and

---

[18] R. W. Connell, *Masculinities* (Cambridge: Polity Press, 1995), p.84.
[19] Connell, p.90.

medical definition. This is what makes sex a particular site of ethical and political concern - and of fear and loathing.[20]

Don Juan's sexual expression brings into relief the tensions of the society within which he lives - between men and women, our primary concern here, but also between generations and classes.

The way in which I propose to trace the shifts in such tensions is to examine in detail, not only don Juan himself but the female characters and the way in which they relate to him. The female characters, indeed, will receive the greater emphasis. It might perhaps seem strange to discuss the crisis in male identity by concentrating on the women, but as Giddens suggests, the increasing doubt about male identity is reflected in part in a greater antagonism towards women, and how men see women may tell us a great deal about how men see themselves. Defining oneself as male or female cannot be done in isolation: an *other* is always implied, and self-definition as male is intricately intertwined and symbiotic with definitions of women. As is by now a commonplace of literary criticism, women's portrayal in literature is often negative and at times indeed harmful, as a result of entrenched patriarchal views; but I will also propose that these depictions of women also indicate that patriarchy is not as secure and inevitable as sometimes supposed. The alterations in men's attitudes to and treatment of women, while sometimes hostile (with often very negative consequences for women), also implies a sense of underlying weakness and doubt. By studying some female characters in don Juan works, I believe we can pinpoint some of these underlying insecurities, and the shifts in depiction of donjuanian women over the centuries should indicate that these insecurities became increasingly critical.

---

[20] Jeffrey Weeks, *Sexuality and its Discontents: Meanings, Myths and Modern Sexualities* (London: Routledge and Kegan Paul, 1985), p.44.

The figure of don Juan has often rendered all women, whether noble, peasant, married or single, as equally the victims of seduction. Don Juan apparently reinforces popular notions of women as naturally weak and untrustworthy, without exception. But it should become clear from our study that the don Juan genre does not derive from a simple male/female dualism. Far from all women being indistinguishable, some female characters retain their individual personalities and experiences. The main contention that I will examine here is that the portrayal of women becomes more negative the closer the don Juan tradition comes to the twentieth century. An increasingly negative portrait of women in literature seems to go against the many developments that have occurred to improve women's lot in life. Some women, at least, have acquired greater political, economic and social freedom over the last couple of centuries. But male efforts to rein women in have also become more overt:

> ...the unequal relationship between women and men, present at the beginnings of history in Europe, intensified as time went on. The early nineteenth century marked the nadir of European women's options and possibilities. In earlier centuries, alternative authorities and customs, as well as regional, governmental, and religious variations created a range of circumstances that enabled some European women to achieve relative independence and relative dominance. Gradually, however, changes in government, law, economy, and religion tending toward centralization, rationalization, and uniformity worked to further limit women's lives and deprive most of them of powers and opportunities available to some women in earlier eras.

> The centuries from the Renaissance through the Enlightenment broadened the possibilities for men, giving more men access to

education and choices in occupation. They did the opposite for women.[21]

Anderson and Zinnser trace a trajectory of hostility that perhaps culminates in the overtly pathological perceptions of women at the end of the nineteenth century that has provided the focus of many studies, of which those of Elaine Showalter and Bram Dijkstra are among the best known.[22] Again, we see the growth in antagonism between the sexes that Giddens posited. I will hypothesize, then, that this increase in hostility reflects the instability of male individual identity, which in turn manifests itself in the way women are viewed and dealt with. Don Juan's own individuality and sexual identity – the way he defines himself as male – will thus be reflected in his negotiations with the female characters.

The role of the other male characters will not, however, be neglected. I believe that the comparatively consistent way in which they are portrayed as weak and ineffectual can provide us with a clue to why treatment of female characters becomes more malign as literary history passes. The unchanging nature of patriarchy in the works studied here implies that the reason for the growing hostility towards women lies elsewhere, in the increasingly problematic nature of the male individual.

One object of the study of female characters is to reappraise the contribution of Tirso to the don Juan canon. In the coda of the final chapter I will argue that his comparatively positive portrayal of women in *El burlador* means that we cannot dismiss the play so easily as an overly didactic work, as some *donjuanistas* have been wont to do. The way in which Tirso depicts women should allow us a chance to reassess his standing in the don Juan canon.

---

[21] Bonnie S. Anderson and Judith P. Zinsser, *A History of Their Own: Women in Europe from Prehistory to the Present*, Vol. 1 (London: Penguin, 1988), p.xxii

Sex and gender as historical phenomena

The emphasis of this study, then, rests not so much on theoretical elaboration but instead on the alteration of interpretations of gender relations over time, on the 'historicity' of such relations. That gender relations do change over time may at first appear obvious, but many who have written about the sexes and their relations have often taken sex and gender as immutable givens, seeing biology as the determining, and indeed dictating, factor. This is particularly so when discussing women: some sexologists may have discovered new facts and outlined new ideas about female sexuality and the different ways in which women live in society, but they also have tended to take as given that women are inherently weaker and more emotional. They argue, in fact, that the female nature is prescribed by what is 'natural', biologically given: the consequence of this is not only that women's nature cannot change, but that we should not attempt to change it. What is 'natural' is itself clearly open to interpretation. Foucault proposes that our perception of sexuality and gender is very much a historical, a diachronic entity:

> Sexuality must not be thought of as a kind of natural given...It is
> the name that can be given to a historical construct: not a furtive
> reality that is difficult to grasp, but a great surface network in
> which the stimulation of bodies, the intensification of pleasures,
> the incitement to discourse, the formation of special knowledges,
> the strengthening of controls and resistance, are linked to one
> another...[23]

---

[22] Elaine Showalter, *Sexual Anarchy: Gender an d Culture and the* fin-de-siècle,(London: Virago, 1992); Bram Dijkstra, *The Idols of Perversity* (New York: Oxford University Press, 1986).
[23] Foucault, pp.105-6.

This position has been elaborated further by Weeks,[24] who suggests that sexuality is not a given but a process of historical negotiation, so that what seems normal and what seems perverse changes over time. 'Sexuality', Weeks argues, 'is as much a product of history as of nature. Shaped by human action it can be transformed by social and political practice'.[25] Furthermore, Weeks does not see sex as an entity which underlies or is separate from the rest of our lives, but one that interacts with other spheres:

> ...sex, far from being resistant to social ordering, seems peculiarly
> susceptible to it. We know that sex is a vehicle for the expression
> of a variety of social experiences: of morality, duty, work, habit,
> tension release, friendship, romance, love, protection, pleasure,
> utility, power, and sexual difference. Its very plasticity is the
> source of its historical significance.[26]

Weeks's writings stress sexuality and sexual identity. In drawing on his ideas, I do not wish to insist that sexuality is synonymous with identity (nor do I think Weeks himself is saying that). But I would like to take up his concept of historical dialectic and relate it to a sphere closely allied to that of sexuality: that is, gender relations. Gender and sexuality are not the same thing by any means, but equally clearly the two overlap and affect each other. The validity of the notion of historical change becomes apparent with an examination of the literary history of the don Juan phenomenon. Don Juan's sphere of activity encompasses the sexual but also encompasses the wider sphere of interactions between men and women. Many commentators on the don Juan phenomenon have concentrated on the notion of don Juan as seducer; but not all don Juans do in fact seduce. Later don Juans - in this study we will be looking specifically at those of George Bernard

---

[24] Weeks, *Against Nature; Sexuality and its Discontents; Sex, Politics and Society: the Regulation of Sexuality Since 1800* (London: Longman, 1981).
[25] Weeks, *Sexuality and its Discontents*, p.96.
[26] Weeks, *Sexuality and its Discontents*, p.122.

Shaw and Max Frisch - do not necessarily pursue women. However, don Juans are more closely and consistently involved in gender relations; in fact, I would claim that we cannot understand don Juan without reference to such relations. But these interactions also change over time, as the work of Weeks amply demonstrates.

My specific hypothesis is that gender relations, as expressed in different don Juan works, reflect a growing historical recognition of man (but not woman) as an individual. In don Juan literature, the entities of gender, and more specifically of sexual expression, are closely related to don Juan's search for individual identity, as I shall argue in greater detail in the following chapter. Weeks again has discussed the relationship of individuality to sexuality, claiming that 'Sex...is part of the eternal battle of individual and society'.[27] He links the notion of man as individual to his sexual nature: 'The idea that "man" was a coherent product of inner propulsions and drives...made it possible to specify sex as the most vital energetic force in the individual'.[28] Weeks also notes: 'Since at least the time of Rousseau it [sex] has been the assertion of self against the preternaturally distorting effects of modern, and later industrial civilisation; sex, that is to say, is the essence of our individual being which asserts itself against the demands of culture...'.[29] Giddens has also commented on the link between sexuality and individual identity: 'Sexuality becomes a property of the individual the more the life-span becomes internally referential and the more self-identity is grasped as a reflexively organised endeavour'.[30] He also links the issues of identity and gender relations: 'The enquiries which men carried on into the nature of women were not just an expression of traditional sexual otherness; they were investigations into unacknowledged arenas of self-identity and intimacy, as reordered areas of social

---

[27] Weeks, *Sexuality and its Discontents*, p.81.
[28] Weeks, *Sexuality and its Discontents*, p.121.
[29] Weeks, *Sex, Politics and Society*, p.12.
[30] Giddens, *Transformation*, p.175.

life to which men had little entry'.[31] Taking together these comments of Giddens we can deduce the complex interrelation of three entities which will concern us here: sexual activity, gender relations and individual identity.

Don Juan himself is marked out very much as an individual, as a being distinct from the society that surrounds him from his very creation - Sullivan uses don Juan as an instance of Tirso de Molina's propensity to structure his plays in the opposition of the one, the protagonist, against the many, the society that surrounds him or her.[32] It is significant that Foucault refers to don Juan (to him a form of the mythical figure) as: 'the individual driven, in spite of himself, by the somber madness of sex',[33] highlighting again the role of don Juan as individual. The link between individuality and sexuality, that Weeks suggests arose over the course of history, is significant given that don Juan begins his literary life as a seducer. But Weeks also points out that the sense of man as an individual is itself a historical phenomenon subject in consequence to change:

> All societies, of course, have ways of specifying individuals, through names, position or status, but they are not necessarily specified as *individual subjects*, unique entities with a distinct consciousness of self, who have the will and power to constitute social order and make moral judgment. Other societies have conceived of individuals through the dense network of obligations, duties and responsibility they owe: as lords and masters, priests and laymen and so on. Since at least the seventeenth century, however (and many argue that it occurred much earlier), the west has prioritised individual will and responsibility as the starting point of speculations on society. 'Man' exists prior to society. 'His'

---

[31] Giddens, *Transformation*, p.178.
[32] Henry W. Sullivan, *Tirso de Molina and the Drama of the Counter Reformation*, (Amsterdam: Rodop, 1976), pp.101ff.

activity with others founds society. 'He' is the measure of all things.[34]

Weeks does not, in fact, need to mark off the masculine indicators in this passage with inverted commas, for until very recently, and certainly in terms of the don Juan phenomenon, the individual has been synonymous with the male. Part of my hypothesis is that as male individuality comes more and more to the fore of don Juan works, so a sense of women as individual people diminishes. We may observe Weeks's emphasis on a shifting perception of the individual from the seventeenth century - the era when don Juan first appeared on stage - to the present.[35] Not only do significant changes occur in notions of individuality, but they do so at a time when authors took up the character of don Juan and rewrote his story time and again.

Don Juan: discourse or myth?

If we suppose don Juan to be a form of historical discourse subject to change, we run up against the difficulty that many if not most don Juan scholars consider him to be not a historical figure but a mythical one. They dispense altogether with don Juan's longitudinal development to treat don Juan as one unchanging entity outside history. Even Foucault perceives don Juan as an ahistorical figure rather than a historical one that of necessity changed:[36] this is ironic, given that Foucault's emphasis on sex as historical discourse. Further commentators, however, have actually made it their desired object to render don Juan ahistorical. They do this by describing don Juan in terms of myth, thereby suggesting that there exists some 'essential' don Juan against which all literary renditions of the

---

[33] Foucault, p.39.

[34] Weeks, *Sexuality and its Discontents*, p.121.

[35] Richard J. Pym argues that 'the interrogation of the nature of the self and its potential modalities' was an integral part of the Spanish *comedia*. See Pym, 'The Subject in Spain's Seventeenth-Century *comedia*', *Bulletin of Hispanic Studies*, LXXV/3 (1998), 273-292; p.277.

figure can be measured. James Mandrell dissects the use of the term *myth* in don Juan critique, pointing out that treatment of the figure as a myth is strongly associated with the 'popularization' of don Juan that divorces him from any specific literary text: 'the designation of Don Juan as a mythical figure...depends on (and develops out of) the gradual emancipation of the fictional character of Don Juan from any specific text or from the domain of the written word'.[37] The conception of don Juan as myth, according to Mandrell, neglects the aspect of rewriting, the need of each author to tell the story afresh, and diminishes the importance of don Juan's historical development within literature. He rightly points out that the use of myth as a tool with which to study and describe don Juan, devalues the specific literary texts that go to make up the don Juan genre. [38]

The use of myth as a concept with which to frame discussion of don Juan carries difficulties: it implies, as Mandrell comments, 'some form of the essential Don Juan and his story against which every manifestation of the character must be measured'.[39] In other words, don Juan exists essentially beyond the literary texts through which we get to know him. But the essential, mythical don Juan remains very much in the mind of any critic who uses this term: we have no point of authority outside the very texts which the mythical don Juan is supposed to transcend - even the texts of those critics who attempt to reduce him to a myth. Immediately, therefore, we can appreciate that perceiving don Juan as myth, and thus as ahistorical, does not necessarily bring us any nearer to an understanding of the figure, or indeed of specific literary works, beyond the fact that don Juan's character and story has attrached many authors.

---

[36] Foucault, pp. 39-40.

[37] Mandrell, p.17.

[38] Mandrell himself prefers to treat don Juan not as literature but specifically as *text*. Such an approach leads him to describe don Juan as a *mythology* or a *mythography* rather than a myth, for he believes these terms incorporate the desire of authors to rewrite the story. He accentuates rewriting rather than retelling. This approach seems in one sense merely to put the difficulty of myth at one further remove, since mythology still emphasizes unity rather than difference. But mythology does allow for the possibility of historical development.

But this is not the only problem. The need to synthesize don Juan in critical terms in order to be able to provide analysis of the character, and the inevitable problems entailed in such an approach, has led to the rise of the term *myth* to give unity to the don Juan canon and thus allow don Juan to be discussed as if he were one single figure instead of a myriad of characters. However, the differences between don Juan works may prove just as significant as the similarities: distinction, as well as unity, plays an important role in the study of don Juan's literary development. To think of don Juan as an eternal myth means an inability to conceive him as a discourse that develops over time: any differences between different texts become merely variations on a theme,[40] and the import of these differences will be missed. Thus if we wish to consider the significance of the changes to don Juan's masculine identity – my concern here – we cannot very well adopt a mythical approach, which stresses unity at the expense of history.

This study, taking as it does a diachronic approach, thus emphasizes the differences rather than the unity of the don Juan phenomenon. But to take a differential approach carries difficulties of its own. Although myth disregards historical nuances, it does at least provide a measure of unity, which is still necessary if we are to consider don Juan effectively. If don Juan carries the potential to change, how can we recognize a work of literature as a don Juan work? The difficulty in discussing don Juan lies precisely in the need to simplify, i.e to give some measure of unity to the figure in order to overcome the problem of the sheer number of don Juans, *in conjunction with* the simultaneous need to differentiate between individual characters (as well as bearing in mind the sense of don Juan as a popular archetype). Somehow any discussion of the don Juan phenomenon must encompass Tirso's play, for example, with the approaches of such dramatists as Zorrilla and Frisch. The aims of these dramatists were very

---

[39] Mandrell, p.17.
[40] 'Variations on a theme' is how Smeed put it in the subtitles to his work.

different, yet we can recognize that their don Juans bear a certain *family resemblance* to each other. Reducing the plays to a list of invariables would not work if we approached don Juan as a myth, for myth would imply an essential don Juan against which some plays would not compare too well. The idea of 'kinship', however, allows us to overcome this difficulty, for members of the same family resemble each other to some extent, and yet have distinguishing characteristics that permit us to mark them out as individuals. Such an approach allows us to understand don Juan works as individual literary entities and simultaneously as contributions to a particular literary tradition. Similarly, we can understand the works as mutually reinforcing and supporting, even though each work has its own distinct character that separates it from the others. The works may be both like and unlike each other. This approach profitably moves us away from the need to distil don Juan into a single mythical figure, and yet enables us to see don Juan as a group, a family, of characters. Don Juan becomes, on such an interpretation, a collective noun.[41]

We can immediately identify recurrent features that occur in most, if not all, plays, poems and novels (not including those that deal with the archetypal figure featured in the work of Byron and others, as I described earlier). Most of the

---

[41] This approach echoes an idea of the philosopher Wittgenstein in his later work *Philosophical Investigations* (trans. by G. E. M. Anscombe, Oxford: Basil Blackwell, 1978), where he uses the notion of a family resemblance to describe language itself as a series of relationships between words. He cites the example of games: games do not have one single common characteristic that defines them as games, but a series of common features, with the result that 'we see a complicated network of similarities overlapping and criss-crossing: sometimes overall similarities, sometimes similarities of detail' (Wittgenstein, p.32). The criss-crossing relationships Wittgenstein describes in terms of a family resemblance:

> I can think of no better expression to characterize these similarities than 'family resemblances'; for the various resemblances between members of a family: build, features, colour of eyes, gait, temperament, etc. et.c. overlap and criss-cross in the same way (Wittgenstein, p.32).

Thus within the don Juan genre various themes and motifs may repeat themselves in some versions of the story and may nevertheless vanish completely from others. We can easily discern variable details in plot and character, which differ from each other and yet are comparable.

works share a common plot or common characters. Often the plot does not deviate much from Tirso's original concept: don Juan seduces various noble and peasant women until dragged to Hell by the statue of the Commander, whom he killed earlier. The number and names of the other characters may vary. Don Juan tends to be nobly born and usually has a servant, though the servant's name and role may differ greatly from play to play - compare, for instance, Leporello in *Don Giovanni* to Ciutti in *Don Juan Tenorio*. But works in the don Juan genre also tend to share common themes as well as plot and character details, and it is possible to trace thematic characteristics common to many plays.

Although in many versions he is accompanied by a servant, don Juan is essentially a solitary character, because he breaks the rules by which society ensures some measure of unity and stability: thus he separates himself from the society in which he lives. His social code is not theirs. This becomes a fundamental characteristic: *Don Juan is defiant of social convention.* The result of such social rebellion may have different results, as we can see from contrasting the protagonists of Tirso and Mozart with Shaw's own earnest don Juan, John Tanner. Mandrell suggests don Juan's complicity in the essentially patriarchal culture against which he appears to rebel: don Juan upholds rather than undermines patriarchal structures and institutions.[42] Nevertheless, don Juan refuses to be bound by the social conventions of his day - though he may, as in the case of *El burlador*, make use of them, using his social position as a noble both to attract his victims and as protection from the consequences of his actions. Moreover, defiance of society may not be totally negative, for the societies themselves are under scrutiny. Tirsian commentators have observed that the Seville of *El burlador* is itself corrupt while the other characters in other plays do not necessarily compare well with the don Juan figure.[43]

---

[42] Mandrell, p.11, p.262.
[43] See, for instance, Bruce W. Wardropper, *'El burlador de Sevilla*: a Tragedy of Errors',

As a consequence of his actions, *don Juan resorts to flight*. He needs to flee his victims before they attempt to demand justice of him, so that flight becomes a natural part of his career. Don Juan's flight, as much as the seductions he may make or the other ways in which he is involved with women, contributes to his role as a figure of movement and action, one that lives eternally in the present, as Kierkegaard suggested. Flight is a vital part of his sexual career, but it is not always a direct result of it, as the need to flee often results from the death of the Commander at don Juan's hands. In the case of Shaw's *Man and Superman* and Frisch's *Don Juan oder die Liebe zur Geometrie*, flight is what impels the protagonist to fulfil his traditional role of the seducer, either through a dream sequence or through one night of indiscriminate seduction. In each case, don Juan flees the prospect of total commitment to a woman and attempts to take refuge in an apparently seductive career. Commentators have not as a rule paid much attention to the significance of don Juan's propensity to flee, but it often indicates his desire to avoid responsibility for his actions and thus any consequent punishment. Obviously flight suggests irresponsibility, but it also gives to don Juan an elusive quality that ensures a struggle on the part of society to keep him contained.

So far we have focused on don Juan's career. But the plays also bring his career to an end in some manner, which is nearly always unpleasant. In some measure don Juan has to receive some form of 'punishment': he must suffer as a consequence of the life he has led. This perhaps implies that he receives punishment in retribution for the social rebellion we considered earlier. Certainly his punishment tends to

Philological Quarterly 36 (1957), 61-71; pp.63-4; P. W. Evans, 'The Roots of Desire in *El burlador de Sevilla*', *Forum for Modern Language Studies* 22/3 (1986), 232-247; p.232 Judith H.Arias, 'Doubles in Hell: *El burlador de Sevilla y convidado de piedra*', *Hispanic Review*, 58/3 (1990), 361-377; p.365; Francisco Ruiz Ramón, 'Don Juan y la sociedad del burlador de Sevilla: la crítica social', in *Estudios sobre teatro español y clásico contemporáneo* (Madrid: Fundación Juan March y Cátedra, 1978), 71-95.

restore some semblance of social order at the end of the play, though the order thus established is not unmitigated, as Sganarelle's cry for his unpaid wages at the end of Molière's *Dom Juan* suggests. Therefore we have another principle of the don Juan tradition - *don Juan is punished*. The punishment itself varies: usually don Juan goes to Hell or receives death through some divine intermediary, but later authors conceived other forms of punishment. Shaw and Frisch, for instance, favoured the trap of domesticity which would prevent their protagonists from pursuing their avowed goals. Ironically, relationships with women become a form of punishment rather than a pastime. Some don Juans, such as that of Zorrilla, receive punishment (death in the case of Zorrilla) but are able to repent and receive salvation, so that punishment is not necessarily don Juan's ultimate end.

The above are all features that frequently recur in don Juan works. Nonetheless, there is one specific characteristic that gives us the common denominator of the don Juan genre; and that characteristic is precisely the object of our study. The impulse for the action in a don Juan play or novel is don Juan's attitude towards and treatment of the women he encounters. The whole purpose of the genre revolves around women in some degree. However, it does not automatically follow that don Juan must be a womanizer. The popular conception of don Juan is that of a seducer, that is, a man with a mysterious power over women so that they cede to his sexual demands. This conception has been established to such an extent that the term 'don Juan' can be applied to any man who is sexually successful with a number of women; and don Juan's name appears in the dictionary with just such a definition.[44] Certainly this idea features strongly in earlier versions of the don Juan story, reaching its height in Mozart and da Ponte's opera, probably the most well-known version, on which most people's idea of don

---

[44] 'Don Juan: a libertine of Spanish legend, subject of plays, poems, and operas in several European languages: an attractive profligate'. Definition found in *Chambers 20th Century Dictionary*, 1983 ed., p.371.

Juan is probably based. Kierkegaard saw in don Giovanni the typical seducer, living for the moment, an idea which he thought was best expressed in Mozart's music:

> ...Don Giovanni is absolutely musical. He desires sensually, seduces with the demonic power of sensuality, he seduces all. The spoken word is no part for him, for that would straightaway make him a reflective individual. He has no substance of this kind but hurries on in a perpetual vanishing, just like music...[45]

But this notion of don Juan as seducer does not tell us everything. Even in earlier versions don Juan was more than this. In Tirso's version - the source of all the others, directly or indirectly - don Juan is not so much a seducer as a cheat, who is not interested in sex so much as trickery. The title of the play tells it all: *El burlador de Sevilla*. Tirsian critics often quote don Juan's description of himself:

> Sevilla a voces me llama
> el Burlador, y el mayor
> gusto que en mí puede haber
> es burlar una mujer
> y dejalla sin honor (II, 269-273).[46]

When Molière came to write his own play, he drew a portrait of a freethinker, who willingly argued against conventional ideas of God and the afterlife - an atheist theologian. Mozart's opera became the basis - not perhaps with much justification - for the new, Romantic interpretation epitomised by Hoffmann, which completely reconceptualized don Juan as a hero in search of the ideal

---

[45] Søren Kierkegaard, 1990. *Either/Or: a Fragment of Life*, trans. by Alastair Hannay (Harmondsworth: Penguin, 1990), p.107.

woman, doomed ever to be disappointed. Twentieth-century writers rejected this idea for new, more philosophical don Juans to whom women were accidental conveniences or nuisances, or entities to be actively shunned.

Mandrell places great emphasis on the notion of don Juan as seducer,[47] echoing the ideas of Shoshana Felman in perceiving language as a mode of seduction. Felman saw don Juan's seductive technique as the making of promises he would not keep.[48] Mandrell argues that through written text (both the works themselves and items such as letters and lists that feature within them) don Juan seduces both his victims and the audience or reader. But Mandrell's use of seduction as an identifying mark of don Juan would automatically exclude some significant incarnations of the character, in particular that of Shaw. And for other don Juans, seduction is almost incidental. When discussing Zorrilla's *Don Juan Tenorio*, for example, Mandrell understands don Juan's letter to Inés to be a tool of seduction, and it is certainly that.[49] The letter engenders in Inés unfamiliar feelings of love which have a strong sensual overtone.[50] Nevertheless, don Juan's ultimate aim is not one of seduction but of salvation, as he perceives Inés not as a victim but as a

---

[46] 'Sevilla loudly proclaims me as the Trickster, and for me the greatest possible pleasure is to cheat a woman and deprive her of her honour'. All references to *El burlador* come from the edition by Edwards.

[47] Mandrell, p.48

[48] Shoshana Felman, *The Literary Speech Act: Don Juan with J. L. Austin, or Seduction in Two Languages* trans. by Catherine Porter, (Ithaca: Cornell University Press, 1983), pp.30-31.

[49] For a rather hyperbolic discussion of the letter as phallus in *Don Juan Tenorio*, see Gustavo Pérez Firmat, *Literature and Liminality: Festive Readings in the Hispanic Tradition* (Durham: Duke University Press, 1986). Mandrell (p. 97) suggests don Juan's pen as a phallic symbol, a subtler image. Mandrell is more preoccupied at this point in his discussion with writing as don Juan's identifying mark. But, when Ciutti describes don Juan as 'gran pluma' (line 32), Mandrell focuses on the writing motif, and seems to miss - or, at most, implies - the implication of don Juan as phallus.

[50] For instance, Inés says: '¿Qué sentimientos dormidos/ son los que revela en mí?/ ¿Qué impulsos jamás sentidos?/ ¿Qué luz que hasta hoy nunca vi?/ ¿Qué es lo que engendra en mi alma/ tan nuevo y profundo afáa?/ ¿Quién roba la dulce calma/ de mi corazon?' (1736-1743). ['What dormant feelings are waking within me? What impulses, never known before? What light that I never saw before today? What is causing such new and deep anxiety in my soul? Who has taken away the sweet serenity of my heart?]

potential saviour. Don Juan's seduction of Inés is therefore incidental to his true purpose, the search for redemption through the love of another.

So don Juan is not necessarily a seducer, contrary to the popular archetype. But whatever path he follows, women and sex play a significant role. In some fashion, don Juan's fate will always be decided through his interactions with women. Whether or not don Juan is a cheat, a Romantic idealist or a victim of female attention, the women are always part of his career. Therefore, an essential part of the don Juan tradition is that *don Juan's career is always dependent on women*, though the manner in which this occurs varies considerably. That is to say, our concern with gender relations, as they are expressed in the sexual sphere, is central to the don Juan phenomenon, and don Juan cannot be properly appreciated without attention to this issue.

This understanding of don Juan, somewhat removed from the archetype, will have significance for our interpretation. Referring again to Kierkegaard, his notion of don Giovanni as the perfect seducer cannot coincide with, for instance, the anguished dithering of Frisch's don Juan, who longs to escape the demands of women in order to study the eternal and impersonal truths of geometry. The don Juan canon tells us something of don Juan's nature through his relationships with women but it does not always reveal to us the sprightly charmer that Mozart was supposed to have depicted. Using the idea of family relationships I referred to above, it is easy to perceive that don Juan's relationship with women essentially defines his career and his progress through his own tale; but that his role as a libertine may or may not be a feature of different works.

Other characteristics of the tradition mentioned above - defiance, flight and punishment - reveal, in addition to our central theme here of the treatment of women, further areas in which male-female relations come under scrutiny. In these areas, the other male characters have a particular role to play. The male characters in general, however, as I shall argue in chapter 6, serve to demarcate the male individual from patriarchy as a whole. Don Juan appears more active than do the other male characters, who seem inadequate and passive. What is also significant for our study is that male society remains equally ineffectual regardless of the shifts in attitudes that occur around women and the individual. Among other things, therefore, the male characters accentuate the arena of change as that of don Juan attempting to establish his own identity in the way he relates to women.

Although the principal focus of this study is the attitudes towards women in the don Juan tradition, and the way in which women are portrayed, some discussion of the principal character is nevertheless essential to an appreciation of how different dramatists treat women in their plays. For all the women have some relationship to don Juan: mostly they are his seduced victims, occasionally his collaborators and sometimes, as the tradition progresses, his nemesis. We saw earlier how don Juan's nature seems elusive because of the difficulty in discussing him comprehensively, and how nevertheless some manner of synthesis might be attempted owing to the family relationship of different plays, which possess both similarities and distinctions. We can distinguish works dealing with the don Juan story from other literary works, and when we discuss the concept we still have some idea of what we mean, even when dealing with the later, modern works. And we are also able to discuss salient characteristics of don Juan works, even though we can also perceive that one common characteristic does not apply in every instance. Our way should now be clear to embark on an examination of don Juan's relationships with women, and how this in turn reveals the growing crisis in male individual identity.

The question of selectivity

Because of the sheer number of don Juan works, any discussion is inevitably selective. This carries its own danger. The need for selectivity leads many commentators to dismiss or neglect any don Juan who does not fit their own criteria for the theme, an issue analysed by Smeed.[51] Thus any conclusions they make about the character can only partially apply. The problem of selectivity occurs most often over *Don Giovanni*, where the protagonist comes to stand for all don Juans. Moreover, the first work in which we encounter don Juan must inevitably influence our understanding of other works when we come across them. Thus, if we already know *Don Giovanni*, we will be influenced by the ideas of Mozart and da Ponte when we see the play by Tirso, who died over a century before they wrote the opera. Ramón Pérez de Ayala argues that it is impossible for anyone to see a don Juan play 'for the first time', as everyone possesses some previous familiarity with the character and story of don Juan:

> Lo que estorba a la inteligencia y emoción del *Don Juan* [by Zorrilla], esto es, lo que impide verle por vez primera, es su leyenda. Estoy por decir que, no ya nosotros, pero ni aun los contemporáneos de Zorrilla, lograron ver por primera vez su *Don Juan Tenorio*, ni los de Tirso de Molina su *Burlador de Sevilla y convidado de piedra*. Con siglos de anterioridad a Tirso de Molina existe la leyenda del muerto, o estatua, que asiste a un convite, adonde sacrílega e impíamente se le brindó por mofa.[52]

---

[51] Smeed, ch. 9.
[52] 'It is don Juan's legend that confuses our intelligence and feeling when seeing [Zorrilla's] *Don Juan*; it prevents us from seeing the play as if for the first time. By this I mean that not just ourselves but Zorrilla's contemporaries were unable to see *Don Juan Tenorio* as if for the first time, nor were Tirso de Molina's contemporaries able thus to see *El burlador de Sevilla y convidado de piedra*. The legend of the stone guest, who attends a banquet where he is sacrilegiously, impenitently and derisively toasted, existed centuries before Tirso de Molina.' Ramón Pérez de Ayala, *Tigre Juan y El curandero de su honra*, ed. by Andrés Amorós (Madrid:

Smeed describes the problem of the don Juan heritage in the following terms:

> As soon as the author of a new version produces his variation on traditional motifs and incidents, the informed member of the audience (or reader) will make the connection and judge the one work against the other; this is likely to be particularly strong in drama, where the events are actually unfolding before his eyes. Here he will experience the new play as a play and will simultaneously respond to it as a contribution to a literary tradition.[53]

Even to understand the tradition in ironic and parodic forms, it is necessary to draw on the tradition in order to understand what is being said.

The weight of the don Juan canon appears such that it is an impossible task to uphold one particular character as representative of the theme as a whole. The tradition therefore creates difficulties for critics and authors alike by undermining attempts at selectivity or attempts to refine or dismantle characters and plot. The innumerable incarnations of the character make comprehensive understanding of him impossible.[54] Yet discussion of the story inevitably entails some measure of synthesis and summary, for there are far too many versions of it for comprehensive treatment to be feasible. Selective criteria, a set of defining principles such as the ones suggested above, become necessary in order to be able to manage such a diffuse character.

Castalia, 1980), p.460

[53] Smeed, p.123.

[54] A further difficulty is the confusion between don Juan as a literary character and the popular womanizing archetype mentioned earlier. Kristeva, for instance, confuses the two concepts. She discusses don Juan as Molière and Mozart conceived him, and then proceeds to discuss a 'case history' of a womanizer whose life bears comparison with don Juan's only in terms of an interest in women. Mandrell discusses this question as part of his refutation of don Juan as a mythical figure.

Six plays provide the focus for the ensuing study. The first main text is clearly that of the original play, Tirso's *El burlador de Sevilla*, particularly since one object of this proposed study is the reassessment of Tirso's status in the don Juan tradition as a whole. Molière's *Dom Juan* and Mozart/da Ponte's *Don Giovanni* also feature strongly. These earlier plays are, as well as significant in their own right, fairly representative of the earlier era of don Juan works. *Don Giovanni*, however, marks a pivotal point in the development of the don Juan genre, and later works begin to show more variation. Of the Romantic don Juan, Zorrilla's *Don Juan Tenorio* has proved the most enduring, being still popular in Spain today and influencing Spanish literature of the nineteenth and twentieth century far more than *El burlador*. In my chapter on the Romantic don Juan, however, I shall also refer to the writings of Søren Kierkegaard and E. T. A. Hoffmann, whose thoughts on Mozart's *Don Giovanni* contributed significantly to the reinterpretation of don Juan in Romantic terms. The Romantic don Juan movement in turn provoked a reaction that culminated in the last two plays presented here for discussion. Shaw's *Man and Superman*, while not conforming to the traditional plot of the earlier era, nevertheless contains characters, themes and details drawn from the tradition, to which it has proved a significant contribution. In particular, its scrutiny of the role of women in sexual relations will be especially relevant for our discussion here. Shaw's play also influenced Frisch's *Don Juan oder die Liebe zur Geometrie*, the last of our plays. Frisch's play takes us into the contemporary post-war era. However, Frisch's attempt to reappraise and dismantle the don Juan genre points us back towards don Juan's origins and brings us in a circle back to Tirso.

This chapter should have served to demonstrate that concepts of gender, sexuality and individuality are entities subject to historical change, and that the don Juan figure embodies these entities and their propensity to change. We have emphasized the study specifically of women in analysis of shifts in attitudes to gender relations. Subsequently we have identified don Juan himself as a historical phenomenon that nevertheless contains essential characteristics that remain persistent throughout the literary centuries, and have marked relations with women as a significant characteristic. Before we proceed, however, to look at the female characters in more detail and trace the shifts in attitudes towards them, we should look first at the protagonist himself, note his purpose in his relations with women, and discover how this affects his construction of himself as an individual.

Chapter 2: The search for identity

In this chapter, I intend to discuss how don Juan attempts to define himself as an individual separate from the society within which he finds himself. An examination of the protagonist of each of the six works selected here for study should demonstrate two of my hypotheses: that don Juan attempts to use the female characters as tools with which to define himself, and that his attitude to his own identity reveals the longitudinal shifts I proposed in the preceding chapter. Don Juan's attempt to demarcate his own identity in defiance of society can be seen in the first instance in Henry Sullivan's concept of the one versus the many within Tirso's plays. Sullivan argues that Tirso's protagonists, including don Juan of *El burlador*, tend to dominate the action of their play and to manipulate the other characters in order to achieve their own aims. He says: 'the fundamental goal of the typical [Tirsian] protagonist is to impose his...will on one person or a group of persons in the attainment of a specific end'. [55] The protagonist wishes to exert control, or, to put it another way, to establish his individual self at the cost of the aspirations of other characters. Tirso's don Juan certainly attempts to do this. Tirso seems however to have set a pattern for the don Juan figure that other dramatists have used, and in the six plays we are studying here, we can perceive don Juan's attempt to mark himself out as separate from the other characters, the 'society' in which he lives and acts - and to attempt to do this at their expense.

Paradoxically, the need to mark out one's own separate existence implies the existence of others against whom one can contrast one's own individual nature. Weeks touches on this point:

---

[55] Sullivan, p.103.

> ...identities must always be about relationships: to ourselves, precarious unities of conflicting desires and social commitments...and to others, who address and call upon our recognition in diverse ways and through whom our sense of self is always negotiated.[56]

Weeks also says: 'Identity is about...what you have in common with some people and what differentiates you from others. At its most basic it gives you a sense of personal location, the stable core to your individuality. But it is also about your social relationships, your complex involvement with others...'.[57]

Don Juan tries to assert his identity by deriving it from women, either through seduction or opposition: but his very attempt to stand out as an individual against the mass of women, underscores his reliance on them in order to assert his individuality. The female characters define don Juan in those cases where he acquires the reputation of a seducer or libertine. He cannot gain a name for womanizing without the presence of women towards whom he can direct his attention. (This is not to say that he must seduce successfully: the protagonists of *Dom Juan* and *Don Giovanni* have arguably little success throughout the course of each work. However, the *existence* of women is essential in order to maintain reputations as seducers). The earlier three plays present this idea in a comparatively straightforward and similar manner: don Juan seduces and abandons women and thus attains notoriety as a womanizer. Two of the later plays also use women as evidence of seduction. The history of conquered women provided by don Juan in *Don Juan Tenorio* (441ff) contributes to his role as the profligate prodigal son. Frisch's don Juan, on the other hand, earns his fame as a seducer almost against his will, and in spite of his true ambition to study geometry, because the women themselves desire him to be a seducer (as I

---

[56] Weeks, *Against Nature*, p.85.

elaborate below). An apparent exception to the seducer/women structure is John Tanner in *Man and Superman*, where the play deals not with a series of sexual conquests but with what seems superficially to be a conventional Edwardian comedy of courtship. However, while Tanner's goal is to follow a new philosophy and become a social 'revolutionary' - a superman, in short - the play reveals his subjection to the conventions of courtship and, eventually, marriage. His existence and actions in the play are defined by Ann Whitefield, the woman who pursues him with the aim of marrying him. Thus his relationship with a woman provides the foundation for the play's action. Moreover, in the dream sequence in Act III, where the characters revert to traditional Mozartian figures, don Juan is again portrayed as a cynical womanizer.

It is no accident that these attempts to establish individuality occur in the sphere of gender relations and, more specifically, that of the sexual. Giddens argues that sexuality 'in the modern sense...became a property of the individual...as eroticism conjoined to guilt was progressively replaced by an association of sexuality with self-identity...'.[58] The link that Giddens posits here between individuality and sexuality has particular application to our study of the don Juan figure, since don Juan asserts his individuality, his defiance of the society in which he lives, in the realm of sexual activity or, more generally, relations with women that encompass the sexual. On the whole, don Juan is the only male character to be sexually active in the six plays I have designated - for, as we shall see in more detail in chapter 6, the other male characters are impotent, figuratively and sometimes literally.[59]

---

[57] Weeks, *Against Nature*, p.184.

[58] Anthony Giddens, *Modernity and Self-Identity: Self and Society in the Late Modern Age* (Cambridge: Polity Press, 1991), p.164.

[59] There are exceptions to this at first sight. The Marquis de Mota in *El burlador* has recourse to prostitutes, don Luis Mejía of *Don Juan Tenorio* keeps a tally of conquests much as don Juan does, and Frisch's Pater Diego has embarked on an affair with donna Elvira. Nonetheless, none successfully rival don Juan in his sexual exploits: Mota is tricked by don Juan and imprisoned for

Some might argue that what defines don Juan is not so much his career of seduction, or his relations with women, but his defiance of divine justice (or social convention, in some later plays) represented in his invitation of the statue to supper. His willingness to face up to death and judgement, and often his refusal to repent, indicates an individual strength of character that challenges inexorable power structures. Don Juan's defiance reiterates individuality and a refusal to conform. Nevertheless, his defiance of God and society plays itself out through his relations with women: he requires them even for his defiance. In *El burlador*, for example, don Juan's rebellion against society, whose members constantly evoke the threat of divine justice, occurs in the form of the seduction and trickery of women. Male characters also become victims, but women are the principal vehicle for his rebellion. In Frisch, on the other hand, don Juan attempts to defy social convention through a retreat into the study of geometry, but he views geometry specifically as an escape from relationships with women. The notion of punishment which, as we saw, forms a component part of the don Juan tradition, does not therefore detract in any way from the key role played by women in the protagonist's efforts to achieve individuality. Regardless of the punitive outcome for don Juan, women still are the raw material of his defiance.

Therefore don Juan's reputation, his identity, is in each play linked to the relations he has with women. But we can say more. While these don Juans actively derive their identity from women, they seek to acquire identity by depriving women of theirs, and by equating them all. Kierkegaard in his discussion of *Don Giovanni* exemplifies the tendency of many *donjuanistas* to perceive the female sex as ultimately an undifferentiated mass. The individual characteristics that each woman might possess count for nothing, as individual identity is subsumed into generalized 'womanhood':

---

the latter's crimes; Mejía is killed by Don Juan; while Pater Diego, as a priest, cannot occupy the same sphere of gender relations that don Juan does.

But what is this force with which Don Giovanni seduces? It is the force of desire, the energy of sensual desire. In each woman he desires the whole of femininity, and in this lies the sensually idealizing power with which he at once beautifies and overcomes his prey. The reflection of this gigantic passion beautifies and unfolds the desired, it irradiates a heightened beauty with its refulgence. As, with a seductive glow, the enthusiast's flame illumines even those not concerned, so Don Giovanni transfigures every girl in a far deeper sense, since his relation to her is essential. So for him all finite differences fade away in comparison with the main thing: being a woman.[60]

Such an attempt to equate the female characters, so that their individual personalities are insignificant compared with their sheer femaleness, holds true for the protagonists of all six plays. Don Juan becomes a device for attempting to rob women of any significance except as a vague symbol, where one woman is interchangeable with another. The woman's personality has no value, for only her sheer female being matters.[61] We can, however, observe shifts in the treatment given to individual female characters of the different plays. In the earlier works, and particularly in *El burlador*, the female characters have quite distinct personalities, suggesting that the dramatists view women more acutely and sympathetically than their protagonists do. We can easily distinguish, for instance, between the aloof Tisbea and the gullible, conventional Aminta; and Isabela, concerned for her reputation, with Ana, who will throw caution to the winds in order to obtain Mota. Gradually, however, this distinction ceases, so that by the time we reach Shaw and Frisch the women indeed seem interchangeable. Ann Whitefield and Violet are concerned only to get married, while Frisch's female

---

[60] Kierkegaard, pp.105-6.
[61] Mandrell (pp. 237-245) notes that Ortega y Gasset and Gregorio Marañón adopt a similar attitude to women: both dismiss efforts towards female suffrage since that is a move away from

characters all want to possess don Juan to some degree. As we go on to consider the treatment by different authors of different female characters, this change of approach, from a more benign appreciation of different, individual women to one which sees them as all the same and all dangerous, should become clear. At this point in the argument, however, it should suffice to perceive that for don Juan, at least, distinction for himself is achieved only by making women indistinguishable. His individuality as don Juan rests on their loss of individuality.

These changes in the treatment of women are related to the changes in don Juan's attitude to himself as an individual: as he shifts in his belief as to what is necessary to define himself as an individual, so his attitude towards the female characters changes. To begin with, in the earlier works - by which I mean those by Tirso, Molière and Mozart - don Juan tries to assert himself by means of seduction, and by establishing a reputation as a womanizer. In doing so he attempts to deprive the female characters of their own identity, by rendering them all equal and thus indistinguishable, as I will elaborate below. This need to render women indistinguishable tends to remain constant in all the plays: but the ways in which don Juan tries to do this will change. As we move into the Romantic era, don Juan's sense of individuality becomes more elevated, and Zorrilla equates don Juan's assertion of his own identity with his redemption and acceptance by God. *Don Juan Tenorio* encompasses, not don Juan's seductive career, but his quest for salvation. At this point, perhaps, the notion of individuality reaches its highest point. After this, Shaw and Frisch view individual identity as problematized, and their protagonists pursue goals that lie beyond their own selves - thus John Tanner/don Juan seeks a purer, higher form of living, and the don Juan of Frisch wishes to study geometry. The latter's sense of individuality is so troubled that he wishes deliberately to lose his identity, by submerging it in geometry's abstractness. Both protagonists perceive women as a threat to their aims, and their

---

woman's ultimate destiny - being essentially woman.

notions of identity are bound up with a sense of opposition to the aims of the female characters.

The earlier works

Weeks argues that the notion of individuality arose in the seventeenth century (and possibly earlier):[62] Don Juan himself first made his literary appearance in the same century. It is clear from the very beginning of the tradition that the don Juan figure embodies struggle and manoeuvre over personal identity. Don Juan in *El burlador* describes himself as 'un hombre sin nombre' ('a man with no name', I, 15), and refuses to name himself to anyone for the first two acts. The first occasion on which he identifies himself is to Aminta, as she prepares for her wedding night. This does not occur until the third act:

> Yo soy noble caballero
> cabeza de la familia
> de los Tenorios, antiguos
> ganadores de Sevilla (III, 235-238).[63]

He does not identify himself to either Isabela or Ana, even though Isabela asks who he is (I, 14), as does the woman at the grille (II, 252) who is either Ana or her maid. He forbids his servant Catalinón to reveal his identity to Tisbea (too late, for Catalinón has already done so; I, 577-8 and 681-2). He also refuses to tell his name to the King of Naples when the latter catches him with Isabela: '¿Quién ha de ser?/ Un hombre y una mujer' ('Who else? A man and a woman', I, 22-3). Nor does don Gonzalo know the identity of the man he challenges to fight. Similarly, the audience needs time to know the name of the protagonist. They may initially

---

[62] Weeks, *Sex, Politics and Society*, p.121.
[63] 'I am a nobleman, head of the Tenorio family, former conquerors of Seville'.

take him to be don Octavio, as Isabela does,[64] and until the encounter with Tisbea (where Catalinón gives the game away), they know no more than that he is the nephew of don Pedro.

Instead, don Juan insists on the name he acquires for himself through his seduction of women. Thus when he says 'Sevilla a voces me llama/el Burlador' ('Seville loudly proclaims me as the Trickster', II, 269-270), he draws attention to the fact that his seductions give him fame and thus identity. Similarly, when Catalinón proclaims 'Guárdense todos de un hombre/ que a las mujeres engaña,/y es el burlador de España',[65] his master replies 'Tú me has dado gentil nombre' ('What a fine name you have given me', II, 441-5). Don Juan's name arises directly from his career with women, and Catalinón equates the two ideas in his speech. Although he refers to his lineage in his speech to Aminta quoted above, don Juan does not actually call himself by his real name until he agrees with the statue on their final rendezvous: 'Digo que la cumpliré,/ que soy Tenorio' ('I promise I will be there, as I am a Tenorio', III, 658-9) as Jean-Yves Masson observes.[66] However, only a few lines earlier don Juan also identifies himself as the statue's guest, 'Mañana tu güésped soy' ('I will be your guest tomorrow', III, 653): this reinforces the link between his assertion of his own name and the final meeting which will lead to his damnation.

Until this point, don Juan has styled himself as the *burlador*, which is to say that he takes his identity from his seduction of women. Once he asserts a different identity, he is doomed. Charles Presberg points out that don Juan begins to assert

---

[64] Isaac Benabu reminds us that this initial scene, though supposed to take place at night, would actually be acted out in daylight as was customary in Golden-Age theatre. Don Juan and Isabela would not face each other, to give credence to the idea that she thought him to be Octavio. Benabu suggests that this would allow don Juan to face the audience, and share complicity with them through gestures and facial expressions. (Isaac Benabu, 'Reading the Opening of a Play: Tirso's *El burlador de Sevilla*', *Bulletin of the Comediantes* 47 (1995), 191-200; p.196).

[65] Everybody beware of the man who cheats women, the Trickster of Spain'.

his own claim to nobility of name and character only once the statue provokes him into doing so at the first supper scene.[67] The statue asks him if he will keep his word and don Juan assents, saying, 'las palabras cumplo,/ porque caballero soy' ('I will keep my word, as I am a gentleman', III, 542-3) and 'Digo que la cumpliré,/ que soy Tenorio' ('I promise I will be there, as I am a Tenorio', III, 658-9). Thus until he is adequately challenged, don Juan prefers his notoriety as a man who steals the honour of women; but once his own honour is questioned by the statue he reverts to the notions of nobility and name that have been latent in his earlier speeches (e.g. II, 259, III, 235-242). Doing this, he sets out on the path to his damnation. Or, if we reconsider Presberg's idea from our particular viewpoint here, we can say that don Juan derives his identity from seducing women, but once he prefers to identify himself differently, through name and nobility, he damns himself in the process.

We can see also that although Tirso's don Juan derives his fame and his essential character from the seduction of women, the question of his name and lineage is also significant, as Robert ter Horst suggests.[68] Don Juan has relatives, male relatives, his father don Diego and his uncle don Pedro. Don Juan refers to his noble lineage in the speech to Aminta quoted earlier, and traces his ancestry back to the reconquest of Seville ('ganadores de Sevilla', III, 238). The emphasis here, as ter Horst points out, is on *patriarchal* lineage, in which women do not figure. Don Juan appears not to have any female relatives, and in particular we do not see his mother. Mothers rarely figured in the *comedia*, but the absence of the mother figure in *El burlador* highlights the idea that identity through lineage neglects the role of women; or, as ter Horst puts it, the female is no more than an empty vessel

---

[66] Sarah Kofman and Jean-Yves Masson, *Don Juan, ou le refus de la dette*, (Paris: Galilée, 1991), pp.17-20.
[67] Charles D.Presburg, 1995. '*El condenado por presumido*: the Rhetoric of Death and Damnation in *El burlador de Sevilla y convidado de piedra*', *Bulletin of the Comediantes* 47 (1995), 223-243; p.231.
[68] Robert ter Horst, 'Epic Descent: the Filiations of Don Juan', *MLN* 111 (1996), 255-274; p.257.

that permits the transfer of the patriarchal name from father to son.[69] Thus don Juan even acquires his name - Tenorio - at the expense of a woman - his mother, who remains unidentified.[70] However, don Juan's eventual insistence on the name inherited from his forefathers, which leads to his damnation, suggests that identity derived from patriarchal society is destructive; but while he derives his identity from seducing women, he continues secure in his career. Patriarchy and heritage do not provide a route to individuality.[71] The male individual is beginning at this point to distance himself from his family and assert himself as individual; and when he abandons this route to identity, resorting to claims of family name, heritage and social position, he damns himself in consequence.

To summarize, then, *El burlador* gives us the initial concept of don Juan as a character who derives his essential nature from his relationship with women: in this case he uses them in order to gain notoriety as a seducer and trickster. As long as he continues to assert his identity in this way he survives, eluding pursuit and justice. But once he begins to assert his identity through the *patriarchal* line of heritage, through his male kin rather than relationships with women, then he is quickly damned. Women rather than men are essential to his survival. Don Juan's need for women in order to maintain his own being resembles that of the vampire figure (such as Dracula), who feeds off the blood of women in particular in order

---

[69] ter Horst, 'Epic Descent', p.258.

[70] The question of the mother figure in Tirso and other plays draws attention to the possibility of Freudian readings of the don Juan figure, particularly when the question is perceived in conjunction with the murder of the 'father' - the Comendador - by the 'son', don Juan. I prefer to avoid a Freudian reading of don Juan for the reason that this tends to neglect the point of view of the women. For Freudian interpretations, see for example Peter Gay, 'The Father's Revenge', in *The Don Giovanni Book: Myths of Seduction and Betrayal*, ed. by Jonathan Miller, (London: Faber, 1990); Evans and Wade. Otto Rank takes a similar Freudian approach to *Don Giovanni*, but interprets the role of the woman more positively.

[71] By historical accident, the issue is further confused in that we cannot be clear about the name of don Juan's father. He is traditionally known as don Diego, but evidence suggests that he was at one point also called don Juan. In an exchange with Gaseno (II, 668-670), Catalinón declares his master to be the younger don Juan Tenorio and not the older one. In the alternative version of the play, *Tan largo me lo fiáis*, don Juan's father is called don Juan the elder. If both names are the same, then don Juan's individual identity depends even more on his seductive career.

to survive, with the result that the women die. (José Monleón specifically compares the vampire to Zorrilla's don Juan Tenorio).[72] Nonetheless, although don Juan maintains his identity by victimizing women regardless of who they are, he does not stress their lack of individuality in the manner of Mozart and da Ponte's catalogue aria, or Molière's speech (I, ii, quoted below) that argues that all women equally merit dom Juan's attention. The 'undifferentiation' of women in *El burlador* is left to other male characters. Octavio wails that 'la mujer más constante/es, en efeto, mujer' ('the most constant woman is still a woman', I, 357-8), Batricio says that Aminta 'al fin es mujer' ('after all is a woman', III, 86), and the King of Naples bemoans the fact that a man's honour rests on the behaviour of fickle women (I, 153-6). Isabela and Tisbea redress the balance somewhat when they comment: '¡Mal haya la mujer que en hombres fía!' ('Woe to the woman who trusts in men!', III, 402 and 408). And although they are all don Juan's victims, contributing to the maintenance of his fame as a trickster, the female characters of *El burlador* retain their own distinct personalities.

The same is true to some extent in Mozart and da Ponte's *Don Giovanni*, and don Giovanni establishes his career in a similar manner to the original don Juan, building up his reputation through victimizing women. Tirso's 'hombre sin nombre' reappears in a more fully developed form in *Don Giovanni*, though we have now lost the ancestral element, for this don Juan has no relatives. Again in *Don Giovanni*, the protagonist is a figure that lacks identity, who enters the stage without being immediately identified by name, and who indulges in disguise and masquerade. Mystery surrounds his identity from the first words he sings: 'Donna folle!..chi son io tu non saprai' ('Foolish woman!...you'll never know who I am', p.34) [73] - a comment reminiscent of the 'hombre sin nombre' of *El burlador*. We

---

[72] José B. Monleón, 'Vampiros y donjuanes (sobre la figura del seductor en el siglo XIX)', *Revista Hispánica Moderna* 48 (1995), 19-30; pp.25-6.

[73] All references to *Don Giovanni* are taken from Wolfgang Amadeus Mozart , *Il dissoluto punito*

can also perceive an indication of a problematic identity in the love of disguise, specifically in the Act II scene where don Giovanni and Leporello exchange clothes (p.272), and don Giovanni's subsequent impersonation of Leporello in the scene with Masetto (p. 289ff). Andrew Steptoe demonstrates that during ensembles, don Giovanni's voice emulates those of other singers, so that his own voice becomes difficult to distinguish from others: 'The hero's music inevitably blends with his antagonist's style rather than asserting a separate identity'.[74]

Bermard Williams has accurately observed that don Giovanni's identity lies purely in seduction, although he does not draw the consequent conclusion that women become essential to his character:

> The opera is named after him, it is about him, it is he who holds together a set of scenes in other ways rather disconnected. He is in a deep way the life of the opera, yet the peculiarity is that such character as he has is not really as grand as that implies; he expresses more than he is. He seems to have no depth adequate to the work in which he plays the central role. He has, in a sense, a character - to a considerable extent a bad one. But we are not given any deep insight into what he really is, or what drives him on. We could not have been: it is not that there is something hidden in his soul. It is notable that he has no self-reflective aria - he never sings about himself, as Mozart's other central characters do.[75] We have

ossia il don Giovanni, Neue Ausgabe sämtlicher Werke Serie II, Bühnenwerke Werkgruppe 5, Band 17 (Basle: Bärenreiter Kassel, 1968).

[74] Andrew Steptoe, The Mozart-Da Ponte Operas: the Cultural and Musical Background to 'Le nozze di Figaro', 'Don Giovanni' and 'Così fan tutte' (Oxford: Clarendon Press, 1991), p.202..

[75] Ironically, this lack of a major aria proved a point of complaint for the singer Luigi Bassi, who created the role of don Giovanni. As Sheila Hodges notes, Viennese opera singers tended to view opera as an opportunity to display their vocal skills, and took little interest in the dramatic implications of opera. Thus, in a sense don Giovanni's lack of identity was noted and strongly resisted by Bassi: it suggests how unusual such a concept was in eighteenth-century Viennese

no sense of what he is like when he is by himself. He is presented
always in action - the action, notoriously, of a seducer.[76]

Don Giovanni thus has no inherent character, except when he acts, and for him
action is seduction. To seduce, he requires women, which means that he cannot
establish his identity without them. But we also see in Leporello's catalogue aria
that to him all women are the same - they are all equally potential victims of his
seductive power.[77] By perceiving them thus, he reduces them to an
undifferentiated mass, neglecting any individual identity each woman might have.
Therefore we can conclude that don Giovanni, in order to establish his own
identity, cannot perceive any identity in women. Indeed, given his active career in
equating all women through his seduction, we might say that don Giovanni
actually tries to rob women of identity. He does not merely comprehend women
as all the same, but acts to ensure that they are. As Leporello emphasizes in the
catalogue aria:

> Non si picca se sia ricca,
> se sia brutta, se sia bella,
> se sia ricca, brutta, se sia bella:

---

opera. This in turn implies the indirect influence of earlier versions of the don Juan theme - and
particularly that of Tirso - on the plot. (Sheila, Hodges, *Lorenzo Da Ponte: the Life and Times of
Mozart's Librettist* (London: Granada, 1985), p.88).

[76] Bernard Williams, 'Don Giovanni as an Idea', in *W. A. Mozart: 'Don Giovanni'*, by Julian
Rushton (Cambridge: Cambridge University Press, 1981), 81-91, p.82.

[77] Robert Donington argues that don Giovanni's lists of conquests reveals an obsession for which
the mother takes the blame: ' Those whose early mothering has been psychologically satisfactory,
especially if supported by good fathering as well, are not prone to such indiscriminate
promiscuity, because they are capable of forming genuine relationships from which they are not
compelled to run away. Those whose sexual experience was ambivalent, perhaps because the
mother seemed at once dangerously possessive and unattainably seductive, may project this image
on to the women they meet, so that no genuine relationship can be allowed to take hold' (Robert
Donington, 'Don Giovanni Goes to Hell', *Musical Times* 122 (July 1981), 448-451; p.447). Such
an approach conveniently removes any responsibility from don Juan himself and makes the

purchè porti la gonnella

voi sapete quel che fa (Mozart, 88-9).[78]

For don Giovanni, women form an essential part of himself. Kristeva terms the women as components of his identity, observing that they lose their individuality.[79] The list that Leporello keeps of his master's conquests is a tangible record of don Giovanni's own character. Thus the latter cannot exist without women, and depends upon them for his own personality to survive. In his short song 'Deh, vieni', he serenades Elvira's maid in the following terms:

Deh vieni a consolar il pianto mio:

Se neghi a me di dar qualche ristoro,

davanti algi occhi tuoi morir vogl'io (Mozart, 286-7).[80]

Beneath the seductive rhetoric of this song lies a note of desperation: without a woman don Giovanni feels sorrowful and close to death. These words underline the true significance of women for the seducer, since he needs them in order to survive. Thus Kristeva points to his comment: 'Sai ch'elle per me son necessarie più del pan che mangio, più dell'aria che spiro!' ('You know that for me women are more necessary than the bread I eat or the air I breathe!', Mozart, 270-1). Women are not a pastime, but more essential than bread and air to ensure his survival. Again, then, he needs them to maintain his identity.[81]

---

mother culpable.

[78] 'It doesn't matter if she's fiery or rich, ugly or beautiful. Rich, ugly or beautiful, if she's got a skirt on, you know what he'll do'.

[79] Kristeva, p.245.

[80] 'Ah! Come and console my lamentation. If you deny me comfort I will die before your eyes'.

[81] Ironically, his need is echoed comically by Masetto, who needs Zerlina to heal the blows he has received from Giovanni. Zerlina, in the suggestive language of her aria 'Vedrai, carino' nevertheless acknowledges the healing, life-giving capacity of women: 'È un certo balsamo che porto addosso' ('It's a certain balm that I carry on me', Mozart, 304). This sense of woman as a restoring power will reappear more strongly in works such as Zorrilla's Don Juan Tenorio, but contrasts with the twentieth-century interpretations of Shaw and Frisch, where women are seen as dangerous and predatory.

Many commentators have pointed out that don Giovanni, despite his reputation and his list of conquests, does not have much success as a seducer during the course of the opera.[82] Rushton, however, reminds us of the need for Giovanni to *appear* to be a credible seducer,[83] and certainly he affects Zerlina powerfully. His seduction of her does not fail through lack of ability. As far as don Giovanni's identity is concerned, he is still seen by all as a womanizer with whom women are not safe, a reputation built up in part from the documented list of earlier victims, a list created before the action of the opera begins. The other characters equate him with the seduction of women, and from this he takes his identity. But the matter of success still has some relevance, nevertheless, since if don Giovanni is not successful he is developing his own personality upon a false premise. He identifies himself as a womanizer, but if he does not succeed in seducing, his claim is false. (Mozart and da Ponte were not, of course, the first to create an apparently unsuccessful don Juan - Molière's protagonist has equally little success. To have an unsuccessful seducer does avoid one problem of staging and presentation, however. All the plays considered here have this in common, the problem of presenting matters of sexuality to public view, at a time when it was unacceptable to stage the sexual act itself. A seducer who fails to seduce is one technique to avoid this difficulty.)

Don Giovanni gives particular emphasis to a feature that also occurs in Tirso and Molière, that don Juan's indiscriminate treatment of women surmounts the barriers of class. He seduces both noblewomen and peasants. The fact that he does not distinguish even by class reveals the extent to which women become undifferentiated in relation to him; but this has a particular resonance for Mozart and da Ponte's contemporary society. Nicholas Till observes that in an eighteenth-century context in particular, the erosion of rank would prove a serious challenge

---

[82] See, for example, Smeed, p.26.
[83] Rushton, pp.58ff.

to established society.[84] Don Giovanni's indiscriminate treatment of women therefore becomes a locus for tension within the class system, and by extension a locus for challenge to identity. Class status is one mark by which to distinguish people: without it, it is hard to tell one person from another. When don Giovanni renders all women equal through seduction, class distinction vanishes. Leporello sings:

> V'han fra queste contadine,
> cameriere e cittadine,
> v'han contesse, baronesse,
> marchesane, principesse,
> e v'han donne d'ogni grado... (Mozart, 79-80).[85]

The protagonists of *El burlador* and *Don Giovanni* therefore derive their identities from women in a similar manner: it is the seduction of women that provides them with fame and a career. But what of Molière? Of the six plays considered here, women feature least strongly in Molière's *Dom Juan*. Instead, we have what seems to be a long debate between dom Juan and his servant Sganarelle on the nature of religion and morality, punctuated by scenes of comedy that sometimes verge on the slapstick. Dom Juan undertakes little seduction, and spends more time perfecting a philosophy of seduction than putting it into practice. However, *Dom Juan* brings to the fore the idea that would later be 'celebrated' in Leporello's catalogue aria, the idea that women are all the same, indistinguishable. If this is true, there is little merit in being faithful to just one woman:

---

[84]Nicholas Till, *Mozart and the Enlightenment: Truth, Virtue and Beauty in Mozart's Operas* (London: Faber, 1992), p.204.

[85] 'Among them there are peasant women, maids and townswomen, countesses, baronesses, marchionesses and princesses; women of every rank'.

...la constance n'est bonne que pour des ridicules; toutes les belles ont droit de nous charmer, et l'avantage d'être rencontrée la première ne doit point dérober aux autres les justes prétentions qu'elles ont toutes sur nos cœurs. Pour moi, la beauté me ravit partout où je la trouve, et je cède facilement à cette douce violence dont elle nous entraîne. J'ai beau être engagé, l'amour que j'ai pour une belle n'engage point mon âme à faire injustice aux autres; je conserve des yeux pour voir le mérite de toutes, et rends à chacune les hommages et les tributs où la nature nous oblige. Quoi qu'il en soit, je ne puis refuser mon cœur à tout ce que je vois d'aimable; et dès qu'un beau visage me la demande, si j'en avais dix mille, je les donnerais tous (I, ii).[86]

The women's own individuality does not matter, because they are seen as women and nothing more. (Dom Juan's references to 'justes prétentions' and 'injustice' in the above speech to describe his indiscriminate treatment, suggest a certain irony: he has no real interest in the rights and just claims of women). What also seems clear, however, is that dom Juan does not need the presence of actual women in order to claim his title as a seducer; their mere existence suffices. Women provide the subject matter for dom Juan and Sganarelle's tales of seduction as well as for dom Juan's philosophy. In consequence, women again become indistinguishable: dom Juan treats them almost as an abstract concept rather than as distinct human beings. Their role as a theoretical idea therefore reduces them to Kierkegaard's notion of sheer womanhood, quoted above, and diminishes any sense that different women have different individual natures.

---

[86] '...faithfulness is only good for the ridiculous: all pretty women have the right to charm us, and the advantage of being first shouldn't rob other women of their just claims on our hearts...my love for one woman cannot force my soul to be unjust to the rest; I continue to see the merit of all women, and render to each the homage and tribute exhorted by nature...I cannot deny my heart to all those I find amiable, and if I had ten thousand hearts, I would give them all if a pretty face demanded it' All references come from [J.B.P. de] Molière, 'Dom Juan, ou le festin de pierre', Œuvres complètes, ed. by Georges Couton, vol. II (Paris: Gallimard, 1971).

Dom Juan sees himself as a conqueror like Alexander the Great, except that the new worlds he wishes to conquer are women's hearts:

> Enfin, il n'est rien de si doux que de triompher de la résistance d'une belle personne, et j'ai sur ce sujet l'ambition des conquérants, qui volent perpétuellement de victoire en victoire, et ne peuvent se résoudre à borner leurs souhaits. Il n'est rien qui puisse arrêter l'impétuosité de mes désirs: je me sens un cœur à aimer toute la terre; et comme Alexandre, je souhaiterais qu'il y eût d'autres mondes, pour y pouvoir étendre mes conquêtes amoureuses (I, ii).[87]

Dom Juan expresses his thoughts in more elevated tones, but his premise is not so far from that of Tirso's don Juan, whose greatest pleasure is to deceive women and deprive them of their honour (II, 269-272). The imagery of conquest, and the consequent notion that women are objects to be conquered like land (the countries conquered by Alexander) in itself suggests a negative attitude towards women; but dom Juan is reliant on such female conquests in order to style himself as a conqueror, as he does here. The desire to be a conqueror of women implies the need or availability of women to be conquered, and accentuates dom Juan's need of women in order to maintain his identity as a libertine.

Of the different don Juan plays, *Dom Juan* has become the specific focus for theories that deal with economic ideas of exchange, and, by extension, the use of language as a tool of exchange and promise.[88] In this context, social relations are

---

[87] 'After all, there is nothing as sweet as triumphing over the resistance of a beautiful woman, and on this point I am as ambitious as conquerors who continually flit from conquest to conquest and who cannot resolve to put a limit on their wishes. Nothing can stop the impetuousness of my desires: I feel I have a heart that could love the whole world; and like Alexander I would wish for other worlds in which to make more amorous conquests'.

[88] See Kofman and Masson; Felman; Michel Serres, *Hermes: Literature, Science, Philosophy*, ed. by J. V. Harari and David F. Bell, (Baltimore: Johns Hopkins University Press, 1982); J-P Dupuy, 'Quasi-objet et échange symbolique: de l'Alidor de Corneille au Dom Juan de Molière', *MLN* 104

interpreted in terms of indebtedness to others and of recompense. Exchange, in terms of a social or sexual relationship, becomes a question of each person's responsibility to the other. The theme of indebtedness arises from the opening speech of the play, Sganarelle's eulogy on tobacco, itself an image of trade and exchange. Sganarelle argues that 'le tabac inspire des sentiments d'honneur et de vertu à tous ceux qui en prennent' ('Tobacco inspires feelings of honour and virtue in all those who take it', I, i). It becomes clear from Sganarelle's speech that dom Juan does not conform to these ideas of exchange, and that women are his principal victims. He seduces women, but does not then 'pay what he owes' by marrying them. An immediate example allows Sganarelle to contrast his master with the principles he has just outlined: he confesses to Gusman that he fears that done Elvire will be 'mal payée de son amour', badly paid for her love. Dom Juan's inability to fulfil his promise is described in economic terms. Sganarelle also uses economic terms to comment on dom Juan's attitude to marriage: 'Un mariage ne lui coûte rien à contracter' ('It costs him nothing to contract a marriage', I, i). He juxtaposes his opening comments on tobacco and right living with fears concerning done Elvire's poor return for her love. In this context, Jean-Marie Apostolidès argues that dom Juan:

> ...transforms people into merchandise, he attributes a quantifiable
> value to them, and he makes them circulate. This process of market
> transformation manifests itself in his relationships as seducer with
> women. What he says about them boils down to this: all women
> are equal and cannot be distinguished except by the time required
> to conquer them.[89]

(1989), 757-786. Not everyone agrees fully with such a reading of Molière. Mandrell, in reference to such theories, argues that both Tirso and Molière wrote before contemporary terms of exchange had been fully developed, so that older systems of sexual arrangement had not yet been superseded. Instead, women became the tokens of exchange through which patriarchy dominated society. Dom Juan nevertheless remains outside this form of exchange as well.

[89] Jean-Marie Apostolidès, 'Molière and the Sociology of Exchange', *Critical Inquiry* 14 (1988),

54

Again we find the element of equation that renders all women as indistinguishable. However, while the theme of exchange is indeed a principal one within the play, commentators tend to overlook the fact that the marriage contract does not conform exactly to the tenets of trade and exchange, because this particular transaction is only supposed to occur once and exclude the possibility of further exchanges. Marriage distinguishes and prefers one woman from all the others. This, of course, runs counter to dom Juan's avowed attitudes towards women quoted above. He uses the promise of marriage, not to distinguish women, but to equate them and thus render them indistinguishable.

From the above it should be clear that in the earlier works don Juan bases his identity on the seduction of women, and thus the women he seduces prove essential to the definition of his identity. Women, however, also have a function in other contexts where he might claim identity, such as lineage, the undermining of class distinctions, and social forms of exchange. Although don Juan cannot in a sense exist without the female characters, his need of them is not necessarily benign. His exploitation of women to obtain his own identity has the intention of depriving them of their own individuality, making them 'all the same' regardless of appearance or social status. The don Juans of the earlier plays therefore share a common attitude towards their female victims, although each dramatist develops this attitude in distinct ways. The later plays, however, reveal a move away from the automatic connection of women with seduction, to suggest fresh ways in which women could contribute to the formulation of don Juan's individuality.

477-492; p.488.

The later plays

In contrast to the earlier plays, the protagonists of the later plays are in quest of more than new victims to add to their lists of conquests. The Romantic era, as we saw in the previous chapter, introduced a more elevated sense of don Juan as a man in search of an ideal. This idealism persists even in twentieth-century works such as the two considered here. Thus don Juan ceases to be merely a seducer, and approaches closer to the notion of a hero in all senses of the word. Nevertheless, his career remains bound up with women in one way or another and, as we shall see, they still contribute to the realization of his identity. What has changed is the way in which the authors present this concept to us.

The opening of *Don Juan Tenorio* apparently takes us away from the notion of women as literally 'character-forming' and seemingly reverts to identity derived through lineage and inheritance. Don Juan, in common with other plays, possesses two father figures, his own natural father and don Gonzalo, his prospective father-in-law. The opposition between fathers and son occupies a primary space in the opening act in the inn, where don Diego and don Gonzalo listen in secret to don Juan's recital of his misdeeds. In rage at what they hear, they both denounce don Juan, and while don Diego refuses to acknowledge his son any more, don Gonzalo breaks off the engagement between don Juan and doña Inés. By doing so they take from don Juan his claim to his name and inheritance (a fact reflected in don Diego's subsequent dedication of his estate to a pantheon into which don Juan is forbidden entry, as the sculptor elucidates in the opening scene of Part 2. Don Juan loses his inheritance literally as well as figuratively).

The argument of ter Horst is that the weakness of the older generation in control of the younger, results in a loss of identity for the son. The picture of the father proves valueless, so that the son cannot understand himself as son, and thus loses a sense of identity and position in the world.[90] The first act demonstrates the inability of father and son to recognize each other. Don Juan does not perceive his father behind the masked figure in the inn until he rips the mask away, while his father tells him: 'no te conozco, don Juan' ('I do not recognize you, don Juan', 767).[91] According to ter Horst, don Juan reacts in the manner of a spoilt bourgeois child trying to gain his father's attention in any way possible. When this fails, he turns to don Gonzalo, begging for his authority: 'en tu casa viviré,/ tú gobernarás mi hacienda/ diciéndome: *esto ha de ser*' ('I will live in your home, you will control my estate, telling me: *this is how it must be*', 2517-2519). The humility before don Gonzalo suggests his need for a father figure who will confer identity upon him by recognizing him in the way his own father has refused to do.[92] Don Gonzalo refuses to grant him forgiveness and authority, however, and instead threatens and harangues him. Eventually don Juan will shoot him.

From the above it should be clear that the two father figures of don Diego and don Gonzalo deny don Juan any identity; but this is not the only way which the opening act brings the protagonist's individuality into question. The character of don Luis Mejía also undermines don Juan's identity by being his virtual double.

---

[90] Robert ter Horst, 'Ritual Time Regained in Zorrilla's *Don Juan Tenorio*', *Romanic Review* 70 (1979), 80-93; p.87.

[91] References come from José Zorrilla, *Don Juan Tenorio*, ed. by David T. Gies (Madrid: Castalia, 1994).

[92] Zorrila's don Gonzalo denies don Juan identity, but in terms of donjuanian discourse he confirms it. One of the few motifs that Zorrilla takes from the don Juan tradition is the statue of don Gonzalo, this time surrounded by the other principal characters in statue form. Only don Gonzalo's statue, however, comes to the obligatory supper scene. This statue resembles many of the other statues that appear in don Juan plays, and in the supper scene and the final encounter in the graveyard (until Inés's appearance) Zorrilla conforms closely to the usual format. Thus ironically, while the son appears to lose his name and thus identity as a result of his father's disinheritance, the father-figure of the statue confers on don Juan his identity within donjuanian discourse. This point can only be perceived in terms of the don Juan genre as a whole, yet *Don Juan Tenorio* occurred at a point when writers had already begun to use the story in a self-conscious fashion. Christopher Soufas suggests that the pantheon symbolizes the don Juan tradition, and observes the fact that don Juan's own statue is included in the cast of statues. The sculptor, in this interpretation, represents Zorrilla. (C. Christopher Soufas, 'The Sublime, the Beautiful and the Imagination in Zorrilla's *Don Juan Tenorio*'. *MLN* 110 (1995), 302-319; pp.312 and 314).

The two characters are hard to distinguish: they have led parallel lives as a result of their bet a year before the play begins, and have drawn up similar lists of their exploits. As the play progresses, the two characters continue to act as mirror images, performing duplicate actions, such as arranging for each other to be taken to prison. On occasion they even use exactly the same words, as for example in their speeches describing their notoriety: 'la razón atropellé,/la virtud escarnecí,/a la justicia burlé,/y a las mujeres vendí' ('I disregarded reason, I scoffed at virtue, I cheated justice and I betrayed women', 502-5 and 612-5). Or they may have parallel conversations which follow the same pattern, as when don Luis talks to Ana and don Juan talks to Lucia (1152-61 and 1416-25).[93] Feal suggests that while Mejía resembles don Juan, he proposes to change: he plans to marry, and thus will reintegrate himself into the social order.[94] But this does not in fact distinguish the two characters, for don Juan was betrothed to Inés at the beginning of the play and we have no indication that he does not plan to marry likewise. Indeed, the first action of don Juan's that we witness is his writing of a letter to the woman he was intended to marry. Thus even on this point the two characters reflect each other: they are both engaged to be married, despite their dissolute lives.

Traditionally don Juan is a solitary character directly opposed to established social norms. He remains alone outside accepted social spheres. In *Don Juan*

---

[93] The similarity of the two characters provides the primary example of Zorrilla's taste for doubling throughout the first act (though as the plot develops the tendency grows less and less). Doubling also occurs with don Gonzalo and don Diego, who enter the inn in similar fashion and react in a similar manner to don Juan's tales of his exploits. Both will also 'disinherit' him in some manner; don Diego by using the land his son would inherit to create the pantheon of statues in the second part, don Gonzalo by depriving him of Inés, who might lead him to a divine 'inheritance' of salvation and redemption. Other pairs of characters who behave in similar fashion are the two friends Centellas and Avellaneda, as well as the two servants Ciutti and Gastón. Only male characters are doubled, however: this might perhaps suggest that the struggle over identity is only a male concern. We could interpret this positively - women have no problem with their identity; or negatively - women's identity does not matter. Don Juan is the only male character to break free from his pairing and survive as a separate individual.

Tenorio the protagonist has a challenger, someone who claims to be as bad as he is. If this were to prove true, then only his name and the notoriety that goes with it (inherited from previous don Juans) distinguishes him from his rival. In the bet, his identity is at stake. We have seen that don Juans usually make use of women in order to provide themselves with some form of identity. They create an identity for themselves as a seducer by equating and undifferentiating all women, making them act in the same way. If we accept that traditionally (i.e. as in the earlier works) don Juan acquires identity only through his reputed exploitation of women, then Mejía as his double proves a further threat to his identity, and must be competed with and beaten, for Mejía also claims to seduce women and uses this fact to maintain *his* reputation. The seduction of Ana therefore acquires a further significance, since through seducing her don Juan reinforces his identity as a seducer and simultaneously deprives don Luis of *his* identity. The rivalry ends when don Juan kills don Luis. With don Luis' death, don Juan has won the struggle between the two characters over identity, and his wild exploits cease at this point.[95]

Don Juan's relations with don Gonzalo, don Diego and don Luis suggest that patriarchy fails to provide him with any sense of individuality: he must struggle against other men in order to define himself. Women, on the other hand, play their part in his efforts to establish identity. Inés fulfils the principal function here, through her association with don Juan's quest for salvation. Don Juan sees her as the path towards which his life may be redeemed and saved, and we can perceive this as simultaneously a quest for identity. His relationship with his *doppelgänger* Mejía therefore acquires renewed significance. In the first scenes the two libertines reflect each other exactly, but don Juan breaks away from this pairing at

---

[94] Carlos Feal, *En nombre de Don Juan: estructura de un mito literario*, (Amsterdam: John Benjamins, 1984), p.37,

[95] Inés must also, of course, influence don Juan's tamer lifestyle from this point since, as he admits in the second part, he has thought of her ever since he fled after killing don Luis and don Gonzalo.

the point at which he begins to desire Inés and searches for salvation. Thus his search for salvation is inseparable from his search for identity.

Men have refused to respond to don Juan's need both for identity and for salvation - don Gonzalo dismisses him with the remark '¿Y qué tengo yo, don Juan/ con tu salvación que ver?' (2554-5). Don Juan believes, however, that Inés represents his chance of salvation:

> No es, doña Inés, Satanás
> quien pone este amor en mí:
> es Dios, que quiere por ti
> ganarme para *Él* quizás (2264-7).[96]

If don Gonzalo denies don Juan possession of Inés, he will simultaneously deprive him of redemption, as don Juan desperately proclaims:

> Míralo bien, don Gonzalo;
> que vas a hacerme perder
> con ella hasta la esperanza
> de mi salvación tal vez (2550-3).[97]

To which don Gonzalo replies that don Juan's salvation has nothing to do with him, as we saw earlier. Thus men strip don Juan of individuality and recognition and disinherit him; he becomes lost, cast out from society. A woman, however, can grant him the opportunity to be 'found' again, to be recognized by the ultimate authority of God the Father. In this way don Juan again finds identity, and salvation, by means of a woman. Again women play a vital role in establishing

---

[96] 'Doña Inés, it is not Satan who instils this love in me but God, who wishes perhaps to save me for himself through you.'
[97] 'Think of it, don Gonzalo, that along with her you may make me lose hope of my salvation'.

the protagonist's individuality, but now Zorrilla casts the search for identity in Romantic terms.

We might at first think that Zorrilla's treatment of Inés suggests a positive approach on the part of the author: how much better to be don Juan's means of salvation than his victim! But in reality the effect of such a treatment is not so benign. Inés herself becomes a sacrifice for don Juan's redemption,[98] and, in a dubious piece of theology, her own salvation will depend on what don Juan decides to do on the point of death. Her fate is dependent on his. She must stake her own soul on that of a notorious profligate; and since Zorrilla bestows upon Inés a powerful aura of saintliness and purity, the implication is that this is what a good woman does. Given the association here of salvation with identity, we could say that a good women risks her soul – her own *identity* - in order to preserve that of the man.

The other female characters also contribute to the realization of don Juan's identity by facilitating his conquest either of Inés, thus leading to his eventual salvation, or of Ana, thus helping him to defeat Mejía and ward off the latter's challenge to his identity. Brígida's main function is to facilitate the meeting of the two lovers, while the abbess serves to heighten the sense that Inés does not belong in a convent. (Inés comments of the abbess: 'en sus pláticas hallé,/ si no enojosos discursos,/ a lo menos aridez', 1525-7).[99] Ana's seduction, on the other hand, allows don Juan to defeat don Luis in the struggle between the two men, and Lucía facilitates the seduction of her mistress. The incident concerning Ana allows don Juan supremacy over don Luis and thus claim to the title of profligate, much in the manner of earlier plays. This victory also helps don Juan to assert his identity in response to the challenge of don Luis. Don Juan, in his description at

---

[98] As suggested by Héctor Romero, 'Consideraciones teológicas sobre la muerte de Don Juan en la obra de Zorrilla', *Hispanófila* 54 (1975), 9-16; p.16.
[99] I found her chats very dry if not irritating'.

the inn of his seductive career, incidentally repeats the motif found in the catalogue aria of *Don Giovanni*, that even class cannot distinguish women:

> Desde la princesa altiva
> a la que pesca en ruin barca,
> no hay hembra a quien no subscriba (486-8).[100]

This summary - reminiscent of don Juan's career in *El burlador* - reinforces the concept, seen in earlier works and most vividly in *Don Giovanni*, that women are all the same, and have no individuality.

This Romantic play sees the protagonist move *towards* a woman in the search for individuality. The modern versions of Shaw and Frisch see the don Juan figure attempt to move *away* from women in order to establish an individual identity. Both these don Juans attempt to attain an abstract ideal - the superman in the case of Shaw, geometry in that of Frisch - and women appear opposed to, and thus excluded from, such ideals. In *Man and Superman*, John Tanner attempts to elude the bourgeois constraints of marriage in order to pursue his philosophical ideals; while in *Don Juan oder die Liebe zur Geometrie* don Juan prefers the study of geometry to dalliance with women. Women do not, therefore, contribute to the protagonist's identity in the same way as in the early works and even in Zorrilla: they are not the seduced victims or the means of redemption. Nevertheless, they provide an essential contribution to the formation of the protagonist's individuality, by *opposing* the quest for identity. In both of the modern plays, don Juan struggles against the women in order to assert himself, and his identity is seen in contrast to them rather than derived from them. Without the female characters, there is no conflict. The presence of the female characters brings out

---

[100] 'From the haughty princess to the woman fishing in a little boat, there is no woman who would not agree'.

his personality in greater relief. What has changed, however, is that both don Juans see women as opponents rather than victims, and such an attitude gives rise to a more overtly hostile attitude on the part of the protagonists. Women have become threatening to them.

We have moved far from the original - and popular - notion of don Juan as seducer. In *Man and Superman*, John Tanner does not seduce: he prefers to flee, and only surrenders at the end because he finds the power of women - a manifestation of what Shaw calls the life force - irresistible. Nevertheless, women still define his career for him. His primary function is to be Ann's husband and father to her children, and his philosophy and revolutionary pretensions cannot help him to avoid this fate. Ann will thus allow him to 'go on talking', indulging his revolutionary beliefs, at the end of the play for, since he will now marry her, he may otherwise do as he pleases. She is indifferent to his philosophy, but not as to whether he marries her. Her comment further suggests that his 'talk' - his revolutionary philosophy - is ultimately meaningless. It has already fallen a victim to the life force that women embody, the female need to reproduce at whatever cost and the ruthlessness of women in their achievement of this aim.

Don Juan/John Tanner does not, however, perceive his identity in terms of women. On the contrary, the impulse to escape female clutches reflects his desire to establish an identity *separate* from woman, and from the society around him which women control. Perhaps his entire career as a revolutionary philosopher springs from this need to be different. As Tanner grew up and became aware of his own distinct identity he withdrew his confidences from Ann, in order to be able to maintain his soul, his identity, separate from female influence:

Tanner [enigmatically]: It happened just then that I got something that I   wanted to keep all to myself instead of sharing it with you.

Ann: I am sure I shouldnt have asked for any of it if you had grudged it.

Tanner: It wasnt a box of sweets, Ann. It was something youd never have let me call my own.

Ann [incredulously]: What?

Tanner: My soul (Shaw, 34).[101]

Don Juan, the *alter ego* of Tanner who appears in the Hell scene of Act III, also touches on the need for separation from women in order to maintain male identity: he loses mastery of himself only once he has experience of women:

Up to that moment [involvement with Woman] I had never lost the sense of being my own master; never consciously taken a single step until my reason had examined and approved it. I had come to believe that I was a purely rational creature: a thinker! I said, with the foolish philosopher, 'I think; therefore I am.' It was Woman who taught me to say 'I am; therefore I think' (p.113).

In this speech, man and woman are opposed in terms of rational thought and living experience. Shaw's emphasis on the female desire to reproduce tends to exclude women's capacity for rational thought. Women embody the Life Force, the basic need to exist and be, for which rationality has not much relevance. Thus Ann can ignore Tanner's philosophy - 'I dont mind your queer opinions one little bit' (p.38) - because they are to her irrelevant. They do not deflect her from her purpose. Men, on the other hand, may occupy the realm of rational thought if they wish, and thus possess the capacity to be the Nietzschean superman of the play's title. Therefore don Juan, as he follows the path to Heaven and the hope of the superman, takes a path that Ana cannot follow: 'I can find my own way to

---

[101] References come from Bernard Shaw, 1931. *Man and Superman: a Comedy and a Philosophy* (London: Constable, 1931). All quotations from Shaw retain his own spelling and punctuation.

Heaven, Ana; not yours' (p. 129). The course of *Man and Superman* follows Tanner's increasingly vain attempts to maintain his separate identity through the realm of philosophy and rational thought. At the end of the play he has failed: he will marry, and become the servant of woman for the purpose of parenthood, like other men. Nonetheless, his philosophical goal is clearly defined in contrast to the aim of the women: and the emphasis on the specifically masculine sphere of the rational excludes women. They do not have access to the higher, rational sphere; and this implies that Tanner/don Juan views them rather negatively.

The question of separate male identity is encapsulated in the matter of the superman. Don Juan's quest for higher forms of life in Heaven is a quest to become a superman:

> I tell you that as long as I can conceive something better than myself I cannot be easy unless I am striving to bring it into existence or clearing the way for it. That is the law of my life. That is the working within me of Life's incessant aspiration to higher organization, wider, deeper, intenser self-consciousness, and clearer self-understanding (p.123).

The value of the superman is ambiguous. The Devil remarks: 'Beware of the pursuit of the Superhuman: it leads to an indiscriminate contempt for the Human' (p.129). Carl Henry Mills and Alfred Turco believe that we should not overestimate Shaw's reliance on Nietzsche's philosophy for his superman motif, since Shaw did not accept the elitism inherent in Nietzsche's notion of the superman.[102] We might remember in this context the portrait of Tanner's chauffeur Straker, and the favourable (or perhaps patronizing?) impression Shaw gives of the 'ordinary' man. But a different form of elitism is involved here,

---

[102] Carl Henry Mills, 'Shaw's Superman: a Re-examination', *Shaw Review* 13 (1970), 48-58; Alfred Turco, *Shaw's Moral Vision: the Self and Salvation* (Ithaca: Cornell University Press, 1976).

however, in which Shaw elevates the rational, philosophical mind of the male over the procreative purposes of the female. Women create men, but men create supermen. Mills argues that the superman 'creates new mind as surely as any woman creates new men'.[103] Women, as we have seen, are excluded in a sphere where reason, not nature, holds sway; and there is no suggestion that women, too, could aspire to the status of superman. On the contrary, don Juan explicitly tells Ana that she cannot follow the same path as he does, as we saw above (Shaw, 129). Women are essential to the Life Force, but their role is still confined to the traditional one of motherhood: they cannot achieve the 'higher' aims of the men. Tanner perceives the forging of the higher, male identity to be feasible only apart from the influence of women and the sphere of gender relations.

Shaw's don Juan/John Tanner thus suggests a move towards a more overtly hostile approach to women. There is no suggestion in the three early plays that men and women occupy distinct spheres, or that the masculine sphere is necessarily a more elevated one than that of the feminine. Moreover, the earlier plays do not share the same insistence of *Man and Superman* on the need for women to confine themselves to their traditional role of motherhood - motherhood, indeed, is scarcely mentioned at all. Yet even Tanner's supposedly revolutionary philosophy enshrines the idea of motherhood, as we can see from his celebration of Violet as a prospective unmarried mother:

> ...she has turned...to the fulfilment of her highest purpose and greatest function - to increase, multiply, and replenish the earth (pp.25-6).

Further hostility is indicated in the perception of Tanner/don Juan that women actively hinder the male individual's pursuit of a higher form of life. Tanner, by trying to flee Ann, implies that the aims of women, marriage and motherhood,

---

[103] Mills, 'Shaw's Superman', p.55

impede a man such as himself from achieving his own higher purposes. He sees women as a threat to himself, describing them as predatory creatures; an idea echoed by don Juan:

> Then the lady, who had been happy and idle enough before, became anxious, preoccupied with me, always intriguing, conspiring, pursuing, watching, waiting, bent wholly on making sure of her prey: I being the prey, you understand (p.112).

This is a far more malign attitude than that of Tirso, Molière or Mozart/da Ponte. A further point to observe here is that women again appear undifferentiated. All women have the same purpose and act in a similar ruthless manner. *Man and Superman*, then, encompasses the opposition of the individual man and the monstrous regiment of women whose own individualities become subordinate to their procreative role.

Of all the dramatists discussed here, however, Frisch is the author that takes the question of the protagonist's identity to its most complex level. In the 'Nachträgliches' that follows the play's printed text, Frisch refers directly to the individual's - don Juan's - troubled sense of male identity:

> Seine Männlichkeit bewegt sich auf der Grenze und ist ihm nichts Selbstverständliches, sondern etwas Kostabares, was er besitzt, also nicht ersetzen muß durch soldatische Pose beispielweise, aber er muß sie verteidigen; seine Männlichkeit ist etwas Gefährdetes (Frisch, pp.168-9).[104]

---

[104] 'His masculinity is pushed to the limit: to him it is not self-evident but a precious possession, so that he cannot replace it with, for example, a military pose: instead he must defend it. His masculinity is under threat'. All qutations come from Frisch, *Gesammelte Werke in zeitlicher Folge*, III, 95-175, ed. by Hans Mayer (Frankfurt: Suhrkamp, 1976).

Here Frisch expresses the growing problematization of individual, male identity which is no longer self-evident but which must be defended. The male individual feels threatened. Identity - a popular theme with Frisch, who featured it in other works such as his novel *Stiller* and his play *Andorra* - features as one of the principal themes of his don Juan play. The depiction of a problematized male identity has particular resonance within the don Juan theme as it has played itself out over time, as Michael Butler observes: 'Durch ein erneut kritisches Durchleuchten einer beliebten Mythe also glaubt Frisch die Deformation der zeitgenössischen Gesellschaft und deren tödliche Auswirkungen auf das Individuum aufzeigen zu können'.[105] Frisch explicitly recognizes the don Juan phenomenon as a field for the questioning of male identity, given not only the troubling nature of gender relations, as we shall see below, but because of preceonceived notions of a don Juan's personality.

The question of don Juan's identity asserts itself from the beginning of *Don Juan oder die Liebe zur Geometrie*, in the first exchange of dialogue:

> *Donna Elvira:* Don Juan? Don Juan?
> *Donna Inez:* Kein Mensch ist hier. (p. 97).

When donna Inez says that nobody is there, her remark suggests the absence of identity that has always been central to the struggle of the protagonist in the don Juan tradition, as has been noted above. When Elvira insists that Juan's horse is in the stable, Inez replies: 'Sie täuschen sich ganz gewiß, Donna Elvira. Was soll ein

---

[105] 'Frisch believed he could demonstrate the distortion of contemporary society and its fatal consequences for the individual, by means of a critical investigation of a popular myth'. Michael Butler, 'Die Flucht in die Abstraktion: zu Max Frischs *Don Juan oder die liebe zur Geometrie*', in *Frischs 'Don Juan oder die Liebe zur Geometrie'*, ed. by Walter Schmitz, (Frankfurt: Suhrkamp, 1985), p. 289.

Mensch in dieser Finsternis?' (ibid).[106] Inez's remarks imply an absence, and therefore a lack of identity; and it is significant that a female character comments on the absence of the central character. Ironically don Juan is in fact present at this scene but as yet unnoticed and unidentified, described in the stage instructions only as 'der junge Mann' (ibid). In the first act, everybody awaits his arrival, eager to welcome him as don Juan, but they do not recognize him. The opening moments of the play herald don Juan's identity crisis that will prove central to the play.

An apparent lack of identity, of presence, does not prevent the other characters from defining the protagonist for themselves and imposing on don Juan the identity they themselves wish to confer. Thus they will hail him as a sexual seducer and heroic crusading warrior while neglecting all the evidence to the contrary. As Butler observes, society wishes to bestow labels which he will do his utmost to deny: 'Eine ganze Reihe Namen werden ihm aufgezwungen, um ihn in den konventionellen Denksystem der Gesellschaft festzuhalten: Bräutigam, Ritter, Held, dann später, Verführer, Schänder, Mörder'.[107] These labels are a convenient way of identifying don Juan, but no one will give him the label he wants, that of a master of geometry. Thus when don Gonzalo lauds his achievement at the crusades, he heralds him as a hero, unaware of his geometrical exploits.

In an early work such as *El burlador*, don Juan takes his identity directly from the women through his seduction of them - therein lies his claim to the title of *burlador*. But in *Don Juan oder die Liebe zur Geometrie* it is the women themselves who insist on don Juan's identity as a seducer, and they are the ones who distinguish him from the rest of society, the weak, ineffectual and often

---

[106] 'You're deceiving yourself for sure, donna Elvira. What would anyone be doing in this darkness?'

[107] 'A whole series of names are forced upon him, in order to fix him in society's conventional way of thinking: bridegroom, knight, hero, then later on seducer, disgrace, murderer'. Butler, 'Die

impotent men. We have in a sense come full circle from Tirso: the female characters of Frisch combine to create the notion of a great seducer just as Tirso's women do. The difference is that the women of Frisch take the initiative and deliberately set out to do this. They foist an individual personality of their own creation on to an unwilling protagonist. Frisch claims that don Juan, generically, is an intellectual, and that his fame as a seducer lies entirely in the minds of women:

> Sein Ruhm als Verführer (der ihn als Ruhm begleitet, ohne daß er sich selbst mit diesem Ruhm identifiziert) ist ein Mißverständnis seitens der Damen. Don Juan ist ein Intellektueller, wenn auch von gutem Wuchs und ohne alles Brillenhafte. Was ihn unwiderstehlich macht für die Damen von Sevilla, ist durchaus seine Geistigkeit, sein Anspruch auf eine männliche Geistigkeit, die ein Affront ist, indem sie ganz andere Ziele kennt als die Frau und die Frau von vornherein als Episode einsetzt - mit dem bekannten Ergebnis freilich, daß die Episode schließlich sein ganzes Leben verschlingt (p.168).[108]

This passage from Frisch's afterword suggests that women bear the blame for miscasting don Juan as a seducer.[109] They have misunderstood his nature. More specifically, women have awarded him his fame: it is a misattribution on their part. It is significant that Frisch argues that don Juan does not *identify* himself

---

Flucht in die Abstraktion', p.293.

[108] 'His fame as a seducer (a fame that accompanies him although he does not identify with it) is a misunderstanding on the part of the women. Don Juan is an intellectual, although of good stature and not bookish. What makes him irresistible for the women of Seville is precisely his intellectuality, his claim to a masculine intellect, which is an affront because it acknowledges other aims than women, and fits women in as episodes – and indeed with the well-known result, that the episodes eventually devour his whole life'.

[109] Frisch also argues here that women find don Juan's very intellectualism attractive. The corollary here is that women themselves have no pretensions to intellect, so that don Juan's quest for intellectual achievement indeed becomes an affront to them. Again, women are all equated.

with his reputation - 'ohne daß er sich selbst mit diesem Ruhm identifiziert'. The notion that women wilfully misinterpret don Juan's essential nature indicates that the female characters, though not perhaps unsympathetic in themselves, exercise a power that is ultimately negative and detrimental to masculine individuality.

According to Frisch in the above passage, don Juan is not a seducer so much as an intellectual, and in the play the intellectualism of don Juan manifests itself in the pursuit of geometry. Don Juan uses geometry as a tool to evade the attempts of Seville to impose identity on him. The beauty of geometry lies in the irrelevance of human identity: 'was heute gilt, das gilt auch morgen, und wenn ich nicht mehr atme, es gilt ohne mich, ohne euch' (p.132).[110] Frisch introduces a new concept: individual identity is something to be avoided at all costs, and a lack of identity is an ideal worth pursuing. While don Juan wishes to cast off the label of seducer imposed on him, he does not want to establish his own distinct personality. Rather, he wishes to have no identity at all, and his study of geometry is an assertion of his desire to have none. He equates geometry with anonymity and with an absence of women, as when he asks the Bishop of Cordoba to provide him refuge in a monastery: 'allda lebe ich mit Brot und Wein, namenlos, vom Weib verschont, still und zufrieden mit meiner Geometrie' (p.147).[111] (Ironically, this image will reappear, distorted, in his eventual life with Miranda: he lives quietly and anonymously, but he cannot study and the wine represents his alcoholism). Butler is therefore wrong to argue that don Juan fears losing his identity: on the contrary, in many ways he longs to lose it.[112] Masculine individuality has now become a burden for him, and his troubled sense of identity will express itself in his fear of women and his desire to be free of them. Peter

---

[110] 'What is valid today is also valid tomorrow, and when I no longer breathe it is valid, without me, without you'.
[111] 'There I could live on bread and wine, nameless, free from women, quiet and content with my geometry'.

Ruppert suggests that don Juan's passion for geometry lies partly in the fact that he wishes to evade choice.[113] The absoluteness of geometry precludes choice: 'Unentrinnbar wie ein Schicksal...So und nicht anders! sagt die Geometrie' (p.132).[114] When he is forced to choose - and the decisions he must make always concern women - he makes disastrous choices. Choice again suggests identity, for to choose means to assert one's own individuality in some measure; and again women are to be found at this moment in which identity is called into question. Don Juan's retreat into geometry is an attempt to evade the need for choice that occurs in his dealings with women (in particular, when he must choose between the dead Anna and the 'living' Anna impersonated by Miranda) and thus the need to assert his identity. The irony is that geometry ultimately provides no escape from his identity crisis, as Butler notes.[115] Even his geometrical feats that allow him to work out the measurement of the Moorish fortress result in a proposed marriage to Anna[116] - thus the flight into geometrical study cannot protect him from, and indeed eventually leads him directly to, the gender relations that bring his own individuality into question.

Frisch makes clear a link between a sense of male identity and a fear of gender relations. Juan equates the demand for identity with the demands of women, an idea also expressed by Frisch in the passage quoted above. The sense still remains in *Don Juan oder die Liebe zur Geometrie,* as it did in *Man and Superman,* that women hinder the higher designs of men. Don Juan believes that masculinity is by definition the pursuit of some goal other than women, and the consequent

---

[112] Michael Butler, *The Plays of Max Frisch* (London: Macmillan, 1985).This suggests a further parallel with Tirso: in *El burlador* don Juan does not identify himself until he encouters the statue at supper, and prefers to disguise himself rather than seduce under his own name.

[113] Peter Ruppert, 'Max Frisch's Don Juan: the Seduction of Geometry', *Monatshefte* 67 (1975), 236-248.

[114] 'Inevitable as fate..thus and not otherwise! says geometry'.

[115] Butler, 'Die Flucht in die Abstaktion', p.294.

[116] See Johannes Werner, 'Ein trauriger Held: Vorgeschichte und thematische Einheit von Max Frischs *Don Juan oder die Liebe zur Geometrie',* in *Frischs 'Don Juan oder die Liebe zur Geometrie',* ed. by Walter Schmitz (Frankfurt: Suhrkamp, 1985), p. 276.

devaluation of the latter: 'jeder Mann hat etwas Höheres als das Weib, wenn er wieder nüchtern ist' (p.121).[117] The use of the word 'nüchtern', sober, implies its opposite, drunk, which in turn indicates a loss of control, similar to the surrender of power to the women. Don Juan also equates the pursuit of geometry with his masculine nature. Having jilted Anna and passed a night of indiscriminate seduction, he can now dispense with female contact and dedicate himself to geometry, which he describes in terms of freedom and masculinity: '...meine Hochzeit ist erledigt. Ich fühle mich frei wie noch nie...leer und wach und voll Bedürfnis nach männlicher Geometrie' (p.131).[118] His rejection of women in favour of geometry confers not only anonymity but masculine status upon him: 'Ich bin ein Mann geworden' (ibid). References to the end of youth underline don Juan's 'accession' to manhood. He tells Roderigo that love is over for him and that it was a short youth (p.134), and later he says that his night of seduction enabled him to kill and bury whatever was 'kindisch', childish (p.135). His rejection of gender relations allows him to perceive himself as an adult male.

The women are again inevitably equated and thus undifferentiated by the fact that don Juan treats them all in the same manner. Their distinct identities carry no significance for him. On this point he does not differ from the other male characters, who also fail to distinguish between women. Even Celestina echoes this idea: 'Frauen von jeglichem Alter und von jeglicher Bereitschaft, verheiratete, unverheiratete, was einer nur will' (p.110).[119] Her remark implies the undifferentiation between women: age and marital status are irrelevant. Thus don Juan confuses his bride with a prostitute. A further equating element is that many of the women sooner or later become widows, usually when their husbands attempt to avenge themselves on don Juan. The image of the widow suggests

---

[117] 'Every man has something higher than woman, if he regains his sobriety'.
[118] '...My wedding's sorted out. I feel free as never before...empty and awake and needful of masculine geometry'.
[119] 'Women of every age and degree of willingness, married, unmarried, whatever you want'.

Shavian overtones of the female predator, and thus don Juan perceives them as they cluster round him, making their demands. The complaint of donna Belisa, that she is the only woman present who is not a widow (p.153), is duly comic, but we may comprehend an underlying suggestion of women's inherently predatory and pathological nature. It is thus no accident that Miranda herself becomes a widow, and the 'escape' she offers don Juan proves false.

The tendency towards undifferentiation becomes clear when don Juan tries to distinguish between different women, and cannot do so. Frisch's character tries to differentiate between his bride Anna and other women. His need to differentiate would be essential to ensure a successful relationship with a woman: 'Ich liebe. Aber wen?' (p.104). He desires to love, but he does not know his bride, and is frightened because he cannot remember what she looks like. This instils ambivalence:

> Ich hatte Sehnsucht nach ihr. Ich ritt immer langsamer. Schon vor
> Stunden hätte ich hier sein können...' (ibid).

His first comment - 'I longed for her' - conflicts with his subsequent remarks: 'I rode slower and slower. I could have been here hours ago'. Underlying any desire for Anna rests a strong fear of a woman, a creature he does not know. His fear of women is bound up with his inability to distinguish between them.

In particular, he confuses Anna with the prostitute Miranda, a confusion that arises from his persistence in believing that all women are the same. Even Anna is to him like the rest: 'ein junges Weib, nichts weiter, Weib wie hundert Weiber in der Finsternis' (p.135).[120] Don Juan also projects his attitude to women on to his bride, and argues that for *her* identity is irrelevant. As she behaved with him when they met at the pool (before the play opens), so she could have behaved with any man. 'Nachdem ich weiß, was alles möglich ist - auch für sie, meine Braut, die mich erwartet hat, mich und keinen andern, selig mit dem ersten besten, der zufällig ich selber war...' (p.122).[121] Again, a woman has called into question the matter of his identity. His night of seduction is a vain attempt to justify his attitudes to women, and thus his right to reject Anna: he attempts thereby to prove that indeed all women are the same. Moreover, his confusion of her with a prostitute suggests that Anna herself, as a woman, is no better than a prostitute. Therefore, if women can be equated with a prostitute, as Juan does, all women lose claim to the higher moral ground, the abstract truths that men such as Juan pursue.

Thus what don Juan appreciates most about his encounter with Anna the night before their wedding is the lack of identity in the encounter:

> Wir trafen einander im Park. Zufällig. Gestern in der Finsternis.
> Und auf einmal war alles so natürlich. Wir sind geflohen. Beide.
> Aber im Finstern, da wir nicht wußten, wer wir sind, war es ganz
> einfach. Und schön (p.119).[122]

At this point, don Juan very much resembles Tirso's 'hombre sin nombre' of Act I of *El burlador*. But when Juan and Anna assume identities and names the next time they meet, on their wedding night, Juan becomes confused at this complex matter of identity and answers 'no' to his wedding vows. When Anna recognizes him as her lover by the pool, she is in a sense bestowing an identity on him: her ability to recognize him in itself suggests identity. In consequence, he rejects her and flees, embarking on a night of seduction in an attempt to obliterate identity.

---

[120] 'A girl, nothing more, a girl like a hundred girls in the darkness'.

[121] 'Now I know what they are all capable of – even her, my bride who waited for me, me and no other; she preferred the first to come along, who just happened to be me myself...'.

[122] 'We met each other in the park. By chance. Yesterday in the darkness. And suddenly it was all so natural. We fled. Both of us. But in the dark, since we didn't know who we were, it was easy. And beautiful'.

Ironically, his action will reinforce the 'false' identity as the seducer, and many women will recognize him as such.

Nonetheless, don Juan's desire to lose identity is not a straightforward matter. He remains a self-absorbed character, an idea suggested in the image of his reflection in the pool (Act III), indicative of narcissism. And Matthews and Matthews note that don Juan's conversation is full of the word 'ich', 'I' .[123] His actions in pursuit of the abstract prove fatal for some characters and disastrous for others, indicating the lack of consideration for others that is part of his self-absorption. His egotism, then, adds a measure of ambivalence to his desire for loss of identity, since he pays more attention to his own self than his desire for abstraction would initially imply. Since he continues to exist in society, he connives with the women in the construction of a false identity as the traditional seducer, an identity that eventually takes on a life of its own while the 'real' don Juan leads a sedentary life with Miranda (now the Duchess of Ronda) at her castle, hidden from public gaze. Although he affects to despise his life as a seducer, he makes deliberate and cynical use of it in order to achieve the way of living he wants, free of the demands of society and particularly of women. He makes use of women in order to be free of them. Specifically, he makes use of his traditional descent to Hell in order to escape the demands of his female victims. Thus his identity as a seducer has value for him, since it grants him the freedom to live as he wishes. He needs some form of identity after all.[124] This suggests a troubled sense of male individuality that contrasts strongly with the attempts of earlier don Juans to define themselves.

***

---

[123] Max Frisch, *Don Juan oder die Liebe zur Geometrie*, ed. by D. G. and S. M. Matthews (London: Methuen, 1979), p.xv.

To conclude this chapter, we can summarize our findings by recognizing the link between gender relations and don Juan's identity as a male individual, by saying that don Juan attempts a masculine assertion of identity by trying to deprive women of theirs, removing their individuality by seeing them as one. He makes himself distinguishable from other men by rendering women indistinguishable. The way in which he does this, however, gradually changes. In the earlier plays the women are his victims, and by seducing them he attempts to make them all equal to each other, all the same, while gaining notoriety for himself as a womanizer. In Zorrilla's play, representative of the Romantic era, women are still the object of pursuit, but now a woman will 'save' don Juan from the damnation of lack of identity into which patriarchal society has cast him. To do this she must imperil her own soul (or identity). We might perceive in this a more negative attitude towards women than in the earlier plays, for while the earlier plays portrayed women as victims they did not suggest that women had to be *sacrificial* victims. Finally, in the modern plays don Juan sees women as a definite threat to his own sense of individuality. We can therefore detect that these later don Juan authors viewed the question of male/female relationships in more pessimistic terms than did earlier dramatists.

This increasing tendency towards a more malign depiction of women has so far been considered only from the point of view of the protagonists, none of whom we might expect to perceive women in a sympathetic way. An examination of the female characters themselves should reveal a more complex picture of attitudes towards women; but nevertheless I will argue that the same drift towards a more overtly hostile stance persists. To begin, I shall now consider the different female characters of the earlier works: *El burlador, Dom Juan* and *Don Giovanni.*

---

[124] Again, this parallels *El burlador*. In Tirso's play, don Juan needs some manner of identity in order to carry out his seductions, and he takes on the false identities of other male characters – Octavio and Mota – in order to achieve his aims.

Chapter 3: The early plays

In the previous chapter I traced the gradual changes in perception of don Juan as a male individual, and now propose that these changes parallel shifts in the understanding of women that each don Juan play gives us. In this and the following two chapters, I intend to examine the female characters in some detail, in order to establish over the course of these chapters that interpretations of women shift towards the negative. In order to demonstrate that such interpretations become more negative, I have first to argue that earlier interpretations are more positive. What constitutes a positive interpretation is itself a matter open to debate: while I will argue that the treatment of women in these 'earlier' works - by Tirso, Molière and Mozart - appears more positive than the later interpretations, I do not necessarily mean that these women are 'emancipated' in the way we would understand the term today. As the work of historians such as Anderson and Zinsser reveals, the lot of most women of the time was mixed but often unpleasant. I do not claim that the situation and fate of the female characters of this chapter directly reflect the position of real women of the era. By positive treatment, I have in mind the ability of the female characters to act and think for themselves, to subvert and survive a patriarchy that seeks to control them, to retain their own identities despite the efforts of a male individual to deprive them of these, and eventually, either to achieve the object of their ambitions (usually marriage to the men they love) or a freedom beyond male control. Tirso, Molière and Mozart acknowledge the validity of these aims by the women's survival and success at the end of each work, the moment of moral closure.[125] Their positive stance, I propose, lies in the nuances and capacity for negotiation of the women's position in contrast to the more simplistic opposition between don Juan and the women that will occur later. It would be dangerous to

---

[125] See my paper, 'Don Juan and Foucauldian Sexual Discourse: Changing Attitudes to Female Sexuality' (2001) for a discussion of female sexuality and moral closure in Tirso and Zorrilla.

assume a proto-feminism on the part of Tirso, Molière and Mozart/da Ponte, but I think the key here lies in the lack of representation of woman as a positively malign and threatening force. When we come to the later works, we should bear in mind that here in the earlier plays we have women who are flawed, less than ideal, but who make shift for themselves with reasonably benign intentions. They achieve a sort of parity with the men in terms of gender relations, that contrasts with what I will argue is the later pathological power of women over men in later works.

How far we can expect a so-called benign depiction of female characters in the Renaissance era, has been a matter open to dispute among commentators, but arguments for positive interpretations have been cogently put forward.[126] Some of this debate has occurred in the field of Golden-Age studies, and from here we can construct a framework within which to study our first three works - *El burlador*, *Dom Juan* and *Don Giovanni*. Women of the Golden-Age drama, the *comedia*, possessed a greater liberty of thought and action than might generally be believed today. Melveena McKendrick has written specifically about women in Golden-Age theatre, the *comedia*; and points out that the Golden-Age dramatist Lope de Vega popularized within his plays the figure of the 'mujer varonil', the woman who existed independently of men - though such a figure had precedents elsewhere in Spanish literature. This figure was on the whole an attractive one, allowing a female audience images of freedom and a challenge to notions of masculinity.[127] There was one qualification to this picture of freedom, however:

---

[126] Over time different directors have interpreted these roles in different ways when staging the plays, demonstrating the flexibility of interpretation of the female roles, which in itself implies the freedom for manoeuvre that these characters in fact possess. See David Whitton, *Molière: 'Don Juan'* (Cambridge: Cambridge University Press, 1995); J. Parakilas, 'The Afterlife of *Don Giovanni*: Turning Production History into Criticism', *Journal of Musicology* 8 (1990), 251-265.

[127] Melveena McKendrick, *Woman and Society in the Spanish Drama of the Golden Age*, (London: Cambridge University Press, 1974). Dawn L. Smith argues that McKendrick's views presuppose a 'monolithic solidarity of the patriarchal system' (Anita K. Stoll and Dawn L. Smith, *The Perception of Women in Spanish Theater of the Golden Age* (London and Toronto: Associated

women were still subject to love for men, and a lover of some sort was still a prerequisite for a happy ending and order restored. Lope's prototype became common in the work of other Golden-Age playwrights, including that of Tirso. The principle underlying female activity, then, was freedom of thought and action with nonetheless the ultimate aim of marriage. Dent - commenting as a critic of *Don Giovanni* - makes the following comment concerning women within Golden-Age drama:

> It is characteristic of the Spanish theatre that married women do not appear in it at all...Once safely married, a woman was regarded as something too sacred to be exposed to stage presentment. But before marriage, Spanish heroines seem to be allowed a surprising amount of liberty; indeed, even Spanish critics have accused Tirso of making his female characters *demasiado sensuales y libidinosas*.[128]

McKendrick contends that the *comedia* showed a realistic and on the whole positive approach to the question of women, given the age when these plays were written. In particular, McKendrick singles out Tirso as a dramatist who portrays women as intelligent and on occasion eccentric: his 'understanding of female psychology was subtler than Lope's and his tolerance of female independence and of female eccentricity greater'.[129]

Everett Hesse, on the other hand, suggests a more equivocal picture. He concurs with McKendrick up to a point by acknowledging the depiction of strong female

University Presses, 1991), p.18). I shall argue in chapter 6 that the patriarchy of all six plays reveals itself to be weak, yet I believe that McKendrick's views still hold good. I would emphasize the need for compromise that is an inevitable part of gender relations – yet within this compromise the women nevertheless achieve more than the men. Other authors in the volume by Stoll and Smith also make use of this 'subvert and survive' model.

[128] Edward J. Dent, *Mozart's Operas: a Critical Study*, 2nd edn, (London: Oxford University Press, 1947), 183-4.

[129] McKendrick, *Women and Society*, 330.

characters who are able to assert control over their own lives, illustrating this from Tirso's *Don Gil de las calzas verdes*, Lope de Vega's *Fuenteovejuna* and Calderón's *La vida es sueño*. Women may, however, also play the traditional role of victim. Hesse cites as examples doña Mencía in Calderón's *El médico de su honra*, murdered by her husband despite her innocence, and Casandra in Lope's *El castigo sin venganza*, who is led to unfaithfulness through her husband's neglect. The difference in treatment of the female characters arises principally from the distinction between comedy and tragedy: the women fare far worse in tragic plays. Hesse sums up the situation of female characters in the following terms:

> En la comedia, la mujer es víctima del abuso masculino por problemas que tienen que ver con el amor y la sexualidad. La comedia condena las faltas tanto de los hombres como de las mujeres, siendo todos humanos. Pero por la libertad sexual concedida al hombre, es la mujer que pierde y sufre más. La comedia demuestra cómo las mujeres agraviadas tratan de defenderse contra su destino tomando la iniciativa en busca de la justicia.[130]

In other words, within the *comedia* women attempt to overcome the disadvantage under which they automatically labour, given established social and patriarchal attitudes towards them. Taking the views of Hesse and McKendrick in conjunction, we have in the Spanish *comedia* an overall portrait of women who undertake an unusual variety of roles and who in different ways strive to maintain an element of power in their own lives, despite the automatic disadvantages they

---

[130] 'In the *comedia*, the woman is the victim of masculine abuse because of problems that have to do with love and sexuality. The *comedia* comdems the faults of men as much as of women, since all are human. But because of the sexual freedom allowed to the man, it is the woman who loses out and suffers most. The *comedia* reveals how wronged women attempt to protect themselves from their fate by taking the initative in seeking justice'. Everett W. Hesse, *La mujer como víctima en la comedia y otros ensayos*, (Barcelona: Puvill, n.d.), 43.

have as a result of their gender - a portrait all the more remarkable given the Spanish society of the Counter Reformation against which background the *comedia* was written. But the struggle for control of their own lives taken up by these characters is not always successful, since they struggle against a very powerful patriarchy: even in positive treatments they cannot function without the love of men, as McKendrick points out. We can thus perceive the treatment of women in the *comedia* as ambiguous. Women do not appear as totally independent of men: even when they take power into their own hands it is often in order to win - or win back - the love and attention of a man. But nevertheless they show the ability to take the initiative and often act in ways that subvert, but do not overthrow, the male-dominated society within which they live. We can regard this capacity to act for themselves as not only subversive but as positive.

The active participation and individual strength of the female characters, is a feature of *Dom Juan* and *Don Giovanni* much as it was in *El burlador*. D. Herwitz would not agree with this, claiming that *Don Giovanni* 'does not show women as active participants in the game of love, which is to say it does not allow them to possess and exhibit the freedom of their own powers in love'.[131] But this is not so. Elvira has no inhibitions about expressing her own feelings, a mixture of anger and love towards don Giovanni, and she actively pursues him, first with the object of 'repossessing' and reclaiming him, later with the hope of bringing him to redemption and repentance: done Elvire follows a similar course in *Dom Juan*. Zerlina and Anna, on the other hand, are capable of exercising their own power of love over Masetto and Ottavio respectively, to the extent on occasion of manipulation. Anna also possesses a strong - perhaps almost obsessive - sense of honour, knowing that vengeance is due in order to appease her own sense of self-worth. While don Giovanni is certainly the catalyst that provokes the action of the

---

[131] D. Herwitz, 'The Cook, his Wife, the Philosopher and the Librettist', *Musical Quarterly* 78 (1994), 48-76; p.50

opera, so that the other characters act in response to what he has done, the women pursue him in order to seek restitution. Elvira may love him, as perhaps does Zerlina - though Zerlina only pursues him in the company of Masetto, to seek justice - but Anna's cry is not of love but vengeance. Bernard Williams acknowledges the fact that the women have freedom of action and thought:

> ...no sensible person could think that [*Don Giovanni*] was a work that represented women as more passive than men, or as deriving the point of their existence only from being the object...of some essentially masculine principle. This is above all because it gives such a powerful sense of the individuality and the desires of the women in it.[132]

Following the approach to female characterization I have sketched here, we can detect the ability in the female characters of *El burlador*, and subsequently of *Dom Juan* and *Don Giovanni*, to survive in and subvert not only the patriarchal society in which they live, but more specifically the attempts of don Juan to deprive them of identity. They have the capacity to act, and above all, to achieve their intentions. They compensate by their ability to act for what they lack in terms of power, thus attaining a sort of parity. Despite don Juan's efforts to seduce and disgrace them, most of the female characters finish their plays betrothed once again to their lovers (donna Anna retaining the option of refusal or acceptance at the end of *Don Giovanni*). While their ambitions remain confined to the sphere of love and marriage, much as McKendrick suggested, they nevertheless achieve their ambitions, and often take the initiative to do so. We shall subsequently see that there are three exceptions to this: Tisbea, done Elvire and donna Elvire, who appear to finish their plays without a partner. We might perceive this to be a negative idea, but their solitary status allows each of these three characters to

---

[132] Bernard Williams, 'Don Giovanni as an Idea', in *W. A. Mozart: 'Don Giovanni'*, by Julian Rushton, (Cambridge: Cambridge University Press, 1981), 81-91; p.84

avoid male control and remain free to act as they wish and speak for themselves. Their situation may be ambiguous: it is not necessarily negative.

Furthermore, women actively achieve their aims despite the efforts of don Juan to prevent them. Williams comments: 'It has been suggested...that there is just one respect in which the seducer...is one who himself affirms the liberty of women: though he exploits or even destroys them, he does decline to imprison them in a possessive institution'.[133] But don Juan does not care at all about the fate of his female victims: he certainly does not seek to set them free. And it is hard to appreciate the idea that exploitation or destruction are forms of freedom in comparison with possessiveness. The positive activity of the female characters lies not through the actions of don Juan, which aim to equate all women in an undifferentiated mass; but in the confusion that arises between the libertine's attitudes to women and those of patriarchal society as a whole. The women are able to exploit the weaknesses that appear in the social order. Susana Pendzik comments:

> The consistent attempts to manipulate, control, submit, shut off, and possess [the female presence], turn the females in the play into a subversive force that challenges the established order, exposes its flaws, disrupts its functioning, and ultimately, confronts it to question and assign responsibility for its abuses.[134]

While ter Horst observes that don Juan exposes the abuse of matrimony, which:

> ...curiously liberates its female victims who survive their seduction with extraordinary strength and vividness so that Isabela, Tisbea, Ana and Aminta compose a startlingly lifelike portrait gallery of

---

[133] Williams, 84-85.

women whose real identity flashes into recognition in the sad, brief
interval between their pseudo-marriages to Don Juan and the final,
binding unions that the king arbitrarily imposes on them (ter Horst,
1996, 268).[135]

Yet although the women act independently, they cannot *live* independently, in the
sense that the boundaries of their existence are defined by a patriarchal society.
Thus Anna must look to Ottavio to carry out the vengeance she desires, and
Zerlina must appease Masetto. Isabela hopes that Octavio will resurrect her lost
honour through marriage.[136] The 'hysterical' women - Tisbea, done Elvire and
donna Elvira - do manage to elude male control, but at a cost. Elvira, for example,
is outside any man's control, but the penalty for this is a label as a hysteric (as
discussed below). It is also possible to assume, from the attitudes of Elvire, Elvira
and Zerlina, that women's attitudes to male-female relationships sometimes
contain an element of masochism, since they both knowingly act in an
unacceptable way with don Juan/don Giovanni, and suffer the consequences.
Zerlina's aria 'Batti, batti' ('Beat me, beat me') suggests an additional element of
masochism. Therefore, the women act within a dialectic of male-female
relationships (rather than the confrontation between men and women that would
arise in the later plays of Shaw and Frisch). We might not appreciate such a stance
as female freedom in a modern sense, but we can nevertheless perceive the
different accommodations and compromises the women make in order to retain

---

[134] Susana Pendzik, 1995. 'Female Presence in Tirso's *El burlador de Sevilla*', *Bulletin of the Comediantes* 47 (1995), 165-181; p.179.

[135] ter Horst, 'Epic Descent', p.268. This comment nevertheless conflicts with his remarks in the same essay that women are merely vessels to assist in the transfer of name and lineage to father and son (as I discussed in the previous chapter).

[136] An apparent contradiction to this argument is Ana in *El burlador*, who goes to the Queen of Castile for sanctuary, thus trusting to a woman to protect her. However, both these women are 'invisible': they do not appear on stage. The visible women – apart from those who retreat into 'hysteria' – all look to a man for restitution. Furthermore, Ana turns to Mota to right the 'wrong' that her father commits in marrying her to another man (don Juan, or possibly Octavio) against her will.

some power and survive within patriarchy. The emphasis is on gender relations as dialectic, rather than as confrontation.

If, as I suggested in the previous chapter, don Juan attempts to attain individual identity by rendering women indistinguishable, without any individuality of their own, the early works clearly suggest that he fails in this - because we can tell the female characters apart quite easily. A first glance at *El burlador*, *Dom Juan* and *Don Giovanni* shows us in fact that the female characters are quite distinct one from another. We cannot confuse Isabela with Aminta, Elvire with Charlotte or Anna with Zerlina or Elvira. Within and amongst these three works, each character has her own individual personality and history which don Juan, for all his efforts to the contrary, cannot obliterate. All the female characters here can be seen to have flawed natures, so that some are greedy or ambitious, some calculating and some uncontrolled and melodramatic. We will not find the idealized woman that Zorrilla will depict in doña Inés. But the faults of the earlier female characters, taken in conjunction with the good qualities that all possess, allow us to see more fully rounded and realistic characters. These women do not necessarily rebel against the patriarchal society in which they find themselves, but as a rule they do subvert it in order to find a way to survive within it. Furthermore, while we saw in the previous chapter how don Juan derives his identity by attempting to deprive women of theirs, by rendering them all equal, we shall see how each female character here nevertheless retains a sense of her own individuality. Despite his efforts, we can see them as distinct personalities, and this contributes to the comparatively positive perception of them that we obtain from these plays.[137]

---

[137] Critics differ as to whether Tirso, in particular, perceived women positively. Armand Singer and Ruth Lundelius argue for his misogyny. (Armand E. Singer, 1981. 'Don Juan's Women in *El burlador de Sevilla'*, *Bulletin of the Comediantes* 33 (1981), 67-71; Ruth Lundelius, 'Tirso's View of Women in El burlador de Sevilla', Bulletin of the Comediantes 27 (1975), 5-14.) R. Conlon claims that we are sometimes too ready to accept the judgement of the male characters such as Octavio and Batricio, who loudly proclaim women's fickleness even though it is not at all apparent

In order to enable convenient discussion of these characters, I intend to divide them into (rather crude) groups, according to different characteristics, while recognizing that not all the characters will fit neatly into a categorized scheme. Tisbea is a prime example of this: she is a peasant character, but shares attributes of hysteria with done Elvire and donna Elvira, as we shall see. It also quickly becomes clear that, while the women are each individuals, some characters are descendants of others and bear a strong resemblance to each other. Ana reappears as donna Anna in *Don Giovanni*, while done Elvire reappears as donna Elvira, as da Ponte adopted and redrew these characters for the opera. Obviously these characters bear some relation to each other but are nevertheless distinct. Commentary on the plays traditionally divides the women into two groups, while nevertheless observing some similarity between the two: these groups are the noblewomen and the peasants. The grouping of two noblewomen and two peasant women, originally established in *El burlador*, facilitates a symmetry of seduction as Mandrell comments,[138] so that don Juan moves smoothly from noblewoman to peasant and back again. Other authors, however, took up the use of both social classes of women as victims without necessarily retaining Tirso's structure. The action of *Don Giovanni* focuses on the seduction of one sole victim - Zerlina, a peasant woman - while the seductions, or attempted seductions, of the other female characters have already taken place before the action of the opera begins. Similarly, dom Juan's efforts at seduction revolve principally around the peasant women Charlotte and Mathurine: for him, the noblewoman done Elvire is already a past event. In all three cases, the blurring of social divisions demonstrates readily enough the fact that for don Juan gender takes priority over class in his

---

that any of the women have been faithless. (R. Conlon, 'The Burlador and the Burlados: a Sinister Connection', Bulletin of the Comediantes 42 (1990), 5-23; 6-7.) Carlos Feal offers what perhaps we might perceive as the most balanced judgement, that Tirso's female characters do retain some measure of culpability, but that they act under the promise of marriage that don Juan gives them. They attempt to fit into the patriarchal social order even as they try to subvert it (Feal, *En nombre de Don Juan*, p.112).

[138] Mandrell, p.59

selection of victims. But a study of the different female characters suggest that class does distinguish them to some degree.

For convenience's sake we will use these groupings of peasant and noblewomen as a starting point from which to study their characters. There are, however, other groupings that we may observe by taking the three works together. I would like to propose another grouping, the 'hysterical' woman that I mentioned above, which covers Tisbea, done Elvire and donna Elvira. I believe this particular group to possess a special significance in this study. The hysterical women all appear overly emotional but nevertheless independent, calling for justice on their own terms and careless of social conventions. They seemingly act outside the patriarchal confines of society.

Noblewomen

We can detect the capacity to women to take action from the very beginning of the don Juan phenomenon and the character of Isabela, who is, not incidentally, the first character of the entire don Juan genre to speak. We can arguably say that the action of *El burlador* springs in the first place from Isabela's attempt to push don Octavio into committing himself in terms of marriage. R. Conlon points out the secret reluctance of Octavio to marry her: thus Isabela yields to someone she believes to be Octavio in a desperate effort to force his hand.[139] Evidence for this lies in her search for reassurance: '¿Mis glorias serán verdades,/ promesas y ofrecimientos,/ regalos y cumplimientos,/ voluntades y amistades?' (I, 5-8).[140] Isabela is asking here not for love but for commitment. Schlossmann further suggests the link, contained within Isabela's request for light at this point, between sexuality and marriage, the latter being a sexual relationship lived in the

---

[139] Conlon, 'The *Burlador* and the *burlados*', p.14.
[140] 'Will I delight in truths, promises and offerings, gifts and commitments, good wishes and good friends?'

legitimate light of the day.[141] The text confirms this: for when don Juan (whom Isabela still presumes to be Octavio) asks her why she needs light, she replies: 'Para que el alma dé fe/ del bien que llego a gozar' (I, 11-12).[142]Isabela again seeks confirmation of the betrothal and marriage she hopes to enjoy in the future.

The immediate results of her sexual surrender do not appear to match her expectations. Having been duped by don Juan, found out and placed under guard, she finds herself not only at the mercy of the King of Naples but also at the mercy of don Pedro and Octavio, both of whom betray her. Don Pedro allows her real seducer to escape and thus prevents her from obtaining justice. Her fate is then decided by the king of another country, who plans to marry her to don Juan, and she is taken to Seville to marry against her will. This hardly seems positive. But we should bear in mind this restrictive framework when assessing Isabela's character, because despite such constraints she makes great efforts to take at least some measure of control over her own destiny. Her original surrender to the man she thought to be don Octavio, and her subsequent insistence on his future promises (as quoted above), indicate that she has tired of remaining the passive partner in this relationship. If she leaves the decisions to Octavio, he will never marry her. If we consider the exchange between Octavio and Ripio in the next scene, revealing Octavio's unrealistic concept of love, we find confirmation of this idea.[143] Thus Isabela may have to take the initiative if she wishes to marry him: she views their relationship realistically, while he views it in idealized, romantic terms. Hampered by many restrictions and constraints, she nevertheless shows an ability to act and to take what opportunities come her way in order to achieve her

---

[141] Schlossmann, 'Disappearing Acts', 1039-40.

[142] 'In order to give credence to the good fortune that I will enjoy'.

[143] Ripio asks Octavio why he does not simply marry Isabela if he loves her so much, a suggestion which Octavio angrily dismisses as vulgar. It is significant that Octavio compares his love for Isabela to a child playing: 'siempre quiere madrugar/por levantarse a jugar,/ que al fin, como niño, juega' ('It [Love] always wants to wake up early, to get up and play, since love plays just like a child'; I, 199-201). The reference to the child might imply Cupid, the god of love, but it could also

aims, rather than allow Octavio to decide. And at the end of the play she has achieved what she set out to do: Octavio agrees to marry her. Thus the course of events set in motion by her original surrender brings about her desired object - betrothal to Octavio.

Isabela's capacity to achieve her aims has brought a fair amount of censure from critics, and allows some of them to reassert the common, if unfortunate, belief that women are secretly 'asking for it', that they long to be seduced even while protesting to the contrary; a notion that the don Juan phenomenon has done much to popularize. An extreme example of such an attitude is Benabu, who suspects her ready familiarity with the palace in the dark, and goes so far as to say 'the brazenness of the courtesan is open for all to see'.[144] This is not so: Isabela's mind in the opening scene is much more set on future marriage than past surrender, and her actions spring not from sexual desire but a need to galvanize a lover, Octavio, who cannot himself act decisively (as I shall elaborate in chapter 6). We should also recognize that Isabela's motivation may spring as much from her genuine love of Octavio as from the desire to marry. She shows none of the disposition to run after don Juan that will characterize done Elvire and donna Elvira in the works of Molière and Mozart; and she laments the loss of Octavio even as she travels to her wedding with don Juan (II, 301-2).

Isabela's own ability to act and to survive has laid her open to the charge of manipulation. Ruiz Ramón describes her as equally manipulative as don Juan himself: 'Ambos, cada uno en su esfera, utilizan a los demás como instrumentos para sus propios fines, reduciendo así a las personas a su puro valor

---

imply the childish nature of Octavio's love for Isabela, far removed from the responsibility of an adult sexual relationship.

[144] Benabu, p.196.

instrumental'.[145] This is not just, either. Ruiz Ramón's argument could apply equally to any of the characters present at the court of Naples (to say nothing of that of Seville), all of whom attempt to manipulate each other in order to remain in control. We might not think of Isabela's actions as ethical, but she is trying to survive a situation compelled on her by Octavio's ineffectiveness, the bad judgement of the king of Naples and the deviousness of don Pedro, compounded by the fact that the king will not let her speak for herself (I, 168ff). The fact that she survives don Juan's attack on her honour, and ends the play with the prospect of marriage and her good name restored, suggests a power that is positive, particularly given the corrupt nature of Naples and Seville. In terms of the *comedia*, Isabela succeeds in marrying the man she loves, which is a perfectly acceptable achievement, as we saw earlier in this chapter.

Doña Ana also attempts to assume some control over her own fate in her planned surrender to Mota. Again, Ana does not appear to act ethically in her intended deceit towards her father but nevertheless she takes active steps in order to obtain the man she desires. Again, if it is a tenet of the *comedia* that women must be subject to men *through love*, that a woman's ultimate purpose is to love a man, then Ana's action may be construed as positive: she acts to avoid being married to someone she does not love. We may observe that she sees her father's act in marrying her off as a betrayal: 'Mi padre infiel/ en secreto me ha casado' ('My betraying father has married me off in secret'; II, 281-2).[146] Ana of all the female

---

[145] 'Both, in their own sphere, use others as tools for their own ends, reducing people to a merely functional value'. Ruiz Ramón, p.82.

[146] Commentators have wondered whether Ana in fact falls victim to don Juan's seduction, as others would later do in the case of donna Anna: J. M. Ruano de la Haza summarizes the evidence for and against, and concludes in her favour. For Ruano de la Haza, a decisive factor is that don Juan continues to insist to Ana that he is Mota, in contrast to his opening seduction with Isabela, where he confesses quite readily that he is not Octavio. This, Ruano de la Haza claims, means that he has not yet succeeded in seducing Ana, and thus continues to rely on his disguise. (J. M. Ruano de la Haza, 'Doña Ana's Seduction in *El burlador de Sevilla*: Further Evidence Against', *Bulletin of the Comediantes* 32 (1980), 131-133).

characters is the least developed, and is never seen. In a sense, she acts as a symbol of her father's honour rather than as a real character; but nevertheless, she has a mind and will of her own and is prepared to oppose don Gonzalo - strong action for an invisible character. As in the case of Isabela, Ana survives the attempts of patriarchy - don Diego, don Gonzalo and the king of Castile - to decide her fate for her, and brings about her desired aim in contrast to the plans they have in mind for her. None of them want her to marry Mota, yet Mota announces their forthcoming marriage at the end of the play. Thus if we take the characters of Isabela and Ana in conjunction, we can perceive that both can take the initiative and survive in a corrupt society that intends them no good or recognizes no freedom to choose for themselves, and that furthermore both succeed in obtaining marriage to the man they love - in the terms of the *comedia*, the most laudable aim they can have.

A comparison between Ana and her later incarnation, donna Anna of *Don Giovanni*, suggests the force that lies behind this character.[147] In *Don Giovanni*, the original character has survived very much intact: as in *El burlador* she calls for vengeance from offstage, and don Juan's attempt to seduce her will bring about his damnation. But now Anna moves onstage to speak and sing powerfully of vengeance (particularly in her aria 'Or sai chi l'onore'). Anna is subject to the limitations of patriarchy far more than Elvira in the opera, hemmed in first by her father and then by don Ottavio: but she reveals a strength of feeling that goes far beyond that of her male protectors. Her independence of thought means that she pursues vengeance more rigorously than her fiancé does, and that she successfully postpones their marriage at the end of the opera. She also shows an intensity of purpose equal to that of her father, as they both intend violence. Anna proves to

---

[147] Hoffmann will reinterpret Ana to be the woman peculiarly fitted to be don Juan's own, and his revision will in turn lead to other Romantic interpretations and especially that of doña Inés in *Don Juan Tenorio*. Hoffmann perceives Anna's character in a radically different manner to conventional readings of *Don Giovanni*: I discuss his interpretation in the next chapter.

be very much her father's daughter in this respect. Peter Gay attempts a Freudian interpretation of the triangular relation between Anna, don Giovanni and the Comendatore, pointing to the 'fierce emotionality pervaded by an air of hysterical overemphasis and compulsive repetition which reveals a very special sort of mourning'[148] to suggest a quasi-incestuous relationship with her father.[149] A simple Freudian approach here, however, leaves too much in *Don Giovanni* unexplained. To perceive Anna solely within the context of a Freudian triangle is to neglect her active pursuit of justice.

As with Isabela and Ana, Anna possesses flaws. Her monomania for vengeance makes her seem cold and, as Dent argues, aloof and self-absorbed.[150] She does not seem sympathetic. Nevertheless, these faults stem from her concentration on vengeance. She possesses a strong character that is accentuated by the rather ineffectual nature of her fiancé don Ottavio. Unable herself to give way to violence, because of her position within society as a noblewoman, she urges Ottavio to avenge her. Her aria 'Or sai chi l'onore' suggests a desire for vicarious violence: 'Rammenta la piaga del misero seno, rimira di sangue coperto, coperto il terreno, se l'ira in te langue d'un giusto furor' (Mozart, 145-6).[151] She seems to relish the imagery of blood. This aria gives us the key to Anna's character. Her quest is vengeance, which she seeks purposefully; and this, in turn, displays an independent turn of mind undissuaded by Ottavio's pleas of love.

Anna's position reveals more ambivalence than most of the other female characters. Her emotional emphasis on violence will reflect the 'hysteria' of

---

[148] Peter Gay, 'The Father's Revenge', in *The Don Giovanni Book: Myths of Seduction and Betrayal*, ed. by Jonathan Miller, (London: Faber, 1990), 70-80; p.75

[149] Strangely, of all commentators it is Rank (ch.1) who argues that the Oedipus theory is useful only as a point of departure for literary interpretation, not as an interpretative framework on its own.

[150] Dent, p.158.

[151] 'Remember the pitiable wound in his breast, behold the ground covered in so much blood, should your anger ever fail in its righteous fury'.

Tisbea, Elvire and Elvira that I discuss below, but her dependence on Ottavio as her instrument of vengeance recalls the dialectic with their lovers that exercises Isabela and Ana. These two contrasting elements are reflected in the outcome of *Don Giovanni*. Anna has achieved what she set out to do in that she has seen her father avenged and her would-be seducer punished. She also has the prospect of marriage to Ottavio - if she wishes to accept it. Her postponement of marriage for a year has troubled commentators and allowed some (Hoffmann is the most notorious example) to assume from this that she secretly loves not Ottavio but don Giovanni. However, I will claim in my discussion of the hysterical women that their emotion allows them liberty beyond male control. Anna's capacity for emotion, which Ottavio cannot match, similarly suggests a covert desire to be free of male restraint. I believe that her ambivalence towards marriage and her emotion give rise to the uncertainty over her future at the end of the opera.

Some commentators have also questioned whether donna Anna succeeds in resisting don Giovanni or not at the beginning of the opera. Hoffmann was not alone in affirming that she did indeed succumb, and some authors have since used this claim to see donna Anna as don Giovanni's true partner.[152] Julian Rushton condemns such a critical response, arguing that her desire for vengeance is quite in keeping with a successful resistance of the seducer - though the claim that Ottavio acts appropriately does not convince, for Ottavio still comes across as a weak character who cannot fulfil Anna's demand for vengeance.[153] However, the ambiguity concerning Anna's fate at Giovanni's hands has given rise to the nineteenth-century tendency to perceive her as the ideal partner for the notorious womanizer.

---

[152] See Ruano de la Haza for a similar debate within *El burlador*.
[153] Julian Rushton, *W. A. Mozart: 'Don Giovanni'*, (Cambridge: Cambridge University Press, 1981), p.60.

These noblewomen all show a certain measure of constraint and decorum in their conduct, but decorum is not always synonymous with the noblewomen. Done Elvire and donna Elvira are also noble, but they have cast away any vestiges of conventional behaviour and allow their passions, alternately their love and their hate for their seducer, to control their actions. They have stepped outside their allotted social role. I prefer to discuss them separately; but I will first turn to the peasant women in the three early works.

Peasant women

In *Dom Juan* and *Don Giovanni* the peasant women provide the central focus for don Juan's seductive campaigns: unlike Isabela and Ana in *El burlador*, the noblewomen of Molière and Mozart's works have already been victims of don Juan's attentions before the action of each work begins. This point is particularly striking in *Don Giovanni*, where the only seduction we witness is that of Zerlina. At first glance, the focus on the peasant women reminds us of their vulnerability, but also serves to underline their greed and stress the importance of such women keeping their place. Aminta, Tisbea (whom I will consider in more detail in the following section on 'hysterical' women), Charlotte and Zerlina all succumb to don Juan's promises of wealth and title, but events reveal them to have been deceived by don Juan, and they return to their 'proper place' as peasants. In order to show the folly of hoping for betterment, the peasant women often come in particularly for ridicule. Thus don Juan laughs at Aminta for calling herself 'doña Aminta' (III, 440-1), and, as Pendzik points out, he deceives her openly in front of witnesses.[154] In fact, these witnesses are her own family and community, rendering the deception even more cruel. Similarly, dom Juan's praise of Charlotte lays her open to ridicule. His particular reference to the beauty of her hands, which turn out to be badly in need of a wash, highlights the comedy, and

---

[154] Pendzik, p.177.

simultaneously the ridicule, that lies behind dom Juan's flattery. The subsequent scene with Mathurine (II, iv) extends the ridicule still further, as both women fight over who will marry a man that does not intend to marry either of them, as the audience knows.

Clearly the peasant characters provide, among other things, an opportunity for comedy, and thus ridicule in some form or other is perhaps to be expected. But the comic element does not disguise the fact that the peasant women show the same capacity for survival and subversion as do their noble counterparts. The peasant women are not merely embodiments of ambition alone: they are more three-dimensional, and possess positive characteristics. These women are shrewder than their noble counterparts, being well aware of the danger that don Juan poses - until ambition dazzles their clearsightedness. Zerlina tells don Giovanni: 'io so che raro colle donne voi altri cavalieri siete onesti e sinceri' ('I know how rarely you gentleman are honest and sincere with women', 110). Aminta also distrusts don Juan, accusing him of being 'lisonjero' ('flattering', II, 733), and later comments: 'No sé que diga,/ que se encubren tus verdades/ con retóricas mentiras' ('I don't know what you are saying, as you cover the truth up with lying rhetoric'; III, 256-8). Charlotte expresses similar sentiments: '...je ne sais si vous dites vrai, ou non; mais vous faites que l'on vous croit' ('I don't know whether you are telling the truth or not, but you make me believe you'; II, ii). She also has reservations about the reputation of noblemen: 'on m'a toujours dit qu'il ne faut jamais croire les monsieux, et que vous autres courtisans êtes des enjoleus, qui ne songez qu'à abuser les filles' (II, ii).[155] (Tisbea, too, shows some distrust: 'sois los hombres traidores' 'you men are treacherous'; I, 935). Because of their instinctive distrust, the women often ask don Juan to swear some sort of oath, or commit himself in some manner or other, before they surrender. Their delight at

---

[155] 'I've always been told that you should never believe gentlemen, and that you courtiers are wheedling characters who only think to take advantage of women'.

the prospect of social betterment does not blind them to the need for insurance. Charlotte asks dom Juan not to deceive her, as she herself is acting honestly (II, ii); and Aminta goes further, demanding an oath of don Juan (III, 271-2 and 276-7) - this is the oath that heralds don Juan's downfall, as he swears that only a dead man (i.e. don Gonzalo's statue) will bring him to justice. Tisbea, for all her passion, only agrees to surrender to don Juan 'bajo la palabra y mano/ de esposo' ('on your word and hand as a husband'; I, 940-1).

Zerlina, Charlotte and Aminta attempt to maintain their dignity in the face of don Juan's attempts to seduce them. Zerlina and Aminta try to remain faithful to their respective fiancés; and Aminta, at least, only yields because she hears that Batricio has already given her up. Charlotte argues that her reputation, even as a peasant, still has value:

> Je suis une pauvre paysanne; mais j'ai l'honneur en recommendation, et j'aimerais mieux me voir morte que de me voir déshonorée (II, ii).[156]

Her speech here suggests a dignity that will reappear more strongly in the beggar who refuses to forswear himself (III, ii); and Charlotte makes this speech in the middle of dom Juan's elevated praise, asserting her own sense of worth in the face of his hyperbole.

The peasant women, like the noblewomen, attempt to make the best of the situations in which they find themselves They do not claim high morals, but try to protect t hemselves as b est t hey c an in a p atriarchal w orld t hat d oes n ot f avour women. They do not rebel against this world, unjust to them, but they do try to subvert it. We can appreciate this by considering Zerlina, particularly her aria

---

[156] 'I am a poor country girl, but I have my honour to recommend me, and I would rather die than be dishonoured'.

'Batti, batti', which provides much ambiguity. Zerlina sings it as a gesture of defiance, since Masetto does not appear to believe her protestations of innocence, but the aria nevertheless contains strong overtones of masochism, as she calls on Masetto to beat her and scratch out her eyes, while she submits like a lamb:

> starò qui come agnellina
> le tue botte ad aspettar...
> Lascerò straziarmi il crine,
> lascerò cavarmi gli occhi,
> e le care tue manine
> lieta poi saprò baciar (Mozart, 164-6).[157]

Zerlina's simple and eventually joyous song beguiles the audience into overlooking the less pleasant implications of domestic violence. But we cannot take this aria to be a straightforward example of masochism, since Masetto does not take her at her word (indeed, he is the one to be beaten black and blue in Act II, at the hands of don Giovanni), and so she ends her song with the prospect of passing their days happily. The aria demonstrates the paradox that Zerlina exercises power over Masetto through her apparent lack of power and vulnerability to physical ill treatment. She retains her hold over Masetto ironically by surrendering control to him; she calls his bluff, knowing perfectly well that Masetto will not harm her. In this way Zerlina uses the social power of men against themselves. Her action in apparent surrender shows her subversive power, for it is obvious that Zerlina holds the mastery over Masetto; and indeed, before the aria is over Masetto is happy again (Mozart, p.169). Masetto himself recognizes the power she has over him: 'Guarda un po' come seppe questa strega sedurmi! siamo pure i deboli di testa!' (p.174).[158]

---

[157] 'Like a lamb I'll wait for you to kick me...I'll let you tear my hair out and dig my eyes out, and I will joyfully kiss your dear hands'.

[158] 'Just look how that witch can seduce me! We're simply weak in the head!'

In the aria 'Vedrai carino' Zerlina shows further power over Masetto by her ability to heal his wounds. The sexual innuendo of the aria is clear, but Zerlina's ability to heal also indicates a further positive capacity to amend and make better the hurts caused by don Giovanni (who has just beaten Masetto). Of all the characters mentioned here, none are able as Zerlina is to rectify what don Giovanni (or any other don Juan) has done:

> Vedrai, carino, se sei buonino,
> che bel rimedio ti voglio dar.
> È naturale, non da disgusto...
> È un certo balsamo che porto adosso... (pp.302-4).[159]

The reference to the 'certo balsamo' that she carries on her suggests not only the sexual nature of her healing, but also that her capacity to amend rests within herself. From this aria, we may perceive that Zerlina's power lies in her sexual nature, hence the innuendo of the words, but that such a power is also positive and nurturing.

Zerlina shows some susceptibility to don Giovanni's charm - although she continues to resist until don Giovanni has repeated his promises of marriage and a change of status (pp.109-10). Richard Stiefel traces how, when she first encounters don Giovanni, she gradually succumbs during the course of their duet, 'Là ci darem la mano': she takes up the musical phrase of don Giovanni, with variations of her own to reflect her uncertainty - ascending notes to suggest excitement, dotted rhythms to suggest hesitation.[160] By the end of the duet the two characters are singing together in harmony. But Zerlina's distrust of don Giovanni increases as Act I continues. Her resistance becomes more positive, and she calls

---

[159] 'If you are good, my dear, you'll see the excellent remedy I'll offer you. It's natural and pleasant. It's a certain balm I carry on me'.
[160] Richard Stiefel, 'Mozart's Seductions', *Current Musicology* 36 (1983), 151-163; p.156.

for help during the finale as don Giovanni tries to seduce her once again. Although a straightforward, cheerful woman on the whole – Hermann Abert describes her as 'an unspoiled peasant girl with a lively temperament, natural grace and, above all, strong, healthy instincts'[161] - she struggles increasingly to retain control over her own situation. As do Isabela and Ana of *El burlador*, Zerlina manages to take charge of her own destiny despite the stupidity of Masetto and the plans made against her by don Giovanni, and succeeds in remaining with Masetto at the finale. Her closing comment reflects her commonsense nature, as she and Masetto sing together of going home to dinner (pp.496-7). In contrast to the uncertain future of donna Anna, Zerlina rests secure in the domesticity she has gained despite the threat to it posed by don Giovanni.

As with the noblewomen, the peasant women survive the attempts of don Juan to render them indistinguishable as seduced women. Dom Juan's attempt to seduce Charlotte fails, when he is forced to flee, and she retains her good name even though she has been deceived. Zerlina and Aminta retain the prospect of marriage to their betrothed partners, Masetto and Batricio, as both the women desire, despite the efforts of don Giovanni/don Juan to separate the couples. Furthermore, the women demonstrate rounded characters of common sense and loyalty - provided they are not tempted too far - and a fair idea of the sort of womanizer they are dealing with. As with the noblewomen, they are not the ideal female figure that we will discover in Zorrilla's *Don Juan Tenorio*, but flawed yet capable, positive portraits of individual women.

---

[161] Hermann Abert, *Mozart's Don Giovanni*, trans. by Peter Gellhorn (London: Eulenberg, 1976) p.76

'Hysterical' women[162]

Each of the three early works we are considering in this chapter includes among its cast of characters what we might term a 'hysterical' woman - Tisbea, done Elvire and donna Elvira. The figure of the hysterical woman came to the fore with donna Elvira in *Don Giovanni*. Her antecedents can be traced immediately back to Molière's done Elvire in *Dom Juan*, but the prototype goes much farther back, to the original play and the character of Tisbea. The difference between the characters seems principally one of social status, since Elvira and Elvire are of noble birth while Tisbea is a fisherwoman. They nevertheless trace the same path through their respective dramatic works: once seduced they give way to exaggerated speeches/arias and set out in pursuit of their seducer. They lose all self-control, becoming emotional and possibly melodramatic and ridiculous. They attract little respect in consequence, and male characters ultimately leave them alone. They have no apparent prospect of marriage at the end. Done Elvire and donna Elvira retire to convents; while the assumption sometimes made that Tisbea will marry Anfriso, is not clear from the text - he has no lines to say in the final scene and his presence is not mentioned.

Overly emotional women, who have moved beyond the boundaries of patriarchal convention, are sometimes popularly termed 'hysterical'. The word is a cruel one, but the cruelty involved in such a perception may indeed be a response to an underlying male fear of a woman who, in her apparent madness, nevertheless evades the control of male society. Even don Juan himself does not have this control. Although he draws these women after him, he cannot shake them off, nor can he control what they say. An example is don Giovanni's attempt to silence

---

[162] I have written in greater detail about the hysterical woman in the don Juan tradition in my essay 'Hysteria: female desire versus male rationality in early don Juan works' in *Selected Interdisciplinary Essays on the Representation of the Don Juan Archetype in Myth and Culture*, eds. by Andrew Ginger, John Hobbs and Huw Lewis (Lewiston: Edwin Mellen Press, 2000).

donna Elvira in the quartet 'Non ti fidar' of Act I. He tells Anna and Ottavio that Elvira has clearly lost her senses, and then tries to calm her down: 'Zitto, zitto, che la gente si raduna a noi d'intorno, siate un poco più prudente, vi farete criticar'.[163] He appeals here to a sense of conventional decorum, implying that she will look a fool in public if she continues her complaints. Her reply is significant: 'ho perduta la prudenza' 'I have thrown caution to the winds'. And with the loss of restraint she can speak as she pleases (Mozart, 130-1). We shall discover that though these three characters come in for disparagement and receive little respect, and though they do not acquire the mark of respectability that marriage endows, as do other women at the end of each work, they nevertheless achieve an independence of thought and action that contrasts with their supposed pathos. Each of these three characters eludes the restraints of patriarchal society to some degree, and nobody can exercise any control over them.

Tisbea of *El burlador* provides the prototype for hysterical women in the don Juan genre. However, her initial appearance does not suggest hysteria so much as coldness, a lack of emotion that leaves her unsusceptible to love. Commentators[164] have noted her pride, in fact her similarity to don Juan as she exults in her power over men:

> a sus suspiros, sorda;
>
> a sus ruegos, terrible;
>
> a sus promesas, roca (I, 432-4).[165]

And:

> y cuando más perdidas
>
> querellas de amor forman,

---

[163] 'Shut up, everyone's crowding round us, be a bit more sensible, or they'll criticize you'

[164] For example, Rogers, pp.49-51; Melveena McKendrick, 'Women Against Wedlock: the Reluctant Brides of Golden Age Drama', in *Women in Hispanic Literature: Icons and Fallen Idols*, ed. by Beth Miller, (Berkeley: University of California Press, 1983; p.129).

como de todo río,

envidia soy de todas (411-4).[166]

The note of pride suggests negativity. However, Evans points out that Tisbea defies the conventions of romanticism and marriage in a positive manner. Far from being a cold character, she revels in the sensuous pleasures of nature: the imagery of food implies indulgence.[167] But we can also detect from her long soliloquy the pleasure she has in her freedom from male constraint:

sola de amor esenta,

como en ventura sola,

tirana me reservo

de sus prisiones locas[...]

segura me entretengo,

que en libertad se goza

el alma que amor áspid

no le ofende ponzoña (I, 379-82; 403-6).[168]

Her references to 'libertad', in conjunction with the suggestion of the 'prisiones' which she has eluded, combine with the images of nature and of plentiful provision to reinforce in us a sense of her freedom and power, as well as the sensuality and indulgence mentioned by Evans. Her pride is also evident, however; she reveals contempt of those who love. In talking of Anfriso, she comments: 'Todas por él se mueren,/ y yo, todas las horas,/ le mato con desdenes' (I, 459-61).[169] This remark demonstrates the scorn she feels not only towards

---

[165] 'Deaf to their sighs, formidable before their pleading, as stone to their promises'.

[166] 'And the more in vain they plead their case of love, I laugh at it all, and all woman envy me'.

[167] Evans, 'The Roots of Desire', p.241.

[168] 'Alone in love as in luck, I keep myself, a tyrant, free of love's imprisonment[...] I remain steadfast, and my soul enjoys freedom untouched by the poison of the serpent love'.

[169] 'All are dying for love of him, while I, all the time, make him die of my disdain'.

Anfriso for loving her, but towards other women for loving *him*. Her pride is not itself a pleasant characteristic, but it also indicates Tisbea's sense of independence.

Although Tisbea remains aloof from love, and thus from subjection to men, she does not lack emotion - she is not cold-natured in the manner of don Juan. We can derive from Tisbea a framework in which emotion equals freedom from men, and in which to come under male control means the loss of feeling. Once don Juan has arrived, Tisbea soon contradicts any original idea that she has no emotions. As soon as he is in her presence, she begins to refer to fire, and tells him that he has sparked off the fire of emotion within her: 'tanto fuego en vos tenéis,/ que en este mío os ardéis' (I, 634-5).[170] However, her surrender to don Juan - when she grants him power over her - entails a lack of emotion and consequent calmness: 'Yo a ti me allano/ bajo la palabra y mano/ de esposo' (I, 939-41).[171] Marriage will mean control by a man and emotions contained as a result. She admits something similar to Isabela when they meet by the sea: 'mas las obras me hicieron,/...ablandarme de suerte,/ que al sol la cera es más robusta y fuerte' (III, 369; 371-2).[172] Her emotional reaction to don Juan may initially lead to her surrender, but as a result of succumbing to him she becomes weaker and more pliable than wax: she becomes less proud and hard ('ablandarme') and in consequence loses independence and control.

Once don Juan has abandoned her Tisbea reveals herself to be 'hysterical', giving way to lamentations in her 'fuego, fuego' speech (I, 985ff). Tisbea herself is burning: 'Fuego, fuego, que me quemo' 'Fire, fire, I'm burning' (985) and 'que se abrasa el alma' 'my soul is on fire' (998), and flings herself in the sea after her

---

[170] 'You have so much fire within you that it lights a fire within me',
[171] 'With your word and hand as a husband, I submit'.
[172] 'With his tricks he softened me[...] wax in sunlight would have been more harder'.

speech in an attempt to quench the flames of her passion. Now her hysteria and lack of restraint become apparent:

> Mas si amor abrasa peñas
> con gran ira y fuerza extraña,
> mal podrán de su rigor
> reservarse humildes pajas (I, 993-6).[173]

Suggestions of a love that can burn rock, and of great anger and unusual force, clearly indicate that Tisbea's hysteria has carried her beyond convention, leading her to the (possibly melodramatic) gesture of throwing herself into the sea.

We can appreciate the connection between hysteria and freedom by considering Tisbea's relationship with the fisherman Anfriso. According to Tisbea, Anfriso loves her desperately, but a closer study suggests that he also desires to exert some form of power over her, control her freedom. His speech that immediately follows Tisbea's declaration of honour destroyed, reveals not so much love but a desire to punish and control:

> ..que en él [don Juan],
> me he de vengar desta ingrata.
> Vamos tras ella nosotros,
> porque va desesperada,
> y podrá ser que ella vaya
> buscando mayor desgracia (I, 1033-8).[174]

---

[173] 'But if, with great rage and strange power, love can burn rock, my own humble thatch is little able to keep clear of its force'

[174] 'Through [don Juan] I can get my revenge on this ungrateful woman. Let us follow her, because she is desperate and may get into further trouble'.

He judges her harshly for her former freedom ('desta ingrata'). Her emotion, her state of desperation leads him to follow her, with the idea of rescuing her from future misfortune, or in other words to establish some sort of control over her. His intent to rescue appears benevolent, but also entails an exercise of power. This appears, however, to be in vain. When we next find Tisbea, she is lamenting and cursing her fate, alone by the sea - suggesting both her emotion and her independence.

Anfriso never apparently achieves mastery over Tisbea. She continues to express her emotion to the very end of the play - her lamentation before the king of Castile (III, 998-1005) contrasts with Aminta's naive confidence in don Juan's promises. Equally, Tisbea appears to retain her independence. She asks that Anfriso might accompany her to the King of Castile, when Isabela accepts her into her retinue (III, 403-5), but Tirso does not mention him by name in the final scene, referring only to 'Tisbea y Isabela y acompañamiento' in the stage directions. And while Octavio, Mota and Batricio each make a speech agreeing to marry the women that correspond to them, Anfriso makes no such speech. This may in practical terms be simply a consequence of Golden-Age actors to double parts, so that the actor who played Anfriso would also play Batricio: both could not therefore appear together in the final scene. But this does not detract from Tisbea's singleness at the end of the play when all other women are reconciled to their former partners. Thus Tisbea's fate is unclear. Her pursuit of don Juan thus undergoes a subtle qualification that distinguishes it from the similar pursuit of Isabela. The King of Castile has destined Isabela to marry don Juan, which will at least satisfy the dictates of society if not her own desires; but Tisbea's search for restitution remains open. Restitution can only come about through marriage, as arranged by the king, and Tisbea's apparent lack of a prospective wedding suggests that she may remain outside the patriarchal social order which the king has now restored. Tisbea thus fits into a framework that can be understood as hysterical, a framework for which only women qualify.

Of all the characters in *El burlador*, Tisbea has by far the most poetical speeches, and her lyricism contrasts with the speech of the men; the terse style of don Juan, the pompous and overlong nature of don Gonzalo's Lisbon speech (I, 721ff), the ridiculous speeches of Octavio or the snide remarks of Mota about the Sevillean prostitutes. However, her very poetry sets Tisbea outside patriarchal discourse. Mark Micale has commented that hysteria is 'not a disease; rather, it is an alternative physical, verbal, and gestural language, an iconic social communication',[175] an idea reflected in Tisbea's poetry. Pendzik observes that many critics see don Juan and Tisbea as similar characters, but she claims that while don Juan uses words to deceive, Tisbea, particularly in her long soliloquy, uses words to express how she feels. Pendzik believes that Tisbea's attempt to speak, to enter into a discourse that is male, represents deviant behaviour.[176] Women should not speak - we may immediately think of Isabela, silenced by the king of Naples - and Tisbea's insistence on speech brings about her downfall. But Tisbea's pleasure in freedom and solitude actually takes her outside male discourse and renders her deaf to men ('a sus suspiros, sorda', I, 432): this also sets her outside patriarchal convention and renders the men deaf to her at this point. When she calls to them to help in the rescue of don Juan and Catalinón from shipwreck, they do not respond, and only arrive after Catalinón has summoned them. Tisbea herself later remarksthat she called and no one heard her: 'di voces, y nadie oyó' (I, 662). Thus Tisbea's emotional discourse excludes her from the unpoetical speech of patriarchy. While this prevents her from speaking to any effect in a society governed by men, Tisbea nevertheless possesses her own

---

[175] Mark Micale, *Approaching Hysteria* (Princeton: Princeton University Press, 1994), p.182; quoted in Elaine Showalter, *Hystories: Hysterical Epidemics and Modern Culture* (London: Picador, 1998), p. 7.
[176] Pendzik, pp.171-2.

form of discourse that enables her to express feelings beyond the comprehension of the male characters. Patriarchy, by excluding her from its discourse, simultaneously frees her from its sterility. She retains her rich, poetic discourse to the end, which indicates that she retains her own sexual desire despite her misfortune. Male discourse in *El burlador* excludes the emotion of female desire, but this desire retains for itself the potential for poetry.

In short, Tisbea proves to be another rounded female character, with flaws in her nature but also the capacity to act, think and speak for herself. Her emotional expression reveals pride, but also a sensual enjoyment of nature, an independence which she refuses to sacrifice and an ability to convey her feelings effectively. While Anfriso may feel that it was time Tisbea 'learnt her lesson' and grew less proud, Tisbea has not in fact learnt the lesson that patriarchy has wished to impose upon her. The intrusion of don Juan into her life has given her new matter for her emotions, but it has not stopped her thinking emotionally, or acting and speaking as she wishes without male control.

Tisbea provides the original model of the hysterical woman: Elvira provides its most outstanding example. In *Don Giovanni*, donna Elvira is a noblewoman, but her behaviour throughout the opera does not suggest the restraint of nobility, and contrasts with the comparative decorum of Anna, Ana and Isabela. Her status within the opera is itself ambiguous. She sings arias written in the *seria* manner that compare with those of donna Anna, but she frequently associates with the *buffa* characters, Leporello, Zerlina and Masetto. Her involvement in the burlesque seduction by Leporello (disguised as Giovanni) brings her into the realm of *opera buffa*, of comedy. This structure reflects her uncertain position in the opera's social hierarchy. She is nobly born, but acts in a way that implies comedy and lack of refinement.

108

Elvira provides us with a clear picture of a 'hysterical' woman. She proves to be abandoned in speech and action as well as in love - the rhetoric of her speeches inspires Leporello to comment that she talks like a book: 'Pare un libro stampato' (Mozart, 74). Her desire for revenge takes a violent tone: 'se ritrovo l'empio, e a me non torna ancor, vo' farne orrendo scempio, gli vo' cavare il cor' (pp. 66-7).[177] Thus when we first encounter Elvira she is threatening death. She also anticipates the role that 'rightly' belongs to the Comendatore, seeing herself as an instrument of divine justice: 'Ma il giusto cielo volle ch'io ti trovassi, per far le sue, le mie vendette' (p. 74).[178] Her claim to divine retribution is exaggerated, as is much about her: not really until the twentieth century, and the work of Shaw and Frisch, among others, would women themselves become the form of punishment meted out to don Juan. However, her cries of hatred in Act I change suddenly and rapidly to love at the beginning of Act II, when between them don Giovanni and Leporello seduce her once again. Donna Elvira's expressions of love are as intemperate as her anger: 'Dunque creder potrò che i pianti miei abbian vinto quel cor?' (p. 284) and 'Son per voi tutta foco!' (285).[179] She spends much of Act II struggling amid conflicting emotions of love and hatred,[180] until she finally pleads with don Giovanni for his repentance at the supper scene (closely following done Elvire of *Dom Juan*).

Elvira's hysteria is reflected in her musical style, as observed by many commentators, including Steptoe :

---

[177] 'If I find this wicked man, and he does not come back to me, I'll murder him horribly, I'll rip out his heart'.

[178] 'But divine justice allowed me to find you and carry out its own vengeance and mine'.

[179] 'Can I really believe that my tears have conquered your heart?'; 'I am on fire for you!'

[180] Abert reminds us that Elvira's aria in Act II, 'Mi tradì', was a later addition to the opera, and believes that it clashes with Mozart and da Ponte's original conception of the character: 'Elvira's aria...dramatically only a stopgap...does not quite fit in with the picture of Elvira's character. Psychologically it can certainly be argued that her former passionate desire to win back her lover might turn to pity for the doomed man: but this attitude does not in any way fit Elvira's true nature. She would be much more likely to express her struggle with all its contradictions and to fight her way through with characteristic fire, than to content herself with this strangely meek acceptance of mental anguish'. (Abert, p.133)

...her music is vividly distinguished from that of the other women...Her line is characterized by irregular, nervous contours, with unusual intervals of pitch and abrupt changes in dynamic...In ensemble, too, her phrases stand out idiosyncratically.[181]

D. Heartz similarly outlines the use of jagged lines of song, dotted rhythms and unexpected orchestral fortes in her arias and ensemble work.[182] Henning, in detailing the use of arpeggio motifs and coloratura to suggest Elvira's strong emotions, compares her music to that given by Mozart to don Giovanni in 'Là ci darem la mano' - simpler, smoother, and ultimately seductive.[183] Such a point would also apply to Giovanni's canzonetta of Act II, 'Deh, vieni alla finestra', which is simple, pretty and ultimately meaningless. The powerful emotions of Elvira are thus contrasted with the comparative lack of feeling in the song of her deceitful lover. Elvira's musical style also adds to the comedy and ridicule of which she is the victim, since it is melodramatic. But as Heartz suggests, her musical treatment does not always imply ridicule: she acquires dignity in the sextet of Act II, through a contrast with the comedy of Leporello, who sings after her.[184]

More, perhaps, than the other women in the early works, Elvira becomes the receptacle for masculine perceptions and wish-fulfilment about women, which at first mitigate against any sense of independence, and indeed individuality, that we might perceive. Lawrence Lipking argues to some effect that donna Elvira reflects male conceptions of women's behaviour:

---

[181] Andrew Steptoe, *The Mozart-Da Ponte Operas: the Cultural and Musical Background to 'Le nozze di Figaro', 'Don Giovanni' and 'Così fan tutte'*, (Oxford: Clarendon Press, 1990), p. 196.
[182] D. Heartz, 'Che mi sembra di morir: Donna Elvira and the Sextet', *Musical Times* 122 (1981), 448-451; 449-50.
[183] Cosmo Henning, 'Thematic Metamorphoses in *Don Giovanni*', *Music Review* 30 (1969), 22-26; p.24.
[184] Heartz, p.451.

110

> The words that flow from the mouth of...Donna Elvira are just
> what a man might imagine a woman would say when deprived of
> his presence. She would, of course, want him back. He knows her
> text by heart because he wrote it.[185]

Elvira's obsession with Giovanni indicates another masculine fantasy, a woman's
inability to live without men, and a need to be subject to them. Kierkegaard
echoes this notion when he comments: 'The spectator is meant to hear [don
Giovanni] inside Elvira, coming out of Elvira...what makes it musical is the unity
in Elvira's passion, in which Don Giovanni resonates while it is nevertheless
through him that her passion is posited'.[186] Thus a woman cannot speak with her
own voice, but merely regurgitates that of a man. Lipking comments upon another
aspect of fantasy, the sexual dimension of Elvira's role as victim: 'one cannot
ignore the element of sexual display or titillation that bedevils any distracted
heroine. Spellbound and self-absorbed, she exposes herself to the leers of voyeurs
on the stage as well as in the pit'.[187] As Lipking goes on to observe, this was an
element in Elvira's character taken up and heightened by Kierkegaard in his
portrait of her in *Either/Or* (187-198), as I discuss in the next chapter.
Furthermore, masculine wish-fulfilment about female behaviour gives scope for
the evasion of responsibility: women who behave as Elvira does merely deserve
the treatment they get. Don Giovanni *appears* less reprehensible since Elvira's
own conduct invites censure. Her hysteria, i.e. her 'exaggerated' reaction to
Giovanni's past treatment of her, diminishes the sense of his own guilt.

These points are not positive ones. But to say that Elvira embodies masculine
wish-fulfilment is not to deny her control over her own destiny. The very conduct
that men both wish for and despise grants Elvira the freedom to act on her own

---

[185] Lawrence Lipking, 'Donna Abandonata', in *The Don Giovanni Book: Myths of Seduction and Betrayal*, ed. by Jonathan Miller, (London: Faber, 1990), 36-47 p.37.
[186] Kierkegaard, p.124.

initiative, without any reference to conventions dictated by patriarchal society. Lipking notes that Elvira's hysteria gives her a certain measure of power:

> An abandoned woman is the slave of her lover. Yet once exiled from his presence she has nothing left to lose and takes the reins into her own hands. Donna Elvira exemplifies this curious relation to power. On the one hand she is Don Giovanni's dupe or chattel, drawn magnetically after him and wilfully co-operating in her own deception. On the other, she acknowledges no authority but her own passion.[188]

Thus Elvira's power and freedom to act lies precisely in her hysteria, which liberates her from conventional expectations which have been set down by a patriarchal society. Her hysteria gives Elvira the impetus to pursue don Giovanni and frees her from the need to act ostensibly through a male agent (as Anna does with Ottavio).

Moreover, her indifference to male judgement allows her to reject don Giovanni's attempt to render her indistinguishable. When she discovers his career of seduction, both Leporello and don Giovanni refuse to accept her anger as justified - not because she has not been wronged, but simply because she is not the first or the last to be treated in this way. Leporello, as he embarks upon his catalogue aria, tells her not to react so badly: 'consolatevi; non siete voi, non foste, e non sarete né la prima, né l'ultima' (Mozart, 75-6).[189] This means that she should accept, in his opinion, the idea that she is a woman like any other; that she is undifferentiated and has no individual value, and therefore no reason to be angry. Her refusal to accept her treatment on the terms of don Giovanni leaves her open to the charge of hysteria. Nevertheless, it also grants her the opportunity to assert

---

[187] Lipking, p.41.
[188] Lipking, pp.39-40.

her own individuality in defiance of don Giovanni's efforts to render her indistinguishable. Her insistence on her anger and desire for restitution is equivalent to a refusal to acknowledge a lack of separate identity. Thus Elvira's hysteria impels her to reject male judgements of what she deserves and what she must put up with; and, instead of conceding defeat, she acts to prevent don Giovanni's continued career as a womanizer.

In attempting this, Elvira acts with great effect. She anticipates don Giovanni's moves, turning up at the most inconvenient times to thwart his desires. Even her first appearance on stage proves frustrating for him, as he had hopes of comforting/seducing the woman he hears lamenting her lost lover. The forlorn woman he intends as his next victim proves to be one of his earlier victims, bent on revenge. She interrupts his seduction of Zerlina, using her own bitter experience to warn her of the danger of trusting him. Scarcely has she led Zerlina off stage, than she reappears to alert Anna and Ottavio of don Giovanni's untrustworthy nature - the ensuing exchange in the quartet 'Non ti fidar' eventually alerts Anna to the identity of her would-be seducer. Neither Anna nor Ottavio, incidentally, feel Elvira to be acting indecorously during the quartet: Anna sings that 'Non ha l'aria di pazzia il suo volto, il suo parlar' (pp.128-9).[190] This indicates that Elvira is able to put her point of view across effectively, even while under great emotional pressure. When she accompanies Ottavio and Anna in their Act I finale confrontation with don Giovanni, Elvira leads the way, exhorting the others to have courage. During this scene, she withstands the emotional pressure much better than Anna.

Elvira does not subvert patriarchal convention (as other female characters do) so much as ignore it. We remember that don Giovanni appeals to her sense of

---

[189] 'Cheer up: you are not, nor were, nor will be the first or the last'.
[190] 'Her countenance and speech does not seem that of a madwoman'.

decorum in the Act I quartet with Anna and Ottavio, telling her not to make a fool of herself in front of them. She brushes aside his arguments and declares herself free of restraint - 'ho perduta la prudenza' (Mozart, 131). Conventional dictates and opinions are for her irrelevant, and whatever society thinks of her does not affect her conduct at all. Her avowal in the finale to enter a convent implies a continued intention to remain free of male and social control. Elvira's comparative power and freedom from male authority may be one reason why, as Parakilas observes, producers, audiences and critics of the nineteenth century preferred to devote their attention to donna Anna.[191] As with the previous characters we have considered, Mozart and da Ponte's approach to Elvira appears equivocal - Lipking's essay that I have quoted indicates the ambiguity of our attitudes towards her - but they allow her a measure of autonomy and capacity for thought and action that appears positive. Elvira may end her days in a nunnery, but don Giovanni is unable to vanquish her contrary spirit.

Some of what we have observed concerning donna Elvira also applies to done Elvire in *Dom Juan*, since da Ponte clearly based his character of Elvira on the corresponding character in Molière's play. As does Elvira in *Don Giovanni*, Elvire appears on stage at a moment of great inconvenience for dom Juan, in this case interrupting his plans to pursue a young fiancée. Both women actively pursue and confront their seducer, alternatively raging at him and pleading with him to confess his love; both beg him to repent at the end, and both will enter a convent once he is dead. Thus Elvire shares in the freedom from decorum and convention that characterizes Elvira. An additional indication of Elvire's independence of men is that she succeeds in locating dom Juan and demanding restitution two acts before her brothers do the same, even though they are supposed to be the guardians of her honour. Furthermore, although they do not wish her to enter the

---

[191] J. Parakilas, 'The Afterlife of *Don Giovanni*: Turning Production History into Criticism', *Journal of Musicology* 8 (1990), 251-265; p.263. But Parakilas does not observe that Kierkegaard focused on Elvira, not Anna, in *Either/Or*.

114

convent in expiation of her dishonour (V, iii), this is what she plans to do regardless of their wishes (IV, vi).

Elvire has much less time on stage to establish her own emotionalism, but she succeeds in doing so very quickly. Her feelings for dom Juan have hitherto blinded her to the cold reality of his faithlessness:

> J'ai cherché des raisons pour excuser à ma tendresse le relâchement d'amitié qu'elle voyait en vous; et je me suis forgé exprès cent sujets légitimes d'un départ si précipité, pour vous justifier du crime dont ma raison vous accusait. Mes justes soupçons chaque jour avaient beau me parler: j'en rejetais la voix qui vous rendait criminel à mes yeux, et j'écoutais avec plaisir mille chimères ridicules qui vous peignait innocent à mon cœur (I, iii).[192]

Clearly she has preferred emotion to rationality, and she resorts to rational judgement only when forced to do so. Elvire has had recourse to wishful thinking, but she also demonstrates that emotion has proved more accurate and practical than reason. The above passage refers to her use of reason - 'raisons', 'excuser', 'sujets légitimes', 'justifier'. She subverts reason - traditionally understood as male - and aligns it with her own emotion; 'du crime dont ma raison vous accusait'. Reason has now become personal, '*ma* raison'; it indicates that Elvire has rejected cool rationality (understood as masculine) for her own reasoning born of passion. In this sense, she has subverted male rationality in favour not only of passion, but also of greater effectiveness and freedom of action.

---

[192] 'I have looked for reasons to justify to my tender heart the slackening of your love that my heart observes; and I have deliberately manufactured a hundred different excuses for your precipitate flight, to clear you of the crime of which my own reason accuses you. No matter what my just suspicions told me, every day: I ignored the voice that rendered you guilty in my eyes, and with pleasure I listened to a thousand ridiculous chimeras that made you out to be innocent in my eyes'.

Thus in this scene she proceeds to appeal to dom Juan's emotions, even while asking him for rational explanations:

> Que ne me jurez-vous que vous êtes toujours dans les mêmes sentiments pour moi, que vous m'aimez toujours avec une ardeur sans égale, et que rien n'est capable de vous détacher de moi que la mort? Que ne me dites-vous que des affaires de la dernière conséquence vous ont obligé à partir sans m'en donner avis; qu'il faut que, malgré vous, vous demeuriez ici quelque temps, et que je n'ai qu'à m'en retourner d'où je viens, assurée que vous suivrez mes pas le plus tôt qu'il vous sera possible; qu'il est certain que vous brûlez de me rejoindre, et qu'éloigné de moi, vous souffrez ce que souffre un corps qui est séparé de son âme? (I, iii).[193]

The cumulative structure of this passage reveals Elvire's passion. Her references to death, to burning and to the notion of soul and body separated and suffering, also indicate the exaggerated emotions she experiences. Dom Juan's cool response that he only left in order to get away from her, contrasts strongly with her melodramatic language to make her appear foolish, but also suggests the coldness of rationality. His philosophy of love that he has just expounded in the preceding scene may have a certain logic, but it is also cruel; and in Elvire we can perceive that emotion will not be denied a voice despite the play's emphasis on reasoning and philosophy. Elvire's embodiment of emotion, in contrast to the pseudo-philosophical dialogue of dom Juan and Sganarelle (though we cannot perhaps say much for the reasoning of the latter), may remind us of the simplistic dualism of male rationality and female emotion. Nonetheless, her emotion also gives her a measure of power that challenges dom Juan's philosophies, and impels her to act

---

[193] 'Will you not swear to me that you still feel the same towards me, that you still love me with unparalleled ardour, and that death alone can part you from me? Won't you tell me...that you surely burn to be by my side again, and that far away from me, you suffer as a body separated from its soul?'

on her own initiative without waiting for the tardy attempts at restitution on the part of her brothers.

This independence of thought and emotion also moves her to return to the convent, from which dom Juan took her before the plays begins. When we next see Elvire, her mood has changed again; and she now uses an elevated tone of piety which nevertheless retains traces of exaggeration in what she says to dom Juan:

> Le Ciel a banni de mon âme toutes ces indignes ardeurs que je sentais pour vous, tous ces transports tumultueux d'un attachement criminel, tous ces honteux emportements d'un amour terrestre et grossier; et il n'a laissé dans mon cœur pour vous qu'une flamme épurée de tout le commerce des sens, une tendresse toute sainte, un amour détaché de tout, qui n'agit point pour soi, et ne se met en peine que de votre intérêt (IV, vi).[194]

While she acknowledges her previous hysteria - the 'transports tumultueux' - her avowed sense of calm and purity does not quite coincide with her references to emotion, 'tendresse' and 'amour'. Even when she claims that she no longer indulges in her former melodrama, she nonetheless employs the image of a flame - 'une flamme épurée' - which implies passion. As in Act I, dom Juan attempts to deflate her emotion with cynicism, in this case his aside to Sganarelle: 'Tu pleures, je pense' ('I believe you're crying'; IV, vi). This remark promptly gives Elvire's speech a note of comedy. In both scenes, however, dom Juan's cynical realism cannot disturb done Elvire's recourse to passion and melodramatic expression. His efforts, cruel as they are, to make her see reality for what it is,

---

[194] 'Heaven has banished from my soul all those unworthy passions that I felt for you, all those tumultuous transports of a sinful attachment, all the shameful behaviour of an earth-bound, vulgar desire; and in my heart is left for you only a flame purified of all sensuousness, a pious affection, a detached love that strives for nothing for itself, and is only concerned for your welfare'.

prove ineffectual. Instead, she unswervingly pursues her course of emotion until the end, when she tearfully begs him to repent. When in response he asks her to stay, and thus attempts to retain some measure of control over her, she refuses and exits. Her plan is to retreat to a convent where she will remain free of such control.

Our study of the hysterical women, in conclusion, implies an ambivalent treatment on the part of Tirso, Molière, and da Ponte and Mozart. Certainly their emotionalism leaves them open to ridicule, and don Juan's treatment of each can at times be very cruel. Nevertheless, these authors also introduce suggestions of freedom in each woman. The fact that Tisbea, Elvire and Elvira dispense with decorum and restraint sets them outside conventional society, and since such society ultimately has its foundation in patriarchy, this therefore sets them outside male control as well. To us, the embrace of hysteria as a way to elude male control may seem a bleak option. Indeed, the choices that the women can make are undeniably limited - marriage or hysteria. However, the different paths taken by all the women to subvert the patriarchy that tries to order their lives, does in part mitigate the sense of dualism and determinism that will feature more strongly in the later plays.

It is worth observing that of all the female characters, Elvire and Elvira are the ones who confront dom Juan/don Giovanni face to face with his crimes. Though the other women actively pursue justice, they do not have the opportunity to challenge don Juan within the confines of the conventional society in which they are trying to accommodate themselves. The hysterical women, however, remain outside the decorum of conventional society, and their freedom from convention allows them the capacity to express the anger and pain of all the women - and Elvire and Elvira convey this directly to the seducer himself. Moreover, the hysterical women can express the pain and outrage of all don Juan's victims in a way that other female characters cannot, since the latter must compromise with social convention if they are to redeem themselves through marriage. Thus the emotional cries of these three characters can be understood to represent the distress of all the female victims, even those whom we do not see such as the women who feature in Leporello's catalogue. Walsh describes this idea well, in relation to the specific example of Tisbea: her representative function that he describes, also applies to Elvire and Elvira:

> Her plaint soars with a magnitude not found in the reactions of the noble victims of Don Juan...perhaps because Tisbea was meant to make a main lament and assert the outrage of all the women. She thinks her torment particular, but an audience would find in it the voice of all the dishonored, before her and beyond. Her cry of fire irradiates within the play and prophesies the fire of the finale. Don Juan's last words ['¡Que me quemo! ¡Que me abraso!/ ¡Muerto soy!', III,969-70]...are not borne in metaphor but are...an answer to and echo of Tisbea's rage.[195]

Walsh touches here not only on the sense of representation on the part of the hysterical women, but also on the fact that it is to these women that don Juan must answer. He eludes the censure of other characters, but the demands for justice of these women require a response. While Elvira and Elvire challenge him to his face, Tisbea's demands receive their answer at the edge of Hell itself.

***

---

[195] John K. Walsh, 'Tisbea's "Fire": the Imagery of Tirso's *El burlador de Sevilla*, Vélez de Guevara's *La serrana de la Vera*, and Lope's *La mejor enamorada la Magdalena*', in *Tirso's Don Juan: the Metamorphosis of a Theme*, ed. by Josep M. Sola-Solé and George E. Gingras, (Washington DC: Catholic University of America Press, 1988), 74-85; p.75.

When we come to review the different female characters of Tirso, Molière and Mozart, we can clearly observe that despite the attempts of the male individual protagonist to render them undifferentiated, each character preserves her own individual nature so that we can easily distinguish between them. We have noted that the characters often have some flaw in their personality - for instance, the pride of Tisbea, the dubious morality of Isabela and Ana, the greedy desire of Aminta, Zerlina and Charlotte to better their social status - but hold these flaws in conjunction with a capacity to act and determine the course of their own lives that has a positive resonance today. Moreover, the women succeed either in achieving their aim - the appropriate marriage partner - or in liberating themselves entirely from male control. The ability of the women to accomplish what they set out to do contrasts strongly with the ineffectiveness of the male characters, who plan what to do but fail to carry out their plans. This applies even to don Juan, who fails in his attempt to deprive the women of individuality. As we shall see in due course, later don Juans succeed in rendering women indistinguishable, reducing them in effect to mere female ciphers. That does not happen here. A positive capacity for successful action is, however, not the only element that suggests the benign approach of the dramatists to these characters. After all, we shall discover in the discussion of *Man and Superman* in chapter 5 that the female characters there successfully bring about the marriages they desire, yet I will argue that Shaw's approach reveals a level of hostility towards the women that is not present here. In the early works, the women do not appear pathological or predatory in pursuing their own course of action. The critical comments that the male characters direct at the women - such as Octavio's 'la mujer más constante/ es, en efeto, mujer' (I, 357-8) - focus solely on woman's propensity to be seduced, and *not* on her liberty of thought and action.

In terms of gender relations, we can observe in each work a dialectic in which the female and the male characters negotiate for power, for status and security, in which all (except the hysterical women) attempt to accommodate themselves within the prevailing social order. Within this dialectic, no one gender appears to have any monopoly of power, and the women do not appear weak or inferior to the men - partly because the men themselves can be seen to be flawed but also because the women themselves participate actively in events. There is a greater parity in gender relations than will appear in later plays. I argued in the previous chapter that don Juan looks to women in order to give himself some sense of individuality; but the fact that the women of the earlier plays retain their distinctiveness strongly implies the comparative sympathy with which Tirso, Molière and Mozart and da Ponte understood them. The male individual, in these plays, is not particularly privileged, and the plays end with the opportunity for marriage or the perpetual freedom from men that is the convent - the results that the women on the whole have worked to bring about.

The dialectic of gender relations that we see in *El burlador, Dom Juan* and *Don Giovanni* is not necessarily benign in strictly twentieth-century terms. The mere fact of subversion necessarily implies a tacit recognition of male domination that must be got round rather than overtly challenged. The need for compromise is not always attractive. For example, Zerlina's mastery over Masetto in the aria 'Batti, batti' takes the form of apparent feminine submission: she pretends to conform to preconceived notions of femininity that include a woman's need for physical chastisement. Nevertheless Masetto, in acknowledging the power she has over him, implicitly recognizes the dialectic of gender relations within which men and women make adjustments and concessions, and negotiate for power and space. When we come to contrast this dialectical process with the later don Juan, we shall see a stark dualism come to the fore in the form of outright opposition between women and the male individual of the later plays. There is no compromise, only capitulation by one side - Inés in *Don Juan Tenorio*, don Juan himself in *Man and Superman* and *Don Juan oder die Liebe zur Geometrie*. As

Frisch will put it himself (Frisch, 173): 'Tod oder Kapitulation' - death or capitulation. I do not - I could not - claim that the simplistic male/female dualism did not exist in the eras of the Counter Reformation and the Enlightenment. I do claim that such a dualism becomes more overt and more hostile in the later don Juan plays.

At this point it is worth tentatively suggesting a possible reason for the comparatively positive treatment of the women in the earlier works. The aim of the women is to accommodate their own desires as far as possible within a social order they take for granted; but there is here no threat to the male individual. Don Juan flees from the women in order to evade responsibility for his seductions; but he shows none of the fear towards women that later don Juans experience. The earlier don Juans see women as the raw material for the creation of an identity as a male individual; they do not see women as a threat to that identity. There is therefore none of the sense of men and women as opponents in conflict that will come out clearly in Shaw and Frisch. The emphasis of the earlier works rests with accommodation and compromise, underlining the social nature of the plays - the male individual appears as an aberration that briefly disturbs the equilibrium of society. The Romantic elevation and the modern problematization of the male individual does not occur here. It is to the Romantic elevation that we turn next, where we shall find the male individual in a quest for a more idealized sense of identity - salvation - with the consequence of a loss of female individuality and power.

Chapter 4: The Romantic era

Having studied the treatment of women in the plays by Tirso, Molière and Mozart, and established the comparatively accommodating approach taken by these dramatists towards their female characters, we should now move on to see how interpretations of women changed in the don Juan canon as it moved through the Romantic period. Our principal Romantic don Juan play is Zorrilla's *Don Juan Tenorio*, and we shall focus primarily on this. Before we do so, however, it is worth our while taking a slight literary detour in order to examine the portraits of the don Juan phenomenon by Søren Kierkegaard and E. T. A. Hoffmann. The reason for doing so is not only that their work sheds light on the gradual reinterpretation of gender relations in ways that prove more unequal, which award power in the relations primarily to the male individual and place the women at a distinct disadvantage. The versions that Kierkegaard and Hoffmann give of the don Juan phenomenon act as a sort of pivot whereby interpretations of don Juan change radically. They do this by drawing from the old tradition - specifically, Mozart's *Don Giovanni* - and simultaneously redirecting that tradition into a new path. Therefore, we have here not so much a simple rewriting of don Juan's story, but quasi-philosophical musing that points both forward and back. Mozart and da Ponte were indulgent towards their female characters. The reinterpretation by Kierkegaard and Hoffmann readily reveals a turn towards a more latently hostile approach.

Kierkegaard and Hoffmann: nineteenth-century attitudes

By the nineteenth century, other authors had not only created their own versions of the traditional don Juan plot and thus the female characters within it, but also referred to the earlier works in a conscious way, thus providing not only new versions of the genre but a critique of the older works. If we turn to two of these critiques - those of Kierkegaard and Hoffmann - we should be able to see that these two authors show less of the ambivalence of the earlier authors and a more pronounced tendency to antagonism. This may seem initially surprising, especially in view of Hoffmann's idealized portrait of Anna in his short story *Don Juan*. Nevertheless, both authors reveal a tendency *within themselves* - rather than within the male characters, as the earlier authors had it - to control and seduce women vicariously. A corollary of this is that they provide little actual censure of don Juan (or don Giovanni, since both Kierkegaard and Hoffmann deal specifically with Mozart's protagonist), and both reveal a covert desire themselves to be don Juans. Kierkegaard also shows a marked tendency to render women indistinguishable.

In 1843 Kierkegaard published *Either/Or: a Fragment of Life*. This book brought together a range of different essays concerning either of two ways of life: a life of seduction or a romantic marriage. Kierkegaard attempts to obscure his own views behind a fictitious editor of the essays, who in turn has supposedly gathered the essays written by other authors. Nevertheless, Kierkegaard himself loathed the idea of the duty and drudgery of marriage: Herwitz outlines Kierkegaard's view of marriage as a duty directly opposed to erotic pleasures.[196] Included among the essays is a discussion of don Juan as he manifests himself in *Don Giovanni*. Kierkegaard argues that the opera is the epitome of erotic expression, and that for this reason it is the greatest work of art ever created.

The equation that Kierkegaard makes here between art and seduction carries with it uncomfortable implications for the treatment of women. For Kierkegaard, don Giovanni symbolizes all music and art, the artistic principle within which great art is free but also inevitable. The artist chooses freely to express himself (less often

---

[196] Herwitz, pp.60-61. Shortly before writing *Either/Or* Kierkegaard had broken off his own engagement to Regine Olsen.

herself, in Kierkegaard's time), but the work of art that is the outcome suggests an inevitable whole, and that the artist could have done no other than he did. Kierkegaard applies this principle to don Giovanni, who acts freely but who inevitably desires women. Such a principle, of course, allows don Giovanni to elude any responsibility for his actions; and Herwitz is right to suggest that Kierkegaard is sexist (there can in fact be little doubt about it), since the philosopher uses the notion of great art to justify the seduction, and subsequent cheating, of women.[197] But Kierkegaard also implies by his argument that seduction is itself an art form. Since, as we shall see, seduction for Kierkegaard involves depriving women of identity and power, we can immediately comprehend that his elevated notion of seduction carries negative consequences for women.

Kierkegaard felt that *Don Giovanni* allowed him to understand the feelings of a seduced woman, for the opera itself is seductive. He insists that women are totally subject to don Giovanni, and insists furthermore that this is a good and beautiful thing. He reflects a tendency prevalent in the nineteenth century, which relegated women to a private sphere and subjected their thought and activity to the total control of men (a tendency that appears strongly in Zorrilla's play *Don Juan Tenorio*). Ultimately, Kierkegaard understands women to be totally subject to men, with no minds of their own, and thus he wishes to deprive them of much of the power they possess in the opera itself. Moreover, he insists that the women want it that way: 'Don Giovanni not only has luck with the girls, he makes them feel lucky too - and unlucky, but curiously enough, in such a way that they would have it thus, and it was a foolish girl who did not want to be unlucky in order just once to have been lucky with Don Giovanni'.[198] This idea, of course, neglects the misery experienced by the female victims in *Don Giovanni* and elsewhere; but it

---

[197] Herwitz, pp.48, 71.
[198] Kierkegarrd, p.106.

also suggests a fantasy of the willing victim. Donna Elvira becomes the primary focus for Kierkegaard's rather voyeuristic attitude: Kierkegaard depicts Elvira hurrying through the countryside, so sad, so abandoned and with clothes so interestingly awry:

> her countenance was pale, only her eyes blazed terribly, her body was trembling, her bosom rose and fell violently, but still she hurried faster and faster, her locks flung about and scattered in the wind...her nun's veil was torn in shreds and flew behind, her thin white gown would have betrayed much to a profane glance had not the passion in her face attracted even the most depraved person's glance.[199]

This portrait of Elvira should remind us of Lipking's comments about the sexual implications of Elvira's wildness and vulnerability,[200] as I outlined in my discussion of the character in the previous chapter.

The women's desire for seduction seems clearly to be Kierkegaard's own addition, and implies a wish on Kierkegaard's part for women to be pliant and unresisting. Kierkegaard claims that his view grants men access to feminine feeling and reaction, but he interprets female desire in terms of masculine wish-fulfilment and, according to Herwitz, reaffirms the essential masculinity of the audience. The opera reveals to men 'their capacity to identify with women and hence to love them, to feel those things from the safety of what is in fact an increased sense of masculinity'.[201] Kierkegaard unsurprisingly ignores the matter of how women in an audience would comprehend *Don Giovanni* (and, oddly enough, Herwitz does

---

[199] Kirkegaard, p.191.
[200] Lipking, p.41.
[201] Herwitz, p.57.

not pay the matter much attention either).[202] Neither Tirso nor Molière, nor Mozart and da Ponte, said with such direct force that women wanted to be seduced. Some of the female characters may have listened to don Giovanni's promises of social betterment - Aminta, Charlotte and Zerlina come immediately to mind - but they do not demonstrate obvious sexual desire.

Kierkegaard also believes that don Giovanni pursues an ideal of womanhood, a form of Everywoman represented by every individual woman he encounters. As far as the philosopher is concerned, don Giovanni's quest for ideal womanhood is heroic, a belief inspired (directly or indirectly) by Hoffmann, and a commonplace of *Don Giovanni* appreciation in the nineteenth century. Don Giovanni's constant movement from woman to woman is 'epic', heroic: 'The only way in which Don Giovanni can become epic is by constantly finishing and starting over again...'.[203] To be heroic is, among other things, to assert one's individual personality above those of others; it is to stand out, clearly defined against ordinary society. But don Giovanni's heroism bases itself on treating women as if they themselves have no identity, as Kierkegaard explains, and as I have already mentioned in chapter 2: 'In each woman he desires the whole of femininity...So for him all finite differences fade away in comparison with the main thing: being a woman'.[204] Kierkegaard also remarks that the sensual love which don Giovanni typifies 'can lump everything together. What is essential for it is woman quite in the abstract...'.[205] And more specifically:

---

[202] Herwitz observes that seduction, including its inherent sexism and perceived in the light of Kierkegaard's theories, is not confined to the individual character of don Giovanni, but is a function of the opera as a whole. Herwitz also claims that the opera becomes a metaphor for Mozart and da Ponte's seductive (i.e. successful) career in the sphere of Viennese opera (Herwitz, pp.66-9). Our study of the female characters in the opera does not bear out Herwitz's argument, since in the original work the women elude and subvert any inherent sexism in the attitudes of the male characters (including don Giovanni). But Herwitz's arguments certainly apply to Kierkegaard, who has derived from the opera an attitude to seduction inherently more demeaning to women.

[203] Kierkegaard, p.102.

[204] Kierkegaard, pp.105-6.

[205] Kierkegaard, p.101.

> For Don Giovanni every girl is an ordinary girl, every love affair
> an everyday story. Zerlina is young and pretty, and she is a
> woman, that is the peculiarity she shares with hundreds of others,
> but it is not the uncommon that Don Giovanni desires but the
> general, what she has in common with every woman.[206]

Kierkegaard argues here that all that matters for a woman is her womanhood: any
other defining characteristics she may possess are irrelevant. It is not without
significance that Kierkegaard describes all women as 'ordinary', an indication of
his latent hostility. The inability to distinguish between women coincides with
Leporello's opinion: 'purché porti la gonnella,/voi sapete quel che fa' ('so long as
she's got a skirt on, you know what he'll do'). Kierkegaard's pronounced opinion
contrasts, however, with the greater ambiguity that Mozart and da Ponte brought
to the depiction of the female characters. We can detect a move away from the
dialectic of parity of male-female relations portrayed in the opera, towards a more
definite opposition between don Giovanni and the women, so that women become
for Kierkegaard mere objects of a seductive exercise rather than individuals. To
describe Giovanni's actions as irradiating 'a heightened beauty with its
refulgence'[207] is ingenuous at most. If we compare this with the treatment Elvira
receives from Giovanni, it hardly heightens her beauty or gives her femininity a
greater sense of worth. Such treatment cannot be considered as synonymous with
heroic ideals.

However, his arguments ignore the fact that in the opera the individual female
characters differ greatly from each other, and clearly are not interchangeable. Nor
are the women subject to don Giovanni in quite the way that Kierkegaard
envisages. In the 'early' versions of the don Juan tale - Tirso, Molière and Mozart -
women are pursued, but they also pursue; and (unlike the women of *Man and*

---

[206] Kierkegaard, p.103.

Superman and *Don Juan oder die Liebe zur Geometrie*) they pursue not in order to prey upon men but to exact restitution. All seek don Giovanni in order to hold him to account in some way: even though Elvira's anger weakens through her love for him, she still wishes him to reciprocate her love and hold to the promises he made to her earlier.

Thus Kierkegaard's account of the opera reveals as much about Kierkegaard[208] as it does about don Giovanni. Mozart and da Ponte give the women a good measure of liberty of thought and action in the opera, at least equal to that of the male characters. But Kierkegaard has imposed on the opera an interpretation that dispenses with the individuality of each female character and that insists on the subjection of women to the seducer.

If we turn to Hoffmann's interpretation, we can see similar attitudes. Hoffmann's short story 'Don Juan' concerns a traveller who goes to a performance of *Don Giovanni* and encounters Anna, ostensibly the singer playing the role of Anna in the performance but also possibly the essential spirit of Anna as Mozart and da Ponte imagined her. After the performance, the traveller muses on the natures of Anna and Giovanni. As the clock strikes two in the morning he believes he can smell Anna's perfume: the next day he hears that the singer who played Anna died at that exact hour. The story deals just as much with the feelings towards Anna of the traveller as of don Giovanni, and underlying the language of idealism we can detect a desire towards sexual possession similar to that of a don Giovanni. To the extent that the traveller stands for the thoughts and opinions of Hoffmann - which seems feasible, given that the story is essentially a critique of Anna - the sexual desire is also Hoffmann's.

---

[207] Kierkegaard, p.106.

[208] We must remember, however, the proviso that Kierkegaard is hiding behind two fictitious authors: the anonymous writer of the piece on *Don Giovanni*, and the editor Victor Eremita.

Hoffmann apparently appeals to idealism in setting up Anna as don Giovanni's[209] perfect match:

> Donna Anna ist, rücksichtlich der höchsten Begünstigungen der Natur, dem Don Juan entgegengestellt. So wie Don Juan ursprünglich ein wunderbar kräftiger, herrlicher Mann war, so ist sie ein göttliches Weib, über deren reines Gemüt der Teufel nichts vermochte.[210]

Hoffmann stresses that not only do don Giovanni and donna Anna form a perfect pair, but that Anna herself is pure - 'ein göttliches Weib, über deren reines Gemüt der Teufel nichts vermochte'. The need for purity will be echoed in Zorrilla's character doña Inés, whose purity will ensure don Juan's salvation (as I will discuss below). To be the perfect woman for don Giovanni, Anna must be pure; and thus Hoffmann insists on the highest standards for the woman but not for the man. A look at the description of don Giovanni confirms this difference in standards, for while Anna is 'göttlich', Giovanni is 'kräftig, herrlich' - two qualities that have little to do with purity but quite a lot to do with sexual power.

Hoffmann's description of Anna suggests the traveller's (and thus Hoffmann's?) own sexual desire towards her. The description prefigures Kierkegaard's picture of Elvira:

> Augen, aus denen Liebe, Zorn, Haß, Verzweiflung, wie aus *einem* Brennpunkt eine Strahlenpyramide blitzender Funken werfen, die,

---

[209] Quotations that follow from Hoffmann show that he referred to the male protagonist of Mozart's opera as don Juan. In my discussion of Hoffmann, however, I shall refer to this character as don Giovanni, in order to distinguish the operatic incarnation of the character from other versions of don Juan.

[210] 'Donna Anna is, in view of the highest advantages given her by nature, don Giovanni's opposite. So, just as don Giovanni originally was a particularly strong, splendid man, so is she a divine woman, over whose pure mind the devil has no power'. E. T. A. Hoffmann, 'Don Juan: eine

wie griechisches Feuer, unauslöschlich das Innerste durchbrennen! des dunkles Haares aufgelöste Flechten wallen in Wellenringeln den Nacken hinab. Das weiße Nachtkleid enthüllt verräterisch nie gefahrlos belauschte Reize.[211]

Anna has virtually become one of our hysterical women here: her eyes express strong, contradictory emotions and her hair and clothing are awry. Hoffmann's voyeuristic description of her nightdress should remind us of Kierkegaard's description of Elvira mentioned earlier. The sensuous image of Anna's hair flowing round her neck reinforces the idea of Anna as a sensual woman, as does the imagery of fire and burning (which by this stage of the genre has become a little commonplace in describing the women).[212] The description of don Giovanni which follows again refers to his strength and his manly beauty ('männlich schön', p.68), in contrast to Ottavio who is 'zierlich', dainty and 'geleckt', dapper. It is worth observing at this point that the earlier authors do not dwell with such sexual obsession on the appearance of the female characters. I have to qualify this by saying that the theatre does not facilitate description, and both Kierkegaard and Hoffmann have the advantage that they are writing prose. Nonetheless, we can compare these descriptions with Shaw's portrait of Ann Whitefield, which by contrast reveals the sexual undertone in the portraits that Kierkegaard provided of Elvira, and Hoffmann of Anna.[213]

---

fabelhafte Begenbenheit, die sich mit einem reisenden Enthusiasten zugetragen', *Fantasie- und Nachtstücke*, (Munich: Winkler, 1960), pp.67-78; p.76.

[211] 'Eyes from which blaze love, anger, hate, despair, as if a pyramid of rays and flashing sparks were flung from one single focal point, and which burn indelibly through one's heart like a Greek fire! The dishevelled braids of dark hair flowed in waves down her neck. Her white nightdress treacherously revealed charms observed at one's peril'. Hoffman, p.68.

[212] Later commentators did not share Hoffmann's relish for Anna. Dent (p. 158) describes her as aloof and thoroughly unpleasant. Abert (p.66) refers to her 'virginal tenderness and modesty', and insists on her love for Ottavio. For a description of the changing interpretations of Anna, see Parakilas, pp.263-4.

[213] As an example of Shaw's description of Ann Whitefield:

'Whether Ann is good-looking or not depends upon your taste; also and perhaps chiefly on your age and sex[...]Ann is a well-formed creature[...]she is perfectly ladylike, graceful and comely[...]Ann is one of the vital geniuses. Not at all, if you please, an oversexed person[...]She

When the traveller encounters donna Anna in the theatre, he senses an empathy with her and an appreciation of her which nevertheless contains elements of the sexual. A s h e s ays w hen h e f irst e ncounters h er: 'jeder d araus l euchtende B litz goß einen Glutstrom in mein Inneres, von dem alle Pulse stärker schlugen und alle Fibern erzuckten'.[214] After their meeting, as he watches her on stage, 'ein glühender Kuß schien auf meinen Lippen zu brennen' ('an ardent kiss seemed to burn on my lips', p.72). When the traveller later comes to muse on the opera, he concludes that don Giovanni did in fact seduce Anna before the opera begins, that she could not resist him (and as he thinks this, two o'clock strikes and he smells Anna's fine Italian perfume). Only don Giovanni could achieve her surrender (and not the 'unmännlichen, ordinären Don Ottavio'). When we reflect that the traveller argues for an empathy between himself and Anna, and also a perfect pairing between Giovanni and her, we can deduce that don Giovanni seduces Anna on the traveller's behalf, that the traveller, and thus perhaps Hoffmann, seduces her vicariously.

It should be clear that the two authors share a heightened sense of female sexuality which is far less apparent in *Don Giovanni* itself, and which is also unclear in *El burlador* and *Dom Juan*. Both reveal a voyeuristic attitude to their heroines E lvira a nd A nna, b ut, m ore s ignificantly for o ur d iscussion h ere, t hey demonstrate a sense of the need to control and seduce women that is not present in the earlier works. The sense that women are subject to men comes out strongly here. Tirso, Molière, and Mozart and da Ponte record the seductions of the women, but give no indication that such seduction is a good thing; nor do they themselves reveal any vicarious desire to seduce. The women are individuals,

---

is a perfectly respectable, perfectly self-controlled woman, and looks it; though her pose is fashionably frank and impulsive[...]a woman who will probably do everything she means to do without taking more account of other people than may be necessary and what she calls right. In short, what the weaker of her own sex sometimes callls a cat' (Shaw, pp.15-16).

[214] 'Every radiant flash cast a storm of passion within me, which made all my pulses beat more strongly and all my sinews tingle'. Hoffmann, p.71.

who are threatened by don Juan/don Giovanni because they happen to be women. Kierkegaard and Hoffmann, however, celebrate the power that don Giovanni has over women and link such power directly to sexuality. The desire to seduce, to have sexual power over the women, reveals a move towards a more antagonistic stance towards women within the don Juan genre. This antagonistic stance becomes pronounced in the next three plays we shall look at. The idealism of *Don Juan Tenorio* will prove to contain elements of such antagonism embodied in the need to make women entirely passive and entirely pure, and will reveal a consequent fear of female sexuality. This antagonism, this fear, will develop into outright hostility in *Man and Superman* and *Don Juan oder die Liebe zur Geometrie*. We saw earlier in this chapter how the women attempt to take some measure of control over their own lives: they may live within patriarchy, but are not subordinate to male desire. The work of Kierkegaard and Hoffmann implies a gradual change in attitude, and we will now look at how these changes developed in later plays.

Having seen how the seeming neutrality towards of the earlier works changes to the voyeurism of Kierkegaard and Hoffmann in the nineteenth century, and how in consequence female characters become more sexually dependent on the don Juan figure, we can appreciate how increased opposition and antagonism by (male) authors towards their female creations might come about. An underlying intention of Kierkegaard and Hoffmann appears to be the repositioning of women as the objects of male sexual power, whereby the women's lives are controlled by their seducer. In each case the central female character - Elvira and Anna respectively - lives only for don Giovanni, and is unable to think or act independently. I will argue that this attitude persists in Zorrilla's *Don Juan Tenorio*, and that the elevation of doña Inés to the deserving object of Romantic male desire disguises an equally male desire to render her devoid of independent power. In *Don Juan Tenorio*, don Juan embodies male ambivalence about female sexuality in a manner that is also typical of Kierkegaard and Hoffmann, in the wish both to provoke and to control female desire. Beginning, then, from Zorrilla, we can take up from the previous chapter the indications of the masculine need to control female sexual desire suggested by Kierkegaard and Hoffmann.

Zorrilla and doña Inés

The don Juan figure is popularly regarded as a seducer. The action of many don Juan works (including the three reviewed in the previous chapter) normally follows his career from woman to woman until the figure of the statue appears to bring his career to an end. In *Don Juan Tenorio* the emphasis of the action lies elsewhere. We have a record of seduced women when don Juan produces his list of victims in the first act, and we also witness his arrangements for the seduction of doña Ana. Nevertheless, the focus of don Juan's actions remains Inés, the Comendador's daughter. Zorrilla's portrait of her is sentimental, emphasizing her innocence, purity and pliability. She has little personality. She appears rather as a symbol of inspiration, an ideal towards which don Juan attempts to reach, and a prize which don Juan must become worthy of winning. Zorrilla's development of Inés as a symbol of perfect womanhood inevitably says a great deal about the way in which the patriarchal society of the nineteenth century perceived women. In plays such as *El burlador*, *Dom Juan* and *Don Giovanni* all the characters are shown to be flawed in some way, regardless of their sex. In *Don Juan Tenorio*, however, Inés represents Woman, an idealized being far removed from the pressures of men that drag them towards perdition. It is ironic, however, to note that nineteenth-century literature, more than any other, managed simultaneously to idealize women and yet view them as weak, sensual creatures who posed a threat to rational society. This schizophrenic perception reveals a great deal about nineteenth-century society's own need for a don Juan figure, who carries out vicarious male desires towards women and is nevertheless condemned for it.

Today we might comprehend the portrait of Inés as a little too sentimental for twentieth-century tastes, but male approval of her passive perfection has proved remarkably persistent. In regard to the Romantic perception of women, critics continued to view women in a Romantic haze even when writing in a twentieth-century context. Leo Weinstein's praise of Inés as an excellent female character, and his disparagement by comparison of Tirso's lively women, typifies this. For him, female characters are best when little more than embodied purity: they must not be permitted to display rounded, flawed personalities as male characters can.[215] Zorrilla criticism has woefully neglected the significance of Inés as a symbol of womanhood which lacks personality; and this gap in criticism contributes to a lack, even today, of study of the role of women in the don Juan genre. Mandrell is a notable exception to this, and has discussed female idealization as a method by which patriarchy can control women.[216] The figure of Inés proves to be an important instance of this tendency.

When we turn to consider Inés in more detail, it becomes clear that Zorrilla's perception of Inés is an exalted one, but subconsciously it is not necessarily benign. By idealizing Inés Zorrilla actually distances her from the action: her saintliness is as much a trap for her as is the cloister. A specific example of Inés' uncomfortable role as an inspirer of men can be found in her literal petrification in the pantheon. There the sculptor - a man - has placed her upon a stone pedestal and arranged other men to kneel at her feet in worship. Inés does not, of course, express any doubts about her elevated role, though she does begin to wonder in the cloister whether the life her father has allotted her is what she really wants. However, her pedestal demonstrates the need that men had to raise women to a

---

[215] 'Zorrilla[…]presents some of the most effective portrayals of women in the history of the legend in Inés and Brígida': Leo Weinstein, *The Metamorphoses of Don Juan* (Standford, CA: Stanford University Press, 1959), p.129 – a contrast with the banal corruption of Tirso's women (p.33). Weinstein praises Molière's done Elvire for similar reasons: he applauds the way in which she rises above her initial anger to pray for dom Juan's salvation. Her attitude of sanctity makes her 'a woman of real worth' (p.33).

state of perfection, thus avoiding demands for perfection in themselves. Men admire saintliness, and try to attain it through attainment of a virtuous woman, but they do not themselves try to rise above others in purity. Thus the statues of Mejía and don Gonzalo remain kneeling at Inés' feet.

Yet Zorrilla maintains a strange equanimity at the prospect of this idealized female icon risking eternal damnation, as Inés does, for a character who acts much like a spoiled child throughout the play. That character does not pursue women but Woman. Women not only define don Juan's identity, they are his salvation. It is this very virtue, in ironical contrast to popular expectation of the don Juan figure, that attracts Zorrilla's protagonist to her. However, Zorrilla's don Juan does not prize Inés's purity for its own sake, but because he hopes to benefit from it: his love is not disinterested. Don Juan looks to Inés to ensure his own salvation. Indeed, the first words he addresses to her (in the letter) - 'Doña Inés del alma mía' (1644) and later, 'Inés, alma de mi alma' (1692) - link his soul to hers and suggests that her soul embodies his own. More specifically, and more significantly for Inés' eternal future, he links his salvation to her love for him:

> No es, doña Inés, Satanás
> quien pone este amor en mí:
> es Dios, que quiere por ti
> ganarme para *Él* quizás.
> No, el amor que hoy se atesora
> en mi corazón mortal,
> no es un amor terrenal... (2264-2270).[217]

---

[216] Mandrell, pp.240-1, 244-5.
[217] '.Doña Inés, it is not Satan who instils this love in me but God, who wishes perhaps to save me for himself through you. No, the love that I treasure in my mortal heart for you now is no earthly love[…]'.

In this passage, don Juan makes explicit his belief that Inés represents his redemption: if she will love him, then he will be acceptable to and accepted by God. Their love for each other is a holy love that contrasts with 'amor terrenal' and which will transform his 'corazón mortal'. He believes further that Inés alone can ensure his reform into a good person - 'me siento a tus pies/capaz aún de la virtud' ('at your feet I feel myself still capable of virtue', 2278-79) - and when don Gonzalo refuses to countenance don Juan's marriage to his daughter, he replies 'vas a hacerme perder/con ella hasta la esperanza/ de mi salvación tal vez' ('you will make me lose, along with her, maybe even the hope of my salvation', 2551-53). In the second part of the play Inés is now dead, and don Juan believes that she alone can ensure salvation in Heaven:

> Dios te crió por mi bien,
> por ti pensé en la virtud,
> adoré su excelsitud,
> y anhelé su santo Edén.
> Sí, aun hoy mismo en ti también
> mi esperanza se asegura,
> que oigo una voz que murmura
> en derredor de don Juan
> palabras con que su afán
> *se calma en tu sepultura* (2954-63).[218]

This passage summarizes don Juan's attitude towards Inés as a means of salvation. Her function is to impel the libertine to good behaviour, and it is this inspirational

---

[218] 'God created you for my good; because of you I thought on virtue, I worshipped its exaltedness and longed for its saintly paradise. Even now my hope rests on you, and I hear a voice that whispers around don Juan words that from within your tomb calm his desire'.

quality within her that attracted him to her: 'No amé la hermosura en ella,/ni sus gracias adoré;/ lo que adoro es la virtud,/...en doña Inés' (2500-03).[219]

Through her virtue, therefore, Inés retains responsibility for don Juan's soul - even after her death. Zorrilla's approval of such a state of affairs reveals itself clearly in divine sanction of the arrangement: Inés' own salvation will depend upon don Juan's repentance. God tells her: 'con don Juan te salvarás,/ o te perderás con él' ('you will be saved or be lost along with don Juan', 3006-07). This obviously makes for dubious theology on Zorrilla's part, but it also tells us a good deal about his attitude towards women, that a woman should willingly allow her own soul to hang in the balance for the sake of the soul of an incorrigible man. Zorrilla's proposition is of course romantic in all senses of the term, but we may nevertheless experience some distaste at the notion. The arrangement is hardly a good bargain for Inés, in the possible exchange of the divine grace she merits for the soul of a notorious womanizer. Thus Zorrilla finds a new way in which don Juan makes use of a woman's identity in order save his own. In the eyes of Zorrilla's God, the virtue of a good woman is subsumed into the sin of a libertine. Ines's own identity as a virtuous person counts little: her fate - her own eternal identity - depends on don Juan. And he, in his turn, will gain a new identity as a heavenly being through her intercession. This new way in which he exploits a woman's identity compares badly with those of the three earlier plays. The don Juans of those plays attempted to deprive the women of their individuality (and do not, on the whole, succeed): this don Juan gains control of a woman's very soul.

Feal saw in Inés don Juan's missing mother, a figure noticeably absent from the genre's cast list.[220] Usually within the genre, he argues, the encounter between don

---

[219] 'It was not her beauty or grace that I loved; what I love is doña Inés's virtue'.

[220] Feal, *En nombre de Don Juan,* p.47. I argue earlier that this originally arose in part because of a historical/literary accident: the Golden Age theatre of Tirso's time rarely portrayed mothers on stage. This would not, however, necessarily prevent other authors from making use of this

Juan and the statue indicates a father-son dialogue where the mother is not present to mediate. We can conclude from this, then, that Inés fulfils the mother role to a great extent since she does attempt to mediate between the wrath of her dead father and the desperation of her lover/son; and, moreover, she shows a degree of maternal self-sacrifice in staking her soul on that of don Juan. Monleón's observation of Inés' growing sexual awareness does not preclude a reading along the lines of Feal.[221] In addition, Inés seems very much to represent a figure like the Virgin Mary, giving her a powerful salvatory role (though the comparison does not apply to the extent of staking her own soul).[222] But it would be too simplistic to understand Inés simply as a mother figure, because her symbolism is to be read in a more universal way. Inés represents the aspiration of all women as inspirers of men (at least as a bourgeois society would read it), and while any definition of womanhood must include some notion of maternity, it cannot be confined to it.

Most symbols of womanhood, however, carry contradictory notions of women as something to be both desired and feared. Inés may symbolize innocence, but nevertheless Zorrilla introduces a sexual element to her character at an early stage, an element reminiscent of Kierkegaard and Hoffmann's voyeurism. Brígida depicts Inés aflame for love of don Juan before Inés herself ever appears on stage: 'sus deseos mal dormidos/ arrastraron de sí en pos;/ y allá dentro de su pecho/ han inflamado una llama/ de fuerza tal, que ya os ama/ y no piensa más que en vos' (1300-1305).[223] Don Juan replies by describing Inés in metaphorical terms as a

---

omission and giving it greater significance. Don Juan's lack of a mother has allowed an entry point into the discussion for critics with a Freudian turn of thought. See Rank; and Marina Warner, 'Valmont - or the Marquise Unmasked', in *The Don Giovanni Book: Myths of Seduction and Betrayal*, ed. by Jonathan Miller (London: Faber, 1990), 93-107.

[221] Monleón, pp.27-8.

[222] This may explain one reason why *Don Juan Tenorio* proved popular in Spain but not in other, Protestant countries in Europe, where Marian theology was not so acceptable.

[223] 'Her barely dormant desires pursue her, and in her breast has leapt a flame so strong that now she loves you and can think of nothing but you'.

flower that has not yet opened, an image that strongly implies his intention to awaken her, 'open' her, sexually:

¡Oh! hermosa flor, cuyo cáliz
al rocío aún no se ha abierto,
a trasplantarte va al huerto
de sus amores don Juan (1318-1321).[224]

This metaphor is echoed by the abbess in Inés's opening scene: 'aquí [in the nunnery]a los besos del aura/vuestro cáliz abriréis,/ y aquí vendrán vuestras hojas/ tranquilmente a caer' (1474-7). [225] The abbess's use of the image, however, robs it of any sexual significance and renders it arid: the reference to autumn leaves suggesting death and Inés's life wasted in the cloister. (Inés will later refer to the abbess's words as 'aridez', line 1527). A comparison between the two uses of the flower image favours don Juan's usage with its sexual overtones. Inés may be virtuous, but her virtue must not remain preserved in the safety of the nunnery. It must be available for don Juan to use. Don Juan's reference to an orchard to which he will transplant her indicates ownership: this metaphorical orchard is part of his domain and under his control. Much as don Juan might value Inés' saintliness, then, this does not preclude him from wishing to take full advantage of her growing sexual awareness.

While Inés is to inspire virtue in don Juan, he inspires her sexuality. The strongest statement she makes about her desire occurs at the point where she has just finished reading his letter:

---

[224] 'Beautiful flower, whose calyx has not yet opened to the dew, don Juan will transplant you in his orchard of love'.

[225] 'Here your calyx will open to the kisses of the breeze, and here, quietly, your leaves will fall'.

¿Qué sentimientos dormidos
son los que revela en mí?
¿Qué impulsos jamás sentidos?
¿Qué luz, que hasta hoy nunca vi?
¿Qué es lo que engendra en mi alma
tan nuevo y profundo afán?
¿Quién roba la dulce calma
de mi corazón? (1736-1743).[226]

Inés's reference to 'sentimientos dormidos' mirrors don Juan's earlier metaphor of the awakening flower: in this scene we see don Juan succeed in instilling new and unrecognized feelings within her. The image of the light that she has never seen before that day serves a similar function. Don Juan's letter has inspired these sentiments, and we can recall Ciutti's remark as he watched his master write that letter: 'Es gran pluma' (a great writer – literally, a 'great pen', 32). Don Juan's pen - a clear phallic image - has aroused Inés to hitherto unknown feelings that have an obvious sexual nature, a 'nuevo y profundo afán'.

The above passage also reveals Inés's ambivalent attitude towards these new sensations: they have robbed her of her peace of mind. This indicates that, while for don Juan her sexual awakening is a desired aim, for Inés herself her new-found sexuality is problematic, to say the least. This idea is further strengthened by her references to poison. She calls his letter a 'filtro envenenado' ('posioned philtre', 1732), and later tells him: 'Me habéis dado a beber/ un filtro infernal sin duda' ('You have obviously given me some devillish philtre to drink', 2232-3) and subsequently 'tu aliento me envenena' ('your breath poisons me', 2255). Inés also makes allusions to witchcraft and sorcery: 'algún encanto maldito' ('some evil

---

[226] 'What dormant feelings are waking within me? What impulses, never known before? What light that I never saw before today? What is causing such new and deep anxiety in my soul? Who has taken away the sweet serenity of my heart?'

enchantment', 2104); 'un misterioso amuleto/ que a vos me atrae en secreto' ('a mysterious amulet which draws me secretly to you', 2237-8). Thus while for don Juan female sexuality is a positive thing, to be described in floral terms, for Inés female sexuality appears in negative terms, as a thing to be feared as much as to be desired. Therefore, we can perceive don Juan's search for power over Inés through her sexuality: he wishes to enjoy and control her sexual desires, but this does not mean in consequence that she is free to control and enjoy her sexuality herself.

Such ideas about female sexuality are discussed in a recent paper by José Monleón, who specifically relates the don Juan theme to the vampire figure, suggesting that both figures reflected contemporary social tensions that demanded the confinement of women to a private, domestic sphere. The tensions rest precisely on the question of control of female sexuality. According to Monleón, women in the vampire tradition possess a suppressed sexuality that might rise to the surface if the social order is transgressed. The vampire's victims are predominantly female: he feeds on them in order to maintain his own being in a manner reminiscent of don Juan's exploitation of female identity in order to maintain his own. Despite the fact that both the vampire and the don Juan figure lie beyond nature, they are still sexually desirable: 'la monstruosidad de la figura del seductor consiste en hacerse querer, en convertirse en objeto del deseo femenino',[227] implying in consequence that women's sexuality will attach itself to anything, even unnatural beings, if it is not tamed and reined in. Thus Inés comes to desire don Juan, an idea suggested by recurring imagery of fire and poison, both of which are images suggesting potency and danger. And, as in the case of the vampire, don Juan can only enter Inés' cell if she desires him to come in: the unnatural figure of sexuality can initially only gain power if the female figure

---

[227] 'The monstrousnes of the figure of the seducer consists of making himself loved, in becoming and object of feminine desire'; Monleón, p.28.

assents. Both the don Juan and the vampire figure reveal nineteenth-century attitudes towards women, who were understood as an entry point through which the irrational could infiltrate the rational world. Yet paradoxically, don Juan both usurps male power and reinstates it in the sphere of love, the domain of women. Pérez de Ayala refers to don Juan (a generic don Juan rather than specifically that of Zorrilla) as a usurper who deprives women of their rule over the sphere of love. Don Juan 'éntrase, hazañero y sin escrúpulo, por los dominios en donde la mujer imperaba como soberana, la destrona, la somete y proclama al varón rey del sexo'.[228] Monleón says:

> ¿Qué define al donjuán? ¿Qué le da vida? Al igual que el vampiro,
> Don Juan se alimenta de sus conquistas, y sin la posibilidad de
> repetir su cruel rito, no existirá. Vive de un solo hecho: despojar a
> la mujer de su feminidad (feminidad en tanto que construcción
> social determinanda por el orden patriarchal).[229]

The comparison between don Juan and the vampire provides points of great interest to an exploration of the don Juan genre, for it is undeniable that both figures are parasitic, exploiting women in some manner in order to sustain their own existence - bodily existence in the case of the vampire, personal identity in the case of don Juan. But Monleón misapplies his idea by examining Zorrilla's don Juan to illustrate his idea. He does this presumably to support his link of the vampire obsession with nineteenth-century bourgeois capitalism, since *Don Juan Tenorio* is a principal don Juan work of the nineteenth century. To say that the use of Zorrilla's work is misplaced, is not to deny the validity of Monleón's general

---

[228] 'He enters, dramatically and without scruple, into the dominions where woman reigns supreme; he removes her from her throne, he conqueres her and proclaims man the sexual king'; Pérez de Ayala, pp. 468-9.

[229] 'What defines a don Juan? What makes him live? Like the vampire don Juan nourishes himself from his conquests, and he cannot survive without the ability to repeat his cruel ritual. He owes his existence to one fact alone: depriving women of their femininity (femininity here being a social construct determined by patriarchy'; Monleón, pp. 25-6

hypothesis, but other works would have suggested the vampire figure more clearly. *El burlador* would have fulfilled the task admirably, even though it was not written in an era of bourgeois capitalism. Zorrilla's don Juan, however, does not appear to prey on all women. Throughout the play, he has contact with only three women apart from Inés, and of these, he takes no real notice of two of them - Lucia and Brígida. He may or may not have seduced doña Ana, but we never see him talking to her - his main purpose is not so much to seduce her as to defeat his rival Mejía, to whom Ana is to be married the next day. And the catalogue of conquests with which he opens his claim to wild living in the inn, is now part of the past: for don Juan wishes to reform. The one woman who arrests his attention is doña Inés, and through her he seeks redemption, salvation *after death*, rather than keep himself eternally alive in this world, as the vampire does. It would overtax the imagination to perceive this as vampirical behaviour. Don Juan resembles far more the prodigal son who desires forgiveness and acceptance, which he fails to obtain from his father and don Gonzalo, but which Inés is willing to provide, to the extent of staking her own soul upon his.

However, Monleón uses his study of the vampire to elucidate theories about the need to confine women's sexual desires to the home, and to limit their power to the domestic, private sphere. Here we are on surer ground. Inés epitomizes the female struggle between freedom and the need for safety, which lies in tameness. While the abbess and Brígida compare the character to a bird, the former calls her a '[m]ansa paloma' ('gentle dove', 1462) and the latter a '[p]obre garza enjaulada' ('poor caged heron', 1250), suggesting that Inés simultaneously represents domestic peace and imprisoned sexuality. The use of Monleón's proposed dichotomy of public and private spheres, with women confined to the latter, resolves the apparent contradiction between the clear evidence of Inés's sexuality and her role as a redeeming intercessory for don Juan. Thus don Juan can use Inés to satisfy both his sexual and his spiritual needs, and her life becomes subordinate to his needs. In this light, we may comprehend the opposition between don Juan and don Gonzalo as a struggle to gain or retain authority over women, so that don Gonzalo wishes to confine Inés to her own private sphere of the cloister, while don Juan wishes to remove her to his own home, and thus establish a new private sphere for her. He does not intend to set her free from the potential prison of the cloister, but merely proposes to exchange one enclosed and defined space for another. The murder of don Luis and don Gonzalo may perhaps take on a new significance, because they are the invaders in don Juan's own home, and thus don Juan kills them in defence of his own private world, a sphere which the woman would occupy. The desire to have mastery over the woman reveals itself as well in don Gonzalo's threat to kill Inés rather than let don Juan possess her. We might consider this a relic of an older code of honour more prevalent in Golden-Age theatre, but it does also suggest that don Gonzalo is more interested in Inés as a locus of power rather than as his own child. Patriarchal appreciation of Inés as passive and yet inspirational stems from a perception of men as active, part of the public world, while inspired to act because of women, who occupied their private sphere, confined to the home. Women inspired men merely by *being*, rather than doing: in their passivity lay their perfection. Inés inspires don Juan to seek redemption through her love and later through her intercession; and he pursues his redemption within the female, private domains of the nunnery and the home, and later in the pantheon where the stone statues of men kneel before that of Inés.

Inés's relegation to the private sphere also holds true for most female characters.[230] Zorrilla highlights the restriction of women to the private sphere in the scene that takes place in a *public* sphere, the opening scene at the inn. Don Juan and don Luis's recapitulations of their careers of libertinism, including the

---

[230] But not all. Brígida comes and goes as she pleases: her asexual status ensures her freedom. See my article 'Inés and Brígida: Sexual Presence and Absence in Zorrilla's *Don Juan Tenorio*', *Bulletin of Hispanic Studies*, LXXVI, no. 3 (July 1999), 327-336.

seduction of women, occur in the inn; and there they propose a wager that centres on the conduct of women. But the women themselves have no presence and no voice in the public sphere of the inn, even though they are the subject of the bet. They are conspicuous by their absence.

Furthermore, Ana is a clear example of a woman relegated to the private sphere, confined to the house and guarded by Mejía and his servant in order to prevent don Juan from entering the house. Mejía's protection avails him nothing, for don Juan gains entry to Ana's house through the weakness of a woman, Ana's maid Lucía, who accepts don Juan's bribe. (The conversation between don Juan and Lucía, when the bribery takes place, ironically copies the same poetic metre and rhyming scheme used by Mejía and Ana when Ana swears to keep faith to him). A similar pattern occurs in the nunnery. The abbess emphasizes in her principal speech to Inés the secluded nature of the cloister, that shuts out the world and its dangers, leaving Inés to 'la virtud de no saber' ('the virtue of not knowling', 1489). But again don Juan gains access through the weakness of a woman, this time Brígida, who acts as the go-between of don Juan and Inés. Brígida also indicates the ambivalence of women's sexual nature: she delights in encouraging Inés to surrender to don Juan, and aids and abets the latter as far as she is able; and she takes vicarious pleasure in the thought of Inés's surrender. She also takes delight in don Juan's sexual power. When don Juan proposes to carry Inés away (Inés having fainted), Brígida's reply sounds as if she herself has been seduced:

> ¡Sin alma estoy!
> ¡Ay! Este hombre es una fiera;
> nada le ataja ni altera...
> Sí, sí; a su sombra me voy (1794-7).[231]

---

[231] 'He's taken my breath away! Oh, this man is a wild beast, nothings stops him or upsets him [..]yes, I will follow in his shadow'.

And she later admits that don Juan's letter affected her just as much as it did Inés:

> Y estaba [the letter] en verdad tan tierna,
>
> que entrambas a su lectura
>
> achacamos la tortura
>
> que sentíamos interna.
>
> Apenas ya respirar
>
> podíamos, y las llamas
>
> prendían ya en nuestras camas (2038-2044).[232]

Brígida is ostensibly talking about a fire that broke out in the nunnery, the fiction she gives out as the reason why don Juan rescued Inés and brought her to his house. But we have seen in other contexts the idea that fire represents passion and sexuality; and Brígida's phrase 'las llamas/ prendían ya en nuestras camas' has a strong sexual undertone. But we may also observe that both women share these passions. Don Juan controls Brígida through her sexuality just as much as he does Inés. Zorrilla uses Brígida as a way of suggesting to the audience the waywardness of female sexuality and the need, and ability of a man to control it - without making Inés herself too overtly sexual, which would then conflict with her status as a virtuous woman.

The above discussion of Inés should serve to demonstrate that symbolizing women as figures of purity, ideals to be attained, was and is a complex matter. It indicates the ambiguity in men's perception of women. She becomes a locus of aspiration for men, a sanctified prize to be attained, but also something that must be destroyed, killed lest it fall into the wrong hands, as don Gonzalo argues (736-39). While Zorrilla's understanding of women does not explicitly define women

---

[232] 'And in fact the letter was so tender, that we both held it responsible for the torture we felt inside. We could hardly breathe, and the flames were taking hold in our beds'.

as dangerous and predatory in the manner of Shaw and Frisch in the next century, he has removed from Inés any sense of humanity that enlivens Tirso's female characters, and he has removed from her any vestiges of power. The other female characters, however, do not merit even the ambiguous elevation that Zorrilla bestows on Inés. For don Juan, Ana, Brígida and Lucía are merely means to an end. He does not perceive them as women in their own right but merely as tools to achieve his goals. Despite his reputation as a libertine he does not attempt to seduce Brígida (even though she seems willing to be seduced), and he bribes rather than seduces Lucía.

As for Ana, we never see don Juan talk directly to her, and they never appear together. We do not see her succumb. This total lack of onstage contact makes it that much harder for Ana's seduction to seem credible. His use of her thus is perfunctory, a duty to be fulfilled before returning to Inés, his main interest. Don Juan's true purpose in Ana's seduction is not to make a victim of Ana but of Mejía, his real target. We have seen elsewhere that don Juans usually make use of women in order to provide themselves with some form of identity. They create an identity for themselves as a seducer by equating and undifferentiating all women, making them act in the same way. If we accept that don Juan lacks identity, and acquires it only by his reputed exploitation of women, then Mejía as his double proves a further threat to his identity, and must be competed with and beaten, for Mejía also claims to seduce women and uses this fact to maintain his reputation. The seduction of Ana therefore acquires a further significance, since through seducing her don Juan reinforces his identity as a seducer and simultaneously deprives don Luis of *his* identity.

Zorrilla's portrait of women in *Don Juan Tenorio* therefore reveals notions of women that are less benign than might at first be supposed. Inés is worshipped and revered but she cannot think or act for herself, and her wishes and desires all arise from the controlling power of men - don Juan and her father. Don Gonzalo wants to keep her imprisoned in a cloister where she no longer feels happy: don Juan claims to 'liberate' her from her cell, but she merely exchanges one enclosed sphere for another, don Juan's house and later her tomb. In terms of divine forgiveness, she is not allowed to profit from her own goodness and purity of character, but must surrender it in exchange for the salvation of don Juan, thus allowing the latter to evade responsibility and penitence for his own sins. Thus Inés becomes the sacrificial victim of don Juan. Zorrilla's idealized picture of Inés nevertheless permits him to introduce a note of sexuality, thus satisfying the voyeuristic desires of himself and the audience (along the lines of Kierkegaard and Hoffmann) while simultaneously insisting on the need for masculine control of female sexuality.

Thus with the Romantic era we can see a clear change in interpretation of gender relations. The male individual has gained in stature, and the contest between him and his female counterparts has become more unequal. Women are more obviously sexually available, and more obviously subject to don Juan rather than equal players in the sexual arena as formerly. As with Tirso, Molière and Mozart, the Romantic don Juan attempts to find his own identity by depriving women of theirs, but this don Juan has far more success in his endeavour, rendering the female characters less distinctly themselves and more overtly subordinate to him. The male individual himself reaches his most ideal position at this point: he can be truly equated with the hero in all senses of the word. He attains his highest goal with Zorrilla's play: redemption and eternal existence (a goal not attainable to male society as a whole - Romanticism in this case favours the individual rather than patriarchy as a whole). I think that the link between increasing subordination of the female characters and the simultaneous strengthening of the male individual, the protagonist, should be quite clear. In the twentieth century, however, Romantic ideals faded and men's sense of themselves became more overtly troubled. We shall see in the following chapter what this entails for some authors' perceptions of gender relations.

Chapter 5: The twentieth-century plays

So far we have observed the ability of the earlier female characters to 'subvert and survive', achieving their individual aims despite the attempts of don Juan to seduce them and thereby establish his own identity by rendering them indistinguishable. Subsequently, we have observed the elevation of male individual identity to divine heights, and the consequent subjectivation of the female characters. In the plays of Shaw and Frisch the male quest for identity moves to a new field: the twentieth-century don Juans look for individuality within abstract fields of social philosophy and geometry. In this chapter I intend to show that the negative treatment of women continues and grows to more overt levels. In contrast to *Don Juan Tenorio*, the female characters in the modern plays resume the ability to act positively in the manner of the earlier plays, but now their independence of action is recast in more malignant tones. Both plays end with marriage or domesticity, but instead of restoring order, as in the earlier works, marriage now becomes a form of punishment or damnation for don Juan. Domesticity is a mark of failure for the male individual. While Zorrilla's don Juan understands his quest in terms of woman, the protagonists of the two twentieth-century plays see their quest in terms of separation from woman. As I discussed in chapter 2, and will elaborate further here, the protagonists of Frisch and Shaw perceive the higher, abstract entities which they seek as domains separate from women, where women do not belong, and their quest for these entities occurs in tandem with an opposition to the desires of women. The tendency of Zorrilla to confine women to a private sphere becomes stronger in these plays, and we should be able to observe an increasing sense of mutual exclusiveness between the male and female spheres within the twentieth-century plays, which in turn underscores the notion of opposition between the women and the male individual. It also gives rise to the greater malevolence towards the women.

Zorrilla's play depicts its central female characters in elevated tones that nevertheless incorporate a great deal of the sexual. Shaw and Frisch, however, dispense with sentimental or voyeuristic notions of women, and cast their female characters as menacingly strong, pathological, in danger of overwhelming the male characters and particularly the don Juan figure. Frisch depicts his women as sexual, but female sexuality is now eminently undesirable and don Juan flees it. For Shaw, women's sexuality becomes subordinate to their maternal instinct, and men merely become a means for reproduction. In practice, this means that Shaw's female characters pose a strong threat to the male characters, and the pursuit of their desire for marriage and motherhood results in a malign interpretation of women that makes the protagonist, John Tanner, recoil and flee in desperation.

The suggestion that *Man and Superman* does not portray women in a good light does not coincide with Shaw's avowed championship of women's emancipation. In his political writings he espouses the cause of equality for women, and many of his plays feature strong female characters. He attempts to strip away the romantic ideas that have weighed down the depiction of women in a bid for a more realistic perception of women's position in society. Barbara Bellow Watson observes this:

> When Shaw thinks about women, something remarkable happens.
> He makes no assumptions. It would be wonderful enough to make
> no assumptions about what women are fitted for, what their place
> in society should be. The real wonder is to begin thinking about
> women without assuming that there is any mystery at all. Shaw
> does so and, instead of wearing himself out trying to solve a

mystery that does not exist, sets to work observing the life around him.[233]

According to Watson, Shaw places women at the centre of the drama; and many of Shaw's plays concern a women's quest to realize her own potential. Our consideration of *Man and Superman* will reveal that Shaw does not observe as objectively as Watson suggests; and Watson herself appreciates difficulties of seeing the female characters of the play in a radical light, given the fact that they pursue marriage and use a form of what is popularly considered feminine guile to achieve their purposes. Nevertheless, neither Ann Whitefield nor Violet, the two principal female characters, fit the pattern of conventional romantic heroines within comedy.

Shaw undeniably avowed an appreciation of women that relieved them of the burden of romanticism, which insisted on their passivity while simultaneously requiring that they marry. In his preface to the play he comments:

> Among the friends to whom I have read this play in manuscript are some of our own sex who are shocked at the 'unscrupulousness', meaning the utter disregard of masculine fastidiousness, with which the woman pursues her purpose. It does not occur to them that if women were as fastidious as men, morally or physically, there would be an end of the race. Is there anything meaner than to throw necessary work upon other people and then disparage it as unworthy and indelicate...we ourselves throw the whole drudgery of creation on one sex, and then imply that no female of any

---

[233] Barbara Bellow Watson 'The New Woman and the New Comedy', *Shaw Review* 17 (1974), 2-16; p.2.

womanliness or delicacy would initiate any effort in that direction. There are no limits to male hypocrisy in this matter.[234]

And further:

> Woman must marry because the race must perish without her travail: if the risk of death and the certainty of pain, danger, and unutterable discomforts cannot deter her, slavery and swaddled ankles will not. And yet we assume that the force that carries women through all these perils and hardships, stops abashed before the primness of our behavior for young ladies.[235]

The hypocrisy of such a belief is echoed by John Tanner in his reaction to the news that Violet is expecting a baby, apparently out of wedlock:

> Here is a woman we all supposed to be making bad water color sketches, practising Grieg and Brahms, gadding about to concerts and parties, wasting her life and money. We suddenly learn that she has turned from these sillinesses to the fulfilment of her highest purpose and greatest function - to increase, multiply, and replenish the earth. And instead of admiring her courage and rejoicing in her instinct...here you are...all pulling long faces and looking as ashamed and disgraced as if the girl had committed the vilest of crimes.[236]

Ann echoes Tanner's accusations of hypocrisy towards women in the final act, in discussion with Octavius. She tells him that Violet is 'as hard as nails', and when he counters that his sister is still 'womanly at heart', she replies in exasperation: 'Is it unwomanly to be thoughtful and businesslike and sensible?' (p. 153). She

---

[234] Shaw, xviii-xix
[235] Shaw, xx.
[236] Shaw, 25-6.

envies Violet the ability to achieve her aims 'without having to make people sentimental about her' (ibid), or, in other words, having to resort to 'feminine' guile in order to do as she wishes.

Thus far, Shaw's perception of the female characters seems positive enough, coinciding with his radical thinking about women's position in society. He apparently wishes women to be released from the sentimentality that so imprisons Inés in *Don Juan Tenorio*, and asks that we judge them on their own merits rather than by romantic criteria devised by men (for the men are sentimental while the women are not). Not all critics have accepted Shaw's feminism at face value, however. Elsie Adams points out that while Shaw professes strong support for female emancipation in his political writings, in his literary work he reverts to basic female stereotypes of temptress, goddess and mother; to which we can add that of the huntress.[237] Ann and Violet engage in a single-minded hunt for husbands, homes and potential fathers, failing to be deflected from their somewhat ruthless aim by the romanticism of such characters as Octavius and Hector Malone. The comparison throws new light on the concept of women as the possessions of men, or the loci of male power, as in *Don Juan Tenorio*. Shaw neatly reverses this idea, so that men become the possession of women. Critics such as Apostolidès have proposed theories of the don Juan figure that view women as tokens of exchange, goods with which men can barter between each other (don Juan interrupts conventional exchange relationships that exist between men).[238] Applying this model, the women of *Man and Superman* do not function as tokens of exchange. Instead they themselves actively participate in the matrimonial marketplace, and they are the 'buyers' who initiate the exchange. The men have now become the goods bought and bartered.

---

[237] Elsie Adams, 'Feminism and Female Stereotypes in Shaw', *Shaw Review* 17 (1974), 17-22; pp.17-18.
[238] Apostolidès, p.448.

The image of woman as huntress gives us a starting point with which to examine the antagonism that we will find beneath Shaw's claim to reappraise women in a juster, more positive light; for Shaw's overt celebration of women is not the whole picture. It hides a hostility towards women that underlies the entire play. One indication of this is Shaw's reversal of male and female roles in love and courtship, so that in Shaw's variant of the don Juan tradition, the women are the pursuers, the men the pursued. The idea of female pursuit features implicitly in earlier versions, such as the portrait of donna Elvira in *Don Giovanni*; it is not as novel in the don Juan genre as some critics suppose. But for Shaw, women's pursuit of men is blatant, and he introduces the idea for different reasons - to show, not the need to be subject to a man's control, but that women see men as merely a means to an end. They do not pursue men out of a need for love or for justice, but in order to fulfil their own maternal instinct.

Mandrell argues that pursuit by women follows a tendency within the don Juan tradition to male fantasies about women.[239] Hitherto, the female characters have 'asked for' all they have received from don Juan, if we accept this understanding; they desired the sexual attention he gave them. Now *Man and Superman* takes fantasy to a new level, where the man feigns reluctance before surrendering. Men become passive and women active. Daniel Leary suggests that this is a feature of Shaw's drama elsewhere. He cites the character Charteris in *The Philanderer*, who says 'I loved you from the first, and fled only that you might pursue'.[240] Shaw's inclination to draw strong female characters and weak male ones may underline a possible taste for masculine passivity. Such male passivity and fantasy, however, is not incompatible with a hatred for women. Underlying Shaw's apparent support of women lies a strong hostility, which was noted early on by Otto Rank but few other critics since. Shaw's interpretation of the women as huntresses allows him to

---

[239] Mandrell, p.46.
[240] Daniel J. Leary, 'Don Juan, Freud and Shaw in Hell: a Freudian Reading of *Man and Superman*', *Shaw Review* 22 (1979), 58-78.

use strongly negative images that suggest the threat women pose to men; and their natural maternal instinct becomes a purposiveness which is sub-human.

Shaw often refers to the women as a part of the animal world - the creatures he uses to symbolize women are often unpleasant or dangerous. In the preface to *Man and Superman* he describes women's pursuit of men in monstrous terms that mirror the cruelty of nature, comparing them to spiders:

> It is assumed that the woman must wait, motionless, until she is wooed. Nay, she often does wait motionless. That is how the spider waits for the fly. But the spider spins her web. And if the fly, like my hero, shews a strength that promises to extricate him, how swiftly does she abandon her pretence of passiveness, and openly fling coil after coil about him until he is secured for ever![241]

Tanner compares Ann to a lioness, telling Octavius that 'your head is in the lioness's mouth: you are half swallowed already...she [Ann] breaks everybody's back with the stroke of her paw' (p.22). And to a tiger:

> Oh, the tiger will love you. There is no love sincerer than the love of food. I think Ann loves you [Octavius] that way: she patted your cheek as if it were a nicely underdone chop.[242]

Later, Tanner uses the metaphor of the boa constrictor to describe Ann: 'The boa constrictor doesnt mind the opinions of a stag one little bit when once she has got her coils round it' (p.38). The use of the feminine possessive adjective here is suggestive. These images remind us of the animal savagery of the hunt by stressing the status of the male as the hunted, the prey. Women intend not only to fetter men through marriage but to devour them: man will be subsumed into

---

[241] Shaw, xix-xx.
[242] Shaw, p.24.

woman. This notion reappears in Tanner's conversation with Octavius in Act II: he warns Octavius that he is 'the marked down quarry, the destined prey' (p.52). When Tanner finally realizes that he, not Octavius, is Ann's object, he immediately echoes his words to Octavius, and exclaims: '*I* am the...marked down victim, the destined prey' (p.67). In the Hell scene the protagonist's *alter ego* don Juan also echoes these ideas: 'Then the lady, who had been happy and idle enough before, became anxious, preoccupied with me, always intriguing, conspiring, pursuing, watching, waiting, bent wholly on making sure of her prey: I being the prey, you understand'.[243] He also perceives women as devouring creatures: '...whilst I was in the act of framing my excuse to the lady, Life seized me and threw me into her arms as a sailor throws a scrap of fish into the mouth of a seabird'.[244] Women are therefore fearsome. Tanner tells Ramsden that all must 'cower before the wedding ring' (p.45), the wedding ring being the symbol of women's pursuit of motherhood via matrimony.

We have come far from Shaw's avowed celebration of women in his political writings, and Tanner's ostensible understanding of motherhood (and thus marriage) as a noble ideal, to a perception of women as dangerous, devouring creatures. They are totally alien from men, and, as the spider/fly image indicates, men's natural enemy. The characters of *Man and Superman* reflect this underlying division of the sexes. The male characters are sympathetic, humorous and occasionally ridiculous. None appear dangerous. But Shaw's female characters appear singularly unsympathetic. Of the two principal female characters, Ann is superficially charming but unpleasantly manipulative, while Violet also manipulates but lacks the charm. Watson understood the female's characters activity in a positive light: 'The women are enterprising, audacious, aggressive, and self-assured, and it is they who secure all the desired outcomes through their

---

[243] Shaw, p.112.
[244] Shaw, p.114.

wit and daring'.[245] She neglects, however, to appreciate the negative aspect of female activity in the play: the women dedicate their enterprise to hunt and capture, and we cannot understand this as benign.

This covert malevolence towards women recurs even in Shaw's view of women as mothers. Despite his apparent elevation of the maternal role, Shaw describes mothers in disparaging terms. He considers motherhood the essential work of the human race in his preface, but Tanner nevertheless attacks motherhood in its later stages:

> Look at fashionable society...A horrible procession of wretched girls, each in the claws of a cynical, cunning, avaricious, disillusioned, ignorantly experienced, foul-minded old woman whom she calls mother, and whose duty it is to corrupt her mind and sell her to the highest bidder. Why do these unhappy slaves marry anybody, however old and vile, sooner than not marry at all? Because marriage is their only means of escape from these decrepit fiends who hide their selfish ambitions, their jealous hatreds of the young rivals who have supplanted them, under the mask of maternal duty and family affection.[246]

Shaw marks this speech as ambiguous: he prefaces Tanner's speech with a stage direction that the protagonist is 'working himself up into a sociological rage' (p.96), a comment that somewhat deflates the impact and significance of the speech. Tanner is, it seems, only getting carried away with his ideas. But don Juan says something similar to Ana:

> When your sainted mother, by dint of scoldings and punishments, forced you to learn how to play half a dozen pieces on the spinet -

---

[245] Watson, p.8.

which she hated as much as you did - had she any other purpose than to delude your suitors into the belief that your husband would have in his home an angel who would fill it with melody, or at least play him to sleep after dinner?[247]

This passage reveals a dislike of Ana by her mother, who is well aware that her daughter is no harmonious angel, otherwise she would have no need to delude Ana's suitors. Nonetheless, mother and daughter conspire to trap men, and this reveals that motherhood, too, is not a benign occupation. Eventually, mothers will attempt to trap men for their daughters just as the daughters themselves do. Mrs. Whitefield does not really like her daughter Ann, making disparaging remarks about her at every opportunity. However, even though Mrs. Whitefield does not like Ann, she still wishes her to marry Tanner: 'when it's been put into my head that Ann ought to marry you, what can I say except that it would serve her right?' (p.158). The uncomfortable relationship between mother and daughter lends some support to Tanner's rather malign view; and it also contributes to an underlying sense of hostility towards women as unpleasant, voracious creatures who lack any sense of the higher purposes that inspire men. Violet, the expectant mother, is possibly the most antipathetic character in *Man and Superman*, caring little for the high-minded principles of her husband. We might also observe at this point that other female characters also appear cold, lacking any finer feeling. Miss Ramsden displays a narrow-mindedness in her refusal to help Violet, while Louisa Straker (who does not appear on stage) spurns the advances of Mendoza. Mendoza himself comments (melodramatically) on her lack of empathy for his feelings: 'she...recommended me to marry an accursed barmaid named Rebecca Lazarus, whom I loathed. I talked of suicide: she offered me a packet of beetle poison to do it with' (pp.79-80).

---

[246] Shaw, p.54.

Despite constant references to men as tools for motherhood, the notions of love outlined in the play seem rather asexual. The implications of women as malignant pursuers and the indications of responsibility and commitment for men in consequence, submerge any suggestion of sexual desire. Charles Carpenter suggests that Ann's surname, Whitefield, implies a lack of sexual attraction. He goes on to argue that the final scene with Tanner and Ann in Act IV (Shaw, 162-3) suggests a virtual sexual climax of the two principal characters, as Tanner groans and Ann becomes increasingly breathless.[248] Tanner begins this episode by crying to Ann that he loves her: at this point romantic love and sexual desire become indistinguishable. Nevertheless, Ann here is again manipulating Tanner into marriage. She warns him: 'if anyone comes while we are like this, you will have to marry me' (p.163). And indeed most of the cast do arrive at this point, and Ann immediately announces her engagement, even though, as Tanner himself points out, he never actually asked her to marry him. He sees her use of passion as a way in which to entrap him. Even Ann's sexuality, then, becomes a tool for her to use in order to get her way, rather than an expression of pleasure.

Ann displays an amiability and a coquettishness that mask her determination to make Tanner marry her. Her manipulations bring about the play's action because she has made use of her father's death in order to get Tanner as her guardian. This notion of the daughter 'wishing' the father dead distorts the Oedipal triangle in which two men (father and son) struggle to win control over one woman (the mother): now the woman exercises the control. Thus her father's will, which appoints Tanner Ann's guardian, is in effect Ann's 'will', the embodiment of her wishes, as Tanner recognizes: 'The will is yours then! The trap was laid from the beginning' (p.162). The ambiguity of the word 'will' in his remark implies that all

[247] Shaw, p.116
[248] Charles A. Carpenter, 'Sex Play Shaw's Way: *Man and Superman*', *Shaw Review* 18 (1975), 70-74.

that matters is woman's 'will', her own aims, which are marriage and motherhood. The aims of the male characters count for nothing: she thwarts them all. Octavius asks to marry her but does not; Tanner wants to elude her and does not; Ramsden wants to be sole guardian of Ann but is not. (In a similar way, Violet blocks the proposed aims of the Malones, father and son. The father wishes to stop his son's allowance, the son wants to work for his living. Neither option suits Violet, and in the end her will prevails. The father continues to pay the allowance, the son does not work - all in direct contradiction of their expressed intentions). Shaw points out Ann's ruthlessness in his description of her in the stage directions:

> She inspires confidence as a person who will do nothing she does not mean to do; also some fear, perhaps, as a woman who will probably do everything she means to do without taking more account of other people than may be necessary and what she call right.[249]

What she does call right is usually synonymous with what she wants. This comes across clearly in her opening scene, where Ramsden and Tanner wrangle over the question of their guardianship. Her manipulation of the conversation, so that she confounds both men with her insistence on duty, is comic, but nevertheless remains a strong example of her ability to get what she wants despite the intentions of Ramsden and Tanner. She appears to act submissively towards them, and to the wishes of her dead father, but her submission is false - she controls the entire conversation. Therefore her eventual engagement to Tanner at the end is a victory rather than the conventional happy ending, and Tanner is right to say: 'Ann looks happy; but she is only triumphant, successful, victorious' (p.165).

Ann's *alter ego*, Ana in the Hell scene, shares a similar propensity to disguise her true aims with a cloak of conventional righteousness: when she discovers that she has arrived in Hell nevertheless, she exclaims: 'Oh! and I might have been so much wickeder! All my good deeds wasted! It is unjust' (p.86), and later 'I, who sacrificed all my inclinations to womanly virtue and propriety!' (p.87). This immediately implies that conventional womanly behaviour merely masks a woman's true intentions. Ana also responds to don Juan's philosophical commentary in a deflationary, 'commonsense' manner very reminiscent of Ann, who listens to Tanner's political and social theories with no more than indulgence. Ana, as much as Ann, understands the need to hunt and trap men into the imprisonment of marriage, and in doing so dispenses with notions of sentimentality, much as Ann does when she cries that women ought to be allowed to be practical:

> If you [don Juan] had had the chance, you would have run away
> from me too - if I had let you. You would not have found it so easy
> with me as with some of the others. If men will not be faithful to
> their home and their duties, they must be made to be. I daresay you
> all want to marry lovely incarnations of music and painting and
> poetry. Well, you cant have them, because they dont exist. If flesh
> and blood is not good enough for you, you must go without: thats
> all.[250]

Now that Ana is dead and in Hell, she can express more clearly women's need to pursue and entrap men than Ann can, since Ann must still proceed with guile. Death does not prevent Ana, however, from continuing to follow don Juan even as far as Heaven, or don Juan from longing to escape her company. The struggle for mastery between Tanner and Ann is now revealed as an eternal one: women and men will continue to oppose each other and thwart the aims of each other, even in Heaven and Hell. Men will always flee, women always pursue. Men,

---

[249] Shaw, p.16.
[250] Shaw, pp.112-3.

however, remain one step ahead. Don Juan continues to aspire to a higher, worthier life, and Ana continues to discuss his aspirations in only conventional terms. Hence throughout the entire scene she persists in her conventional perception of Heaven and Hell and her rightful place in the former, despite evidence to the contrary given her by don Juan, the statue and the Devil. Thus women are also eternally unsuitable for the higher goals that Heaven embodies, since they cannot understand Heaven's true meaning.

Ann Whitefield pursues her intended male victim: Violet Robinson has already captured hers. There is a distinct irony in Violet's name: she is hardly the 'shrinking violet' that implies female modesty. Louis Crompton points to the dead bird in her hat (Shaw, 42) as a symbol of her predatory nature.[251] Violet succeeds in doing as she pleases without any hindrance from others. While in Acts I and II other characters insist that she should stay hidden from public view (because of her uncertain marital status), she remains remarkably mobile, mixing confidently in society and joining a car journey which her brother Octavius insisted she should miss. Like Ann she does not accept the idealistic nature of her husband, but while Ann is indulgent towards Tanner's philosophy, Violet is sharply dismissive of Hector Malone's intention to work in order to support them. She aims for a middle-class gentility supported by unearned income, and she gets her way.

Violet demonstrates a capacity for independence and practicality traditionally associated with men. She is well able to take care of herself, and negotiates a marriage settlement independently of her husband (whom she regards as a romantic hindrance). When Tanner defends Violet's purported unmarried motherhood, she turns on him and denounces him for believing her capable of

---

[251] Louis Crompton, *Shaw the Dramatist: a Study of the Intellectual Background of the Major Plays*, (London: Allen and Unwin, 1971); p.87.

such a thing. Not only do women need no protection from men, they may rebuke any attempt at protection that men offer. Tanner's gestures of compassion and support are ironically valueless: their rejection by a woman may suggest another reason to fear women, who reject attempts at fellow feeling. Violet's stance implies that women have little human feeling at all, allowing them to pursue their aims with ruthlessness. In contrast to the female characters of Tirso, Molière and Mozart, who act positively in order to survive and to accommodate themselves the best they can in a patriarchal society, Violet's actions prove more threatening to men. She does not only survive, she secretly controls Malone's life and future, so that he surrenders his power to her.

Since women prove so threatening, Tanner/don Juan shows a desire to escape them: women are to be shunned and eluded as long as possible. Tanner believes that it is 'a woman's business to get married as soon as possible, and a man's to keep unmarried as long as he can' (p.52), introducing the theme of flight and escape. Flight enables Shaw's don Juan figure to assert his individuality *in opposition* to the women. His identity stands out in relief from the monstrous horde of women who all act in the same devouring way. Flight from women becomes essential in order to maintain freedom. Tanner tells Ann that in order to call his soul his own he broke off his childhood confidences with her. 'It happened just then that I got something that I wanted to keep all to myself instead of sharing it with you...It was something youd never have let me call my own...My soul' (p.34). His need to keep his soul free from Ann's control indicates his fear of her pursuit of a husband that disregards any individual identity, and his consequent impulse to elude her control.

A motif in the theme of flight is the car, which appears at the beginning of Act II. Leary notes the significance of the car, and its importance in the mind of Straker,

Tanner's servant and chauffeur.[252] Straker (as is common in the don Juan tradition) remains unencumbered by women, and his desire to break speed records suggests his facility in eluding female pursuit. In this light, we may see a deeper meaning in Straker's comment 'Might as well ave a pram and a nussmaid to wheel you in it as that car and me if you dont git the last inch out of us both' (p.54). The inability to flee will result in parenthood via marriage, hence the reference to the pram. We can also appreciate Tanner's sudden desire to break speed records once he discovers that he and not Octavius is the object of Ann's pursuit. But Ann also has recourse to the car in her pursuit of her victim. The modern industrial age has not altered the situation *vis-a-vis* don Juan and women: it has merely speeded up the chase. Tanner's flight in his car leads directly to the dream sequence that features his subconscious self, don Juan, in which don Juan manages to escape the demands of women in Heaven. His dream ends, however, with the cry of 'Automobile' that announces Ann's arrival in Hector Malone's car: her arrival signifies the end of his dreams of escape. Ironically, Tanner has urged on Ann the significance of the car in female emancipation: 'Break your chains...Get your mind clean and vigorous; and learn to enjoy a fast ride in a motor car instead of seeing nothing in it but an excuse for a detestable intrigue' (p.58). She takes neither of these options, but herself uses the car as a means of pursuit. Tanner cannot outrun Ann. Hector Malone tells him 'Miss Whitefield tracked you at every stopping place: she is a regular Sherlock Holmes' (p.133).

To summarize, then, Shaw's apparent release of women from the confinement of sentimental notions of womanhood masks a clear and strong hostility towards women. Woman's nature appears, quite frankly, horrible. Ann and Violet, the principal female characters, come across to the audience as manipulative and predatory, a point accentuated by Shaw's use of bestial imagery. Even motherhood, the highest aim that women can aspire to, is revealed as mutual

---

[252] Leary, op.cit.

dislike between mother and daughter and yet connivance of the mother in the daughter's matrimonial schemes. The mother preys as much as the daughter does. Women also appear inevitable, inescapable, no matter how hard men flee.[253] We have come very far from Zorrilla's Romanticism in *Don Juan Tenorio*. In that play, the inspiration of woman entailed possession of her: don Juan cannot aspire to goodness if he does not marry her. In *Man and Superman*, however, men can only achieve goodness - or greatness, the way to Heaven - by remaining free of women. Salvation lies precisely where women are not.

Shaw understands the female characters of *Man and Superman* as compelled to follow the Life Force, that is, compelled to marry and reproduce. For women, the Life Force is the compulsion to motherhood: the ruthlessness with which they pursue it appears negative. Their allegiance to the Life Force only functions through the role of motherhood, and they do not participate in Life's higher purpose, what don Juan calls 'Life's incessant aspiration to higher organization, wider, deeper, intenser self-consciousness, and clearer self-understanding' (p.123). Women's work still entails confinement (in both senses); for women cannot aspire to any other ideals. In chapter 2 we saw how men such as Tanner/don Juan can pursue higher, individual goals while women cannot, and here again we see how this diminishes women's activity in the society in which they live. Don Juan argues that men, not women, have created civilization: they have used women for the purpose, but do not allow them to participate actively: 'He has created civilization without consulting her, taking her domestic labor for granted as the foundation of it' (p.107).[254] Shaw's avowed emancipation for women can only occur within a very restricted sphere.

---

[253] Octavius, however, manages to escape. I discuss in more detail how he does this in the next chapter. At this point, it should suffice to observe that he protects himself from women through a romanticism that keeps women at a safe distance.

[254] Don Juan hypothesizes at this point that woman evolved man solely for reproductive purposes, but that, since man has too much energy for use simply as a drone for females, he has been able to create civilisation without her participation or consent. Carl Henry Mills suggests that Shaw took

According to Shaw's don Juan, men must flee women in order to achieve anything of greatness, and indeed he himself has become famous for running away (p.112). His ultimate purpose entails leaving Hell for Heaven in order to follow his philosophical ideals: Heaven is reality while Hell is a fantastical realm of pleasure, a 'Palace of Lies' (p.124). To go to Heaven means to pursue a quest for the Nietzschean model of the superman - Nietzsche himself is to be found in don Juan's Heaven (p.130). It is not coincidental that Heaven contains no eligible women:

> *Don Juan:* ...Commander: are there any beautiful women in Heaven?
> *The Statue:* None. Absolutely none. All dowdies...They might be men of fifty.
> *Don Juan:* I am impatient to get there.[255]

The inevitable conclusion from this passage is that beautiful women are Hell, and freedom from women's attentions is Heaven. Flight from women is, for don Juan, equivalent to a departure for Heaven.

Shaw's disillusioned Romanticism follows on directly from Zorrilla's own Romantic ideals: both see don Juan's life in terms of a quest for Heaven, but John Tanner fails to achieve his. As masculine individuality is perceived increasingly as some sort of divine quest separate from the lower female sphere, and as this divine quest itself is seen to fail, in conjunction with a sense of individuality that appears more and more troubled, it should not surprise us that the consequent disillusionment manifests itself as hostility towards women. The women invade

---

these concepts from the theories of psychologist Lester Ward, who proposed that women rather than men were responsible for the selection of a mate. (Carl Henry Mills, 'Shaw's Debt to Lester Ward in *Man and Superman*', *Shaw Review* 14 (1971), 2-13.)

and overwhelm the higher, more abstract male sphere and intrude on the aspirations of the male individuality with their practical approach to gender relations. This sense of separate spheres, higher and lower, does not really arise in the earlier plays - the don Juans of Tirso, Molière and Mozart involve themselves in gender relations rather than attempt to seal themselves off in a vacuum of celibate abstraction. Only in the later plays do we find the separation into male and female spheres, and the increasingly desperate search on the part of the male individual to maintain salvation or purity in abstract or philosophical thought. The protagonists see the purity of their own individual essence threatened by women, and the negative approach to the female characters is the result.

Fred E. Stockholder echoes the notion of the different spheres of men and women when he argues that Ann's only concern is immediate reality, while Tanner's is for larger issues.[256] Ann's concerns are the ones that coincide and are comfortable with the tenets of Edwardian drawing-room comedy. But then we can perceive that Tanner finds himself 'trapped' in the wrong play: the once famous seducer looks out of place in what seems at first sight to be a conventional comic format. Whether he belongs or not, he cannot escape the domesticating force of society. The use of drawing-room comedy to reinterpret the don Juan theme thus takes on a new significance. It is not a genre in which the womanizer of the older plays could follow his career of seduction, but it is an appropriate vehicle for female pursuit of men, since the women disguise their pursuit under cover of respectability and submissiveness. The very conventionality of the drawing-room comedy implies the inability of the male individual to escape to a higher sphere beyond convention.

---

[255] Shaw, p.126.
[256] Fred E. Stockholder, 'Shaw's Drawing-Room Hell: a Reading of *Man and Superman*', *Shaw Review* 11 (1968), 42-51; p.46.

It might be objected that Shaw's women should be understood in positive terms equal to those of the women of the earlier plays, since Ann and Violet actively work to achieve their ambition, and succeed in their endeavours. Watson comments: 'The women are enterprising, audacious, aggressive, and self-assured, and it is they who secure all the desired outcomes through their wit and daring'.[257] Why do the women of *Man and Superman* receive a more overtly hostile treatment? I believe the answer lies with the way in which perception of the male individual has altered. The earlier don Juans attempt to make use of women through seduction and thus mark themselves out as seducers. Sexual relations and activity are essential to their efforts to identify themselves as individuals. We have since observed the way in which Zorrilla points beyond this idea, so that his don Juan subordinates gender relations to male salvation, with a consequent increase in subjection of women. But in *Man and Superman* don Juan wishes to dispense with gender relations altogether, so that his individual mark becomes his desire to be free of women and his opposition to all they stand for. From this desire arises his hostility towards women.

Frisch

Many of the themes that run through *Man and Superman* recur in Frisch's play *Don Juan oder die Liebe zur Geometrie*, although Frisch does not use the maternal instinct as the focus for his critique of women. He reverts instead to a sense of female sexuality as understood by Kierkegaard, Hoffmann and Zorrilla; but female sexuality no longer provides a need for control or a voyeuristic pleasure for men. Now it is something to be feared and fled much as John Tanner flees the predatory maternal instinct of Ann Whitefield. Frisch does not depict the female characters with quite the hostility of Shaw, but he nevertheless shares with Shaw a concept of women as a danger to men's ultimate, 'higher' goals. In each

---

[257] Watson, p.8.

case the women frustrate the protagonist's struggle to attain to a better way of things. Don Juan is not alone in fearing women, for so do the other male characters of Frisch, with the possible exception of Pater Diego - whose holy office protects him. All the female characters possess strong sexual desires except for Celestina, who nonetheless deals with sex on a daily basis in her brothel. Beside them, the men appear weak and ineffectual, at times even impotent.

In what is by now tradition, don Juan considers all women as equal, liable to be the same and susceptible to the first man that comes along: 'Nachdem ich weiß, was alles möglich ist - auch für sie, meine Braut, die mich erwartet hat, mich und keinen andern, selig mit dem ersten besten, der zufällig ich selber war...'.[258] This assumption that all women are the same leads directly to his rejection of his bride Anna on their wedding night. He is unable to distinguish between Anna and Miranda, thus equating a woman of good family with a prostitute. D. G. and S. M. Matthews, in their edition of *Don Juan oder die Liebe zur Geometrie*, observe that Juan's rejection of Anna arises from his belief that for *her* identity is irrelevant.[259] It is Juan, however, who sees women as all the same, without identity: 'ein junges Weib, nichts weiter, Weib wie hundert Weiber in der Finsternis.' (Frisch, p.135).[260] His night of seduction is a vain attempt to prove himself right about women, and thus right to reject Anna: he attempts thereby to prove that indeed all women are the same.

Frisch believes that generically, don Juan is unfaithful to women in order to maintain his own individuality; but he also suggests that a don Juan does not love women, and that he fears the female nature:

---

[258] 'Now I know what they are all capable of - even her, my bride who waited for me, me and no other; she preferred the first to come along, who just happened to be me myself...'. Frisch, p.122
[259] Max Frisch, *Don Juan oder die Liebe zur Geometrie*, ed. by D. G. and S. M. Matthews, (London: Methuen, 1979), p.xvi.
[260] 'A girl, nothing more, a girl like a hundred girls in the darkness'.

In bezug auf die Untreue, die bekannteste Etikette jedes Don Juan, würde das heißen: Es reißt ihn nicht von Wollust zu Wollust, aber es stößt ihn ab, was nicht stimmt. Und nicht weil er die Frauen liebt, sondern weil er etwas anderes (beispielweise die Geometrie) mehr liebt als die Frau, muß er sie immer wieder verlassen. Seine Untreue ist nicht übergroße Triebhaftigkeit, sondern Angst, sich selbst zu täuschen, sich selbst zu verlieren - seine wache Angst vor dem Weiblichen in sich selbst.[261]

Those who would see in don Juan an example of latent, subconscious homosexuality might find support here in the suggestion of his fear of the feminine within himself. This implies unfaithfulness as a desperate assertion of masculinity. But we may also perceive a dislike of women reminiscent of *Man and Superman*, and thus a dislike of feminine traits. His fear of the feminine in himself may arise as much from a real fear of women as a whole as from any notion of homosexuality; and this is supported by Frisch's preceding comments, 'Angst, sich selbst zu täuschen, sich selbst zu verlieren'. Don Juan fears deception, and this deception lies within women. Thus don Juan does not love women but something else, such as geometry. He flees from each woman in turn, because 'es stößt ihn ab, was nicht stimmt'. This indicates that he finds something in women that is not right, that in some way they are defective. The elevation of an abstract idea above the importance of male-female relations is also, of course, a concept found in Shaw.

The protagonist of *Don Juan oder die Liebe zur Geometrie* has also followed Shaw's John Tanner in, as well as a certain note of hostility and disdain towards

---

[261] 'With regard to infidelity, the most famous label of every don Juan, it would mean that he is not dragged from lust to lust, but is repelled by what is not right. And he must always leave women, not because he loves them but because he loves something else (such as geometry) more than he loves women. His infidelity is not an excessive adherence to instinct, but fear of deceiving himself, losing himself - his wary fear of the feminine in himself'. Frisch, p.169.

women as indistinguishable, a great measure of fear towards them. He confesses this obliquely when he says: 'Ich fürchte mich nicht vor Männern' (p.120).[262] Later, he receives the Bishop of Cordoba with pleasure: 'wie habe ich mich gesehnt...mit einem Mann zu sprechen!...Ich kann keine Damen mehr sehen noch hören...War es nötig, daß es zwei Geschlechter gibt?' (p.146).[263] And in Act V:

> Welche Ungeheuerlichkeit, daß der Mensch allein nicht das Ganze
> ist! Und je größer sein Sehnsucht ist, ein Ganzes zu sein, um so
> verfluchter steht er da, bis zum Verbluten ausgesetzt dem andern
> Geschlecht.[264]

Don Juan implies that women's very existence frustrates man's longing for wholeness and unity of being. Man can never be complete in himself - this indicates the link between the male individual's problematized idea of identity and a growing hostility towards women. The image of blood suggests how women seem to destroy all vestiges of life within men, and reminds us of the bloodthirsty imagery Shaw used to describe women. The motif here is similar: don Juan perceives women as a threat to his life, his individual identity. This reference to blood echoes Roderigo's suicide in Act III: 'In seinem Blute röchelnd hat er Sie verflucht als Schänder seiner Braut' (p.137).[265] Roderigo commits suicide and bleeds to death because Inez, his betrothed, succumbed to don Juan - with great sexual passion, as don Juan relates (p.135). Frisch evokes a sense of women as dangerous in his use of blood as a symbol.

---

[262] 'I'm not scared of men'.

[263] 'How I have longed...to talk with a man!...I can't see or listen to women any longer...Was it necessary to have two sexes?'

[264] 'How monstrous that man is not complete on his own! And the more he longs to be whole, the more accursed he is, standing exposed to the opposite sex until his blood drains away'. Frisch, p.164.

[265] 'With his last breath, covered with his own blood, he cursed you as the defiler of his bride'.

Frisch also emphasizes women and the pursuit of geometry as mutually exclusive, underscoring the concept of women as a hindrance to the quest of the male individual for higher things. As we saw in chapter 2, don Juan wishes to dedicate himself wholeheartedly to the study of geometry. Geometry's abstract nature signifies purity for don Juan:

> Hast du es nie erlebt, das nüchterne Staunen vor einem Wissen, das stimmt? Zum Beispiel: was ein Kreis ist, das Lautere eines geometrischen Orts. Ich sehne mich nach dem Lauteren...Vor einem Kreis oder einem Dreieck habe ich mich noch nie geschämt, nie geekelt.[266]

We should note the emphasis upon purity, 'das Lautere' which is to be found in geometry, in an abstract science that is removed from human relationships. In longing for such purity, don Juan wishes to remove himself from the confusion of his relations with women, who are thus by implication 'impure'. When he states that he has never felt ashamed or repelled by a circle or a triangle, he implies that women, in contrast do repel him. They shame him and make him feel inadequate. Klaus Müller-Salget refers to the idea that don Juan sees science and woman as antitheses:[267] this indicates that they are opposites, and reinforces a popular concept of women as unscientific, unable to grasp mathematical and technological concepts. This reflects the division in *Man and Superman* between men, who can search for higher forms of living and learning, and women, who are shut out from such spheres. In *Don Juan oder die Liebe zur Geometrie* women remain confined to their sexuality; sexuality is their principal characteristic (just as women are defined principally by their maternal instinct in *Man and Superman*). But also, the antithesis of geometry and women implies in consequence that any quality that

---

[266] 'Have you never experienced the sober astonishment of knowing something to be right? What a circle is, for example, the purity of a mathematical locus. I long for purity...I never feel ashamed or repelled in front of a circle or a triangle'. Frisch, pp.131-2.

geometry possesses, women do not have. Thus when don Juan argues that a triangle is a triangle for all time (p.132) he means, among other things, that geometry remains eternally valid and true. If we accept women as the antithesis of geometry, then it follows that women are *not* eternally true. Equally, when he describes a triangle as possessing 'die Hoffnung, das Scheinbare unabsehbarer Möglichkeiten' - the hope of seemingly infinite possibilities - this also implies that women have no such potential. Of course, women are indeed finite creatures, but for don Juan they hold no wonder and no possibility except insatiable female sexual desire.

Women become the pursuers, as they do in *Man and Superman*; but Frisch's female characters possess a more positive sense of sexuality that contrasts with the impotence of some of the male characters such as don Gonzalo and Roderigo. While the men prove ineffective and, in the case of Gonzalo, impotent, female characters seem overcharged with sexuality: they possess a greater sexual self-awareness and self-confidence. The intrusion into the overtly masculine don Juan tradition of Celestina, the procuress from early Spanish literature, suggests a loss of male confidence that develops in proportion to female confidence and power. In the matter of sexual relations, the women are in control. Donna Elvira and donna Inez, who set the scene for us in Act I, immediately introduce the note of sexuality we would normally associate with don Juan. Donna Elvira's first action is to call for Juan, while Inez sounds a note of underlying sexuality in the opening scene:

> Palmen im Wind. Wie das Klingeln eines Degens an steinernen
> Stufen. Ich kenne das, Donna Elvira, ich höre das jede Nacht, und

---

[267] Klaus Müller-Salget, 'Diegos Aster: imagologische Anmerkungen zu Max Frischs *Don Juan oder die Liebe zur Geometrie*', *Arcadia* 22 (1987), 66-69; p.67.

jedesmal, wenn ich ans Fenster trete: nichts als die Palmen im Wind.[268]

The imagery Inez uses of the sound of swords in the night, suggests a sexual awareness within her that draws her to look out of her window each night, presumably in the hope of seeing the male owner of the sword (the sword itself symbolizing the phallus). Each night she is disappointed, and this prefigures the inadequacy and impotence of the male characters. As we later discover, Inez is betrothed to don Roderigo, who shows no inclination to visit her at night. This indicates her sexual frustration, so that when Juan later seduces her, she finds a form of sexual ecstasy even in her vain attempt to defend herself:

> ...nicht ihr helleres Haar und die andere Art ihres Kusses, auch nicht die Lust an ihrem mädchenhaften Widerstand; sie wehrte sich so wild und bis zur Verzückung, schwächer zu sein...[269]

We may remember at this point the voyeurism of Kierkegaard and Hoffmann (and Zorrilla to a lesser extent - his Inés still remains demure even when experiencing sexual passion for the first time), and also the comments of Mandrell about masculine wish-fulfilment.[270] The violent nature of Inez's resistance and capitulation contains a measure of sexual pleasure. The contrast between Frisch and the nineteenth-century authors, however, is that Frisch's protagonist takes no lingering delight in Inez's surrender, and instead reverts to the common cry of many don Juans, that women are all the same: 'in unseren Armen sind alle so ähnlich, bald zum Erschrecken gleich' (Frisch, p.135).[271] Female sexuality is no longer an entity subject to masculine desire, but has a force of its own which don

---

[268] 'Palm trees in the wind. Like the ringing of a sword on stone steps. I know this, donna Elvira, I hear it every night, and each time that I go to the window: just the palms in the wind'. Frisch, p.97.

[269] 'Not her brighter hair and the different way she kissed, nor the pleasure in her girlish resistance; she defended herself so wildly, until she succumbed in ecstasy'. Frisch, p.139.

[270] Mandrell, p.46.

[271] 'In our arms they all seem so similar, it's frightening'.

Juan fears. To him, women are sheer sexuality and as a result are indistinguishable, and their inescapable sexual power terrifies him.

Thus the strong sexual compulsion experienced by Inez also holds true for other female characters, of which donna Elvira is a notable example. Although donna Elvira is Anna's mother, she proves to be her sexual equal: she describes herself as 'bräutlicher...als mein Kind' (p.100), more bridal than her child, and will later be the first to accept Juan as a lover, when he embarks on his night of seduction after jilting Anna at the altar. Although, during the masked ball of Act I, the bride and bridegroom are supposedly the only people without masks, Elvira does not wear one either, and 'hopes' that Juan will not mistake her for his bride (ibid), revealing a barely subconscious desire for him. Elvira's husband, don Gonzalo, proves to be impotent (as he confesses to Pater Diego), but she is not content to remain faithful to a husband who cannot satisfy her, and has previously turned to Pater Diego himself for consolation. Her relationship with Diego, however, is solely on a sexual level, and she does not recognize any further claim he tries to impose on her. When Diego becomes jealous of Elvira's rapt description of don Juan on his horse, she dismisses his jealousy: 'Ich habe nie geschworen, daß ich meine Untreue halte...betrüge ich einzig und allein meinen Gemahl, nicht dich' (p.101).[272] Thus Elvira does not recognize any commitment to Diego: she sees their relationship purely in sexual terms. Elvira also challenges don Juan to run off with Anna - the Anna he met and loved in the park rather than the Anna who is his bride - as he had intended. She immediately highlights his weakness by her challenge. Elvira questions, among other things, don Juan's own sexual commitment to Anna.

Anna's character is more complex than that of her mother: she experiences doubt and confusion about identity just as don Juan does. Don Juan and Anna reflect

---

[272] 'I never swore to stay faithful to you…I deceive only my husband, not you'.

each other: both possess the same fear that they will not recognize each other. They evade the need for identification in their sexual encounter by the pool. But while the anonymity of the occasion is what gave don Juan pleasure, Anna understands the encounter as one of primeval sexuality that does not require labels: 'Ich bin eine Frau...das sind wir: ein Weib, ein Mann!' (p.113).[273] The sexuality is for her the thing that matters, and that allows her to choose where she will commit herself. As with her mother, therefore, her sexual nature is what impels her to act. Her commitment rests with the man with whom she made love, and not to her bridegroom: that is, her commitment is a sexual one, and that fact that her lover and her bridegroom are one and the same don Juan is sheer chance. The black veil worn by Anna, and her dishevelled appearance in Act II, suggest her sexuality, particularly when compared with don Juan, who dresses for his wedding in white, the symbol of purity. With this contrast between bride and bridegroom Frisch underlines the incompatibility between Juan's search for the purity of geometry and Anna's sexual desires.

In his portrait of Anna, Frisch goes a little way towards alleviating the negative sexuality of the other noblewomen: Anna's ability to trust don Juan and commit herself to him proves her to be the stronger and more attractive character. Juan is unable to make the same commitment. Nevertheless, the sexual demands she has made of him prevents him from accepting her as a bride: he uses her sexual surrender to escape from marriage, arguing that she could have surrendered just as easily to any other man who might have met her on that occasion. Out of his own weakness he criticizes her for her strength of commitment and her ability to choose. His reason for rejecting her is that all women will surrender themselves to any man (p.122), and that he cannot therefore tell women apart. He does not know whom he loves. His rejection nevertheless entails a fear of female sexuality, and he does not therefore take the opportunity to run away with Anna as he and she

---

[273] 'I am a woman...that's how we are: a woman and a man!'

had planned and as Elvira subsequently suggests. He refuses Elvira's challenge. In consequence Anna throws herself into the pool where Juan originally led her, unable to live if her sexual passion cannot be satisfied. Anna may be an attractive character but she presents the same negative implications of sexuality that the other noblewomen do.

Thus the three principal noblewomen live lives of (sometimes frustrated) passion; and Act IV confirms that this applies to women in general, when a collection of don Juan's conquests appear at his staged descent to Hell. Frisch accentuates their similarity by having them speak all at the same time, saying more or less the same thing: thus they become interchangeable. Frisch underlines this point further in the fact that don Juan cannot tell them apart, calling them by the wrong names. The noblewomen all pursue sexual satisfaction. It is a different matter, however, in Celestina's brothel, where sex ceases to be a thing of passion but becomes instead a matter of business. Celestina intrudes on the don Juan genre from another well-known Spanish play, Rojas's *La Celestina*, and here as there she acts as procuress for the nobility. Celestina sees her brothel as men's refuge from the demands of conventional society, where they can specifically be free of their false emotions ('falschen Gefühlen', p.110). Celestina does not, however, so much attempt to alleviate men's fear of women as profit by it. And though she proclaims her brothel as an honest place free from conventional sentiment, she nevertheless helps first Miranda to trick don Juan (by sewing Miranda's wedding dress) and then helps don Juan himself by playing the part of the statue in his 'descent' to Hell. A small indication of Celestina's intent to deceive is the shoddy repair work she does to Miranda's wedding dress (which, significantly, does not fit her) - don Juan will only see those repairs once it is too late (p.125). Celestina avows that she helps Miranda only in order to bring the woman to her senses, but their deception works all too well, and in Act III don Juan indeed mistakes Miranda for

Anna. Celestina's cynicism about men is amusing, but it does not hide her contempt for them, or more particularly her willingness to deceive them.

Thus while Celestina does not threaten don Juan with female sexuality, her capacity for deception also places him in an untenable position, as he discovers in Act II when trying to choose between Anna and Miranda. Miranda's deception of Juan, however, is greater than Celestina's. She offers don Juan an escape from the demands of women, claiming that she is the only woman who does not need him (p.145) and thus the only one who can help him. Nevertheless, she also claims that his only way to geometry lies through her (ibid). But her reasoning rests on a false premise, for don Juan cannot escape women by means of women, in order to pursue higher aims. We see the result of her proposition in Act V: he is trapped into a relationship of which the forthcoming child will be a symbol. Thus, when she asks him to trust a woman, herself, just once (ibid), the consequences of the 'escape' she offers merely indicates that women are never to be trusted, even when they seem disinterested.

Miranda's wedding dress becomes a symbol of the deception her promise of rescue contains. While Anna's dress fits her perfectly, Miranda's dress is too tight and requires repairs from Celestina , a sign that Miranda does not fit the role of the 'perfect match' for don Juan. This in turn bodes ill for her promise to him of a pleasant life in the castle of Ronda. In the castle, which Pater Diego describes in rapturous terms as a veritable paradise, don Juan feels trapped. He waits impatiently for Miranda to turn up for dinner, he drinks too much, and at the least provocation breaks out into a diatribe against the fact that creation requires two sexes. His frustration and irritation, in contrast with Diego's pleasure in the paradise of the castle grounds around them, strongly implies that don Juan himself is in Hell. As he says in the previous act: 'eher fahre ich in die Hölle als in die Ehe' -'I would rather go to Hell than be married' (p.144). He in fact manages to do both. Trapped in his life with Miranda, unable to escape since he is hiding from his reputation as a hell-bound seducer, he lives what for him is a Hell. He is faced every day with the emotional demands of a woman, and is no longer his own master. By making him wait for meals, Miranda shows her control over him, and the only respite he has is through alcohol. Miranda's offer of freedom and of geometry therefore proves false, and so a woman creates and forms a vital part of don Juan's Hell. Such an equation of women with Hell, that is, some form of damnation, is a concept shared with Shaw. This attitude towards the female characters reinforces the suggestion latent in both Frisch's and Shaw's works, of a pessimism and hostility in male-female relationships.

Don Juan's childlessness in the tradition is linked to his struggle over individual identity. Having no 'life' of his own he cannot pass it on to others. In his epilogue, Frisch claims that the generic don Juan is a parasite opposing the creative forces of nature itself: the opposition to the creative force of life is again reminiscent of *Man and Superman* where John Tanner attempts to resist the female compulsion towards motherhood:

> Ohne das Weib, dessen Forderungen er nicht anzuerkennen gewillt ist, wäre er selber nicht in der Welt. Als Parasit in der Schöpfung (Don Juan ist immer kinderlos) bleibt ihm früher oder später keine andere Wahl: Tod oder Kapitulation...Sein Widersacher ist die Schöpfung selbst.[274]

Frisch continues by arguing that 'Indem [don Juan] er Vater wird - indem er es annimmt, Vater zu sein -, ist er nicht mehr Don Juan' (ibid).[275] Generically, don Juan robs people - women - of identity: to bestow identity (on children) would be

---

[274] 'Without women, whose demands he is unwilling to recognise, he himself would not exist. As a parasite in creation (don Juan is always childless) he will sooner or later have no other choice: death or capitulation...His adversary is creation itself'. Frisch, p.171.

[275] 'By becoming a father – by accepting fatherhood – he is no longer don Juan'.

a reversal of his own nature, and thus he would no longer truly be don Juan. In the play, however, the prospect of the child fixes don Juan firmly within gender relations: the child acts as a symbol of the way in which gender relations have displaced geometry as the overriding feature of his life. Moreover, to have a child will mean for a don Juan not only a new identity as a father but also a recognition of his own identity and name that he passes on to his child. Again, don Juan must interpret his own individuality through gender relations rather than geometry. And again, Miranda's promise of freedom to lose himself in his geometry proves deceptive, for in fact don Juan becomes more closely enmeshed in the net of gender relations.

In short, then, Frisch has used different motifs to say something fairly similar to Shaw, that woman have strong characters that threaten to frustrate the aims of men, and thus that women endanger men. Frisch therefore reinforces the growing sense of opposition and latent hostility between men and women that is implicit in Zorrilla and overt in Shaw. Women oppose the pure contemplation of eternal truths such as those of geometry, so that don Juan's quest to forgo his individual personality and lose himself in the abstraction of geometry is doomed to failure, given that he cannot escape women. Miranda recognizes his failure to live up to his abstract ideals, for women have prevented him: she asserts that he was originally 'ein Mann, der ein Ziel hat. Hast du es noch? Es war die Geometrie. Lang ist es her! Ich sehe dein Leben: voll Weib, Juan, und ohne Geometrie' (p.144).[276] Juan acknowledges she is correct, but argues that nevertheless he has not married, which should mean that women still do not control him. However, by the next and final act we see that Juan is finally caught: Miranda has tamed and imprisoned him, so that his only escape is alcohol. The news of the forthcoming child is the ultimate announcement of domestic imprisonment.

---

[276] 'A man with an aim. Do you still have it? It was geometry. It's long gone! I can see your life, Juan, full of women and no geometry'.

Women threaten don Juan in one of two ways. They may have strong sexual desires, such as those of Anna, Elvira and Inez. Their passions divert don Juan away from the study of geometry into a career as the womanizer of tradition. Don Juan takes no interest in sexual matters, spending his time in Celestina's brothel by playing chess, a significantly cerebral game. Nonetheless the women impose a life of sexual 'pleasure' on him, leading him so far astray of his chosen path that he resorts to faking his own death and damnation in order to escape them. Celestina and Miranda pose an alternative threat that in the end proves more powerful, that of deception. The promise of release and sanctuary that Miranda holds out to him proves false, thus suggesting that the potential of gender relations is illusory. Miranda cries 'Warum ist alles, was wir tun, nur Schein!' ('Why is everything we do only appearance', p.126), suggesting that their ultimate purpose is to deceive. Thus the female characters offer don Juan either overpowering sexuality or deception, both of which Frisch depicts as a threat to don Juan's attempt to lose himself in the purity of geometry.

Frisch clearly does not intend us to understand his protagonist in the same affirmative way that Shaw does John Tanner. Tanner is, like Zorrilla's don Juan, a hero in both senses of the word, but Frisch's don Juan is only a protagonist. Frisch stresses don Juan's weaknesses, his inability to choose, and the fact that his pursuit of geometry masks a fear of human relationships. Thus we do not have a situation such as in *Man and Superman*, where the women appear uniformly manipulative and unpleasant while the men appear sympathetic. Frisch emphasizes the feebleness of his male characters (and particularly of don Juan) as much as he does the strong sexuality of the women. Nevertheless, women again seem by their strong passions to threaten don Juan, to the extent that he wants to dispense with women altogether, rather than channel and control women's sexual impulses as Zorrilla's don Juan does with Inés. Frisch's play demonstrates, as

Shaw's does, the gradual shift in attitude towards women that occurs in conjunction with a shift in attitudes towards male individual identity.

***

By now it should be clear that the plays of Zorrilla, Shaw and Frisch contain a much more negative approach to the function of women in the don Juan tradition. The power possessed by the female characters of Tirso, Mozart and Molière seems positive, helping them to be able to survive and sometimes subvert the patriarchal world in which they live. The women of the later plays appear more overtly threatening, so that the relevant don Juans regard them with covert fear and a desire to control in the case of Zorrilla, and downright hostility in the case of Shaw and Frisch. I have argued that this alteration in approach to the female characters parallels the changing ways in which the male individual attempts to establish his identity. As he moves from seduction to more abstract domains in order to mark himself out as an individual, so he defines himself in opposition to women rather than through sexual involvement with them.

This change from a comparatively positive treatment of the women to the more hostile approach lies as much with the authors as with the protagonist (though Frisch shows a measure of sympathy towards Anna). Don Juan never deals with women benignly in any of the plays. Seduction as a technique of identity in the earlier plays suggests negative attitudes to women: when don Juan of *El burlador* remarks that 'el mayor/gusto que en mí puede haber/es burlar una mujer/ y dejalla sin honor' (II, 270-3)[277] we cannot interpret this as a positive attitude towards women. But Tirso's attitudes towards his female characters differ markedly from those of his protagonist. The authors of the later plays, however, seem to coincide more with the thinking of their protagonists in regarding women as fearful

---

[277] 'The greatest pleasure I can have is to deceive a woman and deprive her of her honour'.

creatures that need to be contained, confined or avoided. Thus the hostility of the twentieth-century don Juans finds an echo in the thoughts of Shaw and Frisch in their preface and epilogue.

So far we have been able to trace the development of more negative treatments of the female characters, and link this to an elevation and subsequent problematization of masculine individuality. The worsening of relations between the women and the individual do not, however, take place in a social vacuum, but in a context of patriarchal society. The male individual is not synonymous with or totally representative of the patriarchy from which he emanates; and, as we shall see in the next chapter, the parallel developments concerning women and the male individual do not necessarily hold true for patriarchy as a whole. Ironically, we can see this most clearly in the twentieth-century plays, which embody the strongest hostility towards women. Shaw and Frisch, for all their antagonism towards the female characters, do not allow us simply to assume their support of patriarchal mores. Both dramatists themselves held views and beliefs that attacked their own conventional (and thus patriarchal) societies. Shaw, in particular, expresses very contradictory ideas: *Man and Superman* does not depict women in a favourable light, but Shaw nevertheless professed himself to be a feminist and did not accept conventional notions of women. It seems highly unlikely that he would wish to protect a patriarchal status quo. Frisch, as well, challenged social norms in his writings. Both authors use their don Juan plays to attack conventional society - Tanner's speeches about the world around him have their point, as does don Juan's description of Hell. These complex attitudes on the part of Shaw and Frisch suggest that dislike of women cannot be simply equated with a straightforward embrace of patriarchal principles.

I wish to argue that these shifts in gender relations emphasize the male as individual rather than as part of a patriarchal structure. I do not argue that patriarchy inside and outside the don Juan phenomenon is without effect. But I believe that the historical shifts in gender relations are a feature of masculine individuality and not of patriarchy as such. Patriarchy itself is not monolithic, and has often demonstrated itself to be insecure: fear and hatred of women often results from such insecurity. Nevertheless, the patriarchy of the don Juan plays does not respond to the longitudinal shifts I have detailed above. It shows itself to be unchangingly and unremittingly weak. In the next chapter, I shall examine some of the male characters that go to make up the donjuanian patriarchy: its lack of development in the genre should indicate that the shifts in gender relations are linked with male individuality rather than masculinity as a whole.

Chapter 6: The male characters

The last three chapters have studied the female characters of the six don Juan works, examining their relationship to the protagonist and the way in which they give him identity: we have also traced an increasing hostility towards the women on the part of the later authors. These works reveal the establishment and development of a don Juan/women dialectic, in which the close relationship between the don Juan figure and women persists, but the nature of it changes. Nevertheless, the dialectic covers only half of the *dramatis personae*: all six works use male characters apart from that of don Juan, and some of these characters are major ones. This chapter looks at the function of the other male characters, and how their function affects the don Juan/women dialectic, if at all. Since the primary focus of the study has been the female characters, this chapter does not aim to be so exhaustive in its treatment of the male characters. However, certain recurring figures and patterns can be seen in the different plays, and we shall consider these. One figure not discussed in this chapter is that of the statue, but I shall examine the function of the statue in the next chapter.

The relationships between the women and don Juan represent a sphere that subverts, or, in the case of later plays, threatens the generally accepted patriarchal order. On an immediate level, the male characters represent various facets of that patriarchal order, including the division into social class; and both noblemen and working/peasant men appear on the stage in each case. In the conflict between don Juan and the women, the other male characters seem to impinge little: don Juan is the protagonist, the self trying to become an individual, the women are the Other that don Juan tries to render equal and undifferentiated in order to establish his own identity. The other male characters do not seem to have a part in this conflict. They are the spectators, unable to influence the outcome in any way (apart from the Commander figure, once he has metamorphosed into the statue).

Much of our study in this chapter will be of the different ways in which the male characters are rendered powerless, regardless of their social status, and how their actions and speech become ineffective, so that they exert no control over events. Unlike the women, they cannot act for themselves.

The idea of a feeble masculine society might strike us in the first instance as unusual. We popularly suppose male society to have formed itself into a patriarchy, a society in which the male point of view is accepted as natural, right and self-evident; while the specifically female point of view is aberrant. Patriarchal society privileges and grants authority to the male. Furthermore, we cannot doubt that all six plays emanate from a patriarchal context. Why, then, does the male society of don Juan appear to us as uniformly inadequate, as it undoubtedly does? A first response might be that we need to distinguish between the patriarchy that exists within the plays and that which exists outside of them. While the donjuanian patriarchy might seem enfeebled, the patriarchy that exists in actuality uses the figure of don Juan as vicarious wish-fulfilment. Don Juan performs the acts that other men themselves wish they could do. We have already noted in passing the presence of masculine fantasy within the plays, an idea that Mandrell has in particular taken up.[278] Moreover, the Romantic era, and specifically the work of Kierkegaard and Hoffmann, readily demonstrates the use of don Juan as a vehicle for male voyeurism.

However, while the element of voyeurism undoubtedly exists within the don Juan phenomenon, I believe it is mistaken to argue for the equation of don Juan with the actual patriarchal order. The effect of don Juan's actions is that of emasculation: this clearly applies to the male characters within the plays, but I would argue that this notion also has validity outside of them. For voyeurism and fantasy imply in this instance an inability to act. Thus when Feal Deibe claims

---

[278] Mandrell, p.46.

that in *El burlador* don Juan takes on the role of avenger on behalf of other men against women's perfidious sexual nature,[279] his claim implicitly assumes that the men themselves have no power of vengeance. They cannot take on the role of avenger, but remain as spectators to don Juan's actions. Don Juan may share attributes with other male characters - certainly they all have a malign attitude to women - but don Juan does not in fact *represent* the men. Some commentators have observed a certain measure of collusion between male society and don Juan: *El burlador* is an obvious example, where the Spanish nobility excuse or cover up don Juan's crimes.[280] Nevertheless, the don Juan figure emphasizes the weakness of the patriarchal society symbolized by the male characters. If Feal Deibe's point about vengeance were correct, such vengeance would serve to underline the irony of a patriarchy that cannot defend itself; but in fact we can see don Juan as an avenging figure only with difficulty. If ever he looks to patriarchy it is only to make use of it (as in the use of his noble connections in *El burlador*), or to find it lacking in the support and affirmation required (*Don Juan Tenorio*). Don Juan's primary relations are with women; and though these relations are not benign, they do not take into account the requirements of masculinity in general. The don Juan figure encompasses individuality first and foremost, and while that individuality is inevitably male, it cannot be necessarily thought of as synonymous with patriarchy.

Our ability to distinguish between male society and the male individual is one consequence of this study; for while the male individual alters from one play to the next, male society appears as uniformly feeble and marginal to the action of each play, regardless of when that play was written. We have already observed the shifts in the characterization of don Juan and the role of the female characters. Don Juan metamorphoses from the womanizer of Tirso and Mozart to the

---

[279] Carlos Feal Deibe, '*El Burlador* de Tirso y la mujer', *Symposium* 29 (1975), 300-313; p.301.
[280] See Bruce W. Wardropper, '*El burlador de Sevilla*: a Tragedy of Errors', *Philological Quarterly* 36 (1957), 61-71; 64-5.

Romantic of Zorrilla and the political philosopher of Shaw; while the women gradually exchange their role of survival and accommodation within patriarchal society, for one that threatens the male search for things higher than himself - salvation, utopia, mathematical purity. What does not seem to change significantly is the role of the other male characters. Certainly, in the six plays under consideration here, the male characters remain on the whole weak, not affecting the play's action and outcome to any noticeable extent. The consistent weakness of the male characters is what I intend to demonstrate in this chapter.

There are apparent exceptions to this idea, but further reflection demonstrates even with these exceptions an underlying masculine inadequacy. The most obvious example is the Commander figure, who appears in all six plays. In the first four of these the Commander plays the role that Tirso envisaged: he dies in a duel with don Juan, and returns from the dead in the form of the statue which marks his grave. Having undergone his metamorphosis into stone, the Commander gains the power to pass and execute sentence of judgement over don Juan. I shall have more to say about the statue in the next chapter. At this point, however, it is worth noting that the Commander only gains any power over the course of events once he is dead. The statue has the power the living man does not: indeed, the living man loses the fight between himself and don Juan, and fails to preserve his authority over his daughter. The authority that patriarchy bestows on don Gonzalo cannot prevent don Juan's attempted seduction of Ana; for instance, the don Gonzalo of *El burlador* has successfully carried out a diplomatic mission to Portugal on behalf of the patriarchal authority he represents, the king of Castile, but he fails to defeat don Juan in combat (the phallic symbolism of the swordplay readily suggesting the inadequacy of patriarchy).

Another comparatively strong male character is to be found in Frisch's play: Pater Diego. Unlike the other men, who suffer impotence (don Gonzalo) or sexual inadequacy (Roderigo, who leaves Inez frustrated), Diego carries on an affair with donna Elvira, and reveals clear jealousy of don Juan. Were he not a priest, Diego too could be a good, attractive horseman just like don Juan:

> Wäre unsere spanische Kirche nicht so verbohrt in die Idee der Wohlfahrt, die bald einen Zehntel aller einlaufenden Almosen verschlingt, dann könnte auch unsereiner von einem Schimmel springen, Donna Elvira, anstatt von einem Maulesel zu rutschen.[281]

In the comparison between himself on his mule and don Juan on his white horse, Diego stresses the fact that he too has the capacity to leap athletically from a horse like a hero (the white horse symbolizes heroism - ironically, given that its owner, don Juan, does not match the notions of heroism and romance implied by the white horse). What stops Diego from displaying his athleticism and heroism is his position as a churchman, a 'man in skirts', concerned with the 'feminine' notion of doing good and receiving alms,[282] instead of the masculine pursuit of crusading that is followed by characters such as don Gonzalo. However, by denying, in a sense, his masculinity, Diego escapes the control of women, and escapes death too. The other male characters in Frisch's play - don Gonzalo, Tenorio and Roderigo - die, but Diego survives, and sees himself as existing in a sort of paradise (the castle of Ronda) in the final act. The women of *Don Juan oder die Liebe zur Geometrie* subdue those men who carry out traditional masculine pursuits, be they crusading or scientific study. Diego manages to survive because, in his retreat into the Church, he has escaped the sphere of women, partly by himself taking on 'feminine' characteristics. Don Juan himself points this out when he refuses to marry Anna: 'Er [Pater Diego] versteht mich am

---

[281] 'If our Spanish church wasn't so obseesed with the idea of welfare, which will soon devour a tenth of all the alms coming in, then we too could leap from a white horse, donna Elvira, instead of sliding off a mule'. Frisch, p.101

[282] The Church itself, of course, embodies patriarchal attitudes to a marked degree, but we do not normally perceive the Church as possessing strong masculine connotations.

allerbesten. Wieso hat er denn nicht geheiratet?' (p.121).[283] Diego, then, functions as the exception that proves the rule of masculine weakness in these don Juan plays. The other male characters all suffer to some degree in Frisch's play: to survive as Diego does means to surrender one's masculine nature.

Even the apparent exceptions, then, seem merely to reinforce the notion that the male characters as a whole are weak and ineffectual. We shall now study in more detail the ways in which masculine inadequacy is played out on the stage. I have already observed that such inadequacy encompasses the whole social sphere. Yet while we might expect powerlessness in characters such as the servants and the peasants, other male characters should in theory carry an air of authority, of power. The irony of male powerlessness reaches its height in the kings of Tirso's *El burlador*, but we may also find it in the various fathers that feature in different plays. Male weakness resides at the top of the social hierarchy and, as we shall see, permeates all social levels.

Figures of authority: kings and fathers

We would normally understand patriarchy to encompass not only masculine privilege but masculine power that specifically lies in recognized male authority figures such as kings and fathers: patriarchy acknowledges a specifically male capacity to govern over kingdom or household. Nonetheless, such forms of masculine authority remain severely undermined within the don Juan phenomenon. Commentators have for instance widely recognized the weakness of the kings of Naples and Castile in *El burlador*.[284] These kings cannot bring their authority to bear on don Juan in order to keep him under control. As the king of

---

[283] 'He [Pater Diego] understands me best of all. Why hasn't he got married?'

[284] See, for instance, Wardropper, 'Tragedy of Errors', p.64, and 'El tema central de *El burlador de Sevilla*', *Segismundo* 17/18 (1973), 9-16; pp.12-14.

Naples cries, all their considerable power avails them nothing against don Juan's seductive capacity:

> ¡Que no importan fuerzas,
> guarda, criados, murallas,
> fortalecidas almenas
> para amor, que la de un niño
> hasta los muros penetra! (I, 172-6).[285]

Fortresses and servants - symbols of royal power - cannot prevent don Juan from penetrating the king's defences. Tirso's use of the word 'penetra' adds extra force to the image, given its sexual connotation: don Juan has penetrated the king's defences at the same time, and by the same act, with which he penetrated Isabela. Such an image emasculates the king, so that he appears weak.[286] The inadequacy of royal power persists throughout the play in the ineffectuality of the king of Castile, who cannot cope with the pace of events set by don Juan. Of all the commands and decrees the king issues, the only one that is carried through is the one that creates don Juan the Conde de Lebrija (III, 328, 700-1), an odd reward for don Juan's career of trickery. The king's threats against don Juan (and Mota, for that matter) are not carried out, and none of the marriages he arranges will take place. The marriages that do round off the play are those which other characters had in view long before the king involved himself in their concerns.

A similar ineffectiveness can be found in the different fathers who should in theory wield authority over their children but who have no control in practice. The authors give us many examples of fathers who cannot control their children: there

---

[285] 'Armed forces, guards, servants, ramparts and fortified battlements make no difference to love, for the love of a child can penetrate even the walls!'

is even the example of Ann Whitefield's father, recently dead, who could not resist his daughter's manipulation of his will (Shaw, p.162). The various Commanders prove while alive incapable of defending their daughters' honour, while don Juan's own fathers despair of their sons but do not nevertheless possess the strength to discipline them. The don Diegos of *El burlador* and *Don Juan Tenorio* vacilate between condemnation and forgiveness, and both eventually surrender judgement of their sons to God. This is the example of Zorrilla's don Diego: '...los hijos como tú/ son hijos de Satanás.../me matas..., mas te perdono/ de Dios en el santo juicio' (782-3, 790-1).[287] Don Diego expresses disgust at the way in which his son has turned out, but simultaneously an unwillingness/inability to pass judgement. We can perceive the association here between the abdication of paternal authority and the motif of death which don Diego mentions, implying the loss of masculine power and lack of masculine vitality. The reference to death, 'me matas', also occurs in *El burlador* (here don Diego says: '¿Es posible que procuras/ todas las horas mi muerte?', ('Is it possible that you are continually wishing my death?'; II, 382-3). A further reference occurs in Frisch, when Tenorio says: 'obschon mir fast das Herz bricht' ('although my heart is almost breaking', Frisch, p.116) and later ' Es bricht mir das Herz' ('it breaks my heart', p.123). With his references to the heart Frisch prefigures the father's actual death of a heart attack, which occurs at the end of Act II. Don Juan predicts, and in a sense wishes, his father's death - 'Es bricht dir das Herz, Papa, ich weiß...es würde mich nicht wundern, Papa, wenn du eines Tages stirbst' (p.121)[288] - and Tenorio is unable to prevent this. Thus the fathers prove no match for their sons, their weakness showing clearly in their vacilation between anger

---

[286] The 'niño' of the quotation cannot refer to don Juan, since the king believes Octavio to be the culprit. I remarked earlier that Octavio's use of the word 'niño' in reference to his love for Isabela, indicated the childish nature of his love.

[287] 'Sons like you are sons of the Devil...you are the death of me, but I forgive you: eternal judgement is God's'.

[288] 'It breaks your heart, Papa, I know...I wouldn't be surprised, Papa, if you died one of these days'.

and forgiveness: the references to the death of the father in the different plays suggest the death of the natural male authority of the father over the son.

Dom Louis of Molière initially appears more forceful: though he laments his son's evil deeds as do the Diegos and Tenorio, he does not offer forgiveness until dom Juan makes some signs of repentance. The relationship between dom Louis and dom Juan further reinforces our sense of the inadequacy of male society, as the supposed close kinship between father and son proves to be a mockery: 'nous nous incommodons étrangement l'un et l'autre; et si vous êtes las de me voir, je suis bien las aussi de vos déportements' (IV, iv).[289] The use of the word 'étrangement' indicates the unnatural state of relations between the two characters: dom Louis assesses the state of affairs between himself and his son in a clear-eyed manner, showing no vacilation. While don Diego of *El burlador* uses his position at court to protect his son and mitigate his punishment, dom Louis refuses to countenance such an idea, insisting to dom Juan that nobility must be earned, not merely inherited. This father therefore appears strong. But Dom Louis has his own weaknesses: dom Juan easily fools him by a show of humility, and in fact robs him of his senses (V, i). Moreover, dom Louis prays to God, but his prayers are ineffective. He once prayed for a son to bring him joy, but received instead dom Juan, who brings him only despair (IV, iv); and his prayers that dom Juan might repent remain unfulfilled, for dom Juan humbles himself only in outward appearance. Dom Louis's failed prayers provide an instance of the lack of power of the male voice, a concept I discuss in more detail in the following section on servanthood. He appeals to Heaven in vain, demonstrating in the process his inability to affect and influence the course of events, and thus in turn revealing the loss of his authority.

---

[289] 'We make each oher strangely uncomfortable, and if you are tired of seeing me, I am equally tired of your behaviour'.

These examples suggest immediately that positions of natural male authority - kingship and fatherhood - have lost the power normally vested in them by society: the kings cannot rule and the fathers cannot discipline. These figures at the top of the male hierarchy have lost the authority we would normally expect of them, and plainly indicate the patriarchal malaise developed in don Juan plays. We shall now look to see how men fare at the other end of the social scale.

The servant

In all six plays don Juan has a servant, most of whom are major characters (Frisch's Leporello and Zorrilla's Ciutti are exceptions). In dramatic terms their principal function is to serve as confidante, but frequently they also serve to remind don Juan of the possible consequences of their actions. Catalinón, Sganarelle and Leporello[290] warn their masters that God will punish sin, while Straker warns Tanner of the danger of impending matrimony to Ann. Nevertheless, the servants' warnings prove ineffectual, since their masters suffer damnation/matrimony. If, as Rank suggests in the case of Leporello, the servant acts as the master's conscience,[291] they nonetheless cannot change the way their masters behave. This point strongly implies their powerlessness.

Of course, a servant by his very position has little or no power and authority: his work is not to act for himself, but as others tell him. Given their subordinate position, some of the servants try to influence events as far as they dare. Hence Catalinón, Sganarelle, Leporello and Straker try to remonstrate with their master, and warn him of the consequences of his actions. But the earlier works in particular accentuate the servants' lack of power, so that their role as conscience becomes irrelevant. The servants disapprove of don Juan's actions but

---

[290]Reference to Leporello will in this section always designate Mozart and da Ponte's character.
[291] Rank, ch.2.

nevertheless submit, being powerless to change anything. Molière points this out when he gives Sganarelle the lines:

> ...qu'il me vaudrait bien mieux d'être au diable que d'être à lui...Mais un grand seigneur méchant homme est une terrible chose; il faut que je lui sois fidèle, en dépit que j'en aie: la crainte en moi fait l'office du zèle, bride mes sentiments, et me réduit d'applaudir bien souvent à ce que mon âme déteste (I, i).[292]

A few key phrases in this speech indicate the servant's inadequacy and powerlessness. When Sganarelle says that he must be loyal 'en dépit que j'en aie' ('in spite of myself'), he implies that his own personal resources make no difference once dom Juan commands. His powerlessness to act as he wishes reduces him, ('réduit'), makes him fearful and renders him pathetic. However, even an apparently 'liberated' servant possesses no power. Straker in *Man and Superman* initially appears confident, more master of himself than Tanner is: both Shaw and Tanner are at pains to reassure us of the real superiority of the working-class man. Nevertheless, Straker's power is more apparent than real: he could not be a chauffeur and break speed records, as he desires to do, if Tanner did not enable him to do so by having the money to buy the car. Although Tanner avows that Straker holds him enslaved, nevertheless Tanner remains the master. If, as we saw in the previous chapter, the car which Straker chauffeurs represents flight, only Tanner can flee. The servant merely enables the flight of the master, he does not flee himself. He has not the power of flight. Tanner demonstrates his possession of power by providing or withholding information as he sees fit: 'No, Henry: there are things it is not good for you to know...' (Shaw, p.47). Despite the radical ideas of Shaw on social class and position, in comparison with other don Juan authors, the master - the don Juan figure - still maintains control. In *El burlador*, don Juan stresses the servant's powerlessness with greater directness and force:

> El que se pone a servir
> voluntad no ha de tener,
>
> y todo ha de ser hacer
> y nada de ser decir (II, 318-21).[293]

The servants, as with the male characters as a whole, cannot exercise their own will to any effect, and it is pointless for a servant to hold or express an opinion. The ineffectiveness of speech, 'nada de ser decir' is strongly indicative of the incapacity of the servant (as indeed with other male characters in the plays): and we shall observe in this chapter the recurrent motif of the loss of the male voice, suggestive of powerlessness. Lack of will and voice, then, may be the inevitable fate of the servant, but the inability to think and speak for oneself also indicates the inadequacy of the male figure in general.

The don Juan of *El burlador* follows his speech on servitude by comparing the servant's role to playing games, punning on the double meaning of 'ganar' meaning both to win and to earn. According to don Juan, a servant must work if he is to 'ganar', win/earn. But, as Catalinón adds, a servant may also lose: 'Y también quien hace y dice/ pierde por la mayor parte' ('Those who both do and speak, usually lose', II, 326-7). We have here a link of the loss of speech with losing and with poverty, suggesting that the servant must surrender his power to speak if he is to survive. The consequences of the servant's inability to speak or

---

[292] 'I'd be better off working for the Devil than for him. But a wrongdoing nobleman is a terrible thing: I must be loyal in spite of myself. Fear makes me zealous, curbs my feelings and reduces me many a time to applauding those things I loathe with all my heart'.
[293] He who goes into service has no will of his own, his lot is always to do, never to speak'.

act for himself can extend to the unnatural, as Catalinón goes on to acknowledge in the same scene:

> Digo que de aquí adelante
> lo que me mandas haré,
> y a tu lado forzaré
> un tigre y un elefante.
> Guárdese de mí un prior,
> que si me mandas que calle
> y le fuerce, he de forzalle
> sin réplica... (II, 330-7).[294]

In this speech, Catalinón admits that don Juan can order him to commit the most unnatural acts - hence the implication of sexual acts with animals and churchmen - which suggests that the servant has lost his own strength of will to an extreme degree. Tirso repeats here the references to speech and silence: we can observe that the forcing of the prior is to be done in silence. Catalinón starts the speech with the strong word 'Digo', but he speaks only in order to reiterate don Juan's notions of servitude. He still has no voice or will of his own, but will merely do what don Juan asks, and in silence ('sin réplica'). The equation Tirso posits here of silence with 'unnatural' acts may imply that masculine powerlessness is itself unnatural: it certainly reinforces the notion of male weakness.

The motif of the loss of the male voice as a symbol of male powerlessness, implied in the two speeches quoted above, recurs in other plays. Catalinón is not the only servant to lose his own voice: a particularly vivid example occurs in the Act II opening of *Don Giovanni*, where the master provides the song with which

---

[294] From now on, I say, I will do whatever you tell me, and by your side I will ravish tigers and elephants. And keep me away from priors, because, if you ask me to shut one up and rape him, I'll rape him without more ado [lit. without reply]'.

the servant will woo Elvira. Leporello also loses his voice at other times, notably in the supper scene. Don Giovanni insists that Leporello sing to him, to which the servant replies: 'Non mi lascia una flussione le parole proferir' (Mozart, p.407)[295] - in fact, Leporello's mouth is full with food from don Giovanni's banquet. Don Giovanni has thus tempted Leporello to surrender his own voice in exchange for food, an idea which underscores the dependency of the servant. But the stress on the lack of the male voice occurs with particular force in Molière's *Dom Juan*. We have observed that no servant can state his opinions effectively, merely suffering and having no influence on events. In the case of Catalinón, the servant speaks effectively only when doing his master's will. But a don Juan can also leave his servant voiceless in other ways. As Sganarelle says:

> Ma foi, j'ai à dire..., je ne sais; car vous tournez les choses d'une
> manière, qu'il semble que vous avez raison; et cependant il est vrai
> que vous ne l'avez pas. J'avais les plus belles pensées du monde, et
> vos discours m'ont brouillé tout cela (I, ii).[296]

Speaking the truth avails men nothing, as a don Juan can twist the truth to suit himself (a discovery also made by Lopez in *Don Juan oder die Liebe zur Geometrie*). Don Juan confuses the mind, so that any arguments against him become muddled and ineffectual. Sganarelle is reduced to 'hypothetical' argument in his attempt to convince his master of the evil of debauchery (I, ii): his attempt is comic, but also demonstrates the inability to speak directly. When done Elvire arrives and challenges dom Juan, the latter commands Sganarelle to speak on his behalf, to which Sganarelle replies: 'Je n'ai rien à répondre. Vous vous moquez de votre serviteur' ('I've nothing to say. You're making fun of your servant'; I, iii). We can take this statement at its literal value: Sganarelle has no power to speak,

---

[295] 'Some inflamation prevents me from speaking'.
[296] 'Well, I must say...I don't know; you twist everything around so it seems you're right, and yet just the same you're not. I had the most beautiful thoughts ever, and your talking has confused all that'.

and dom Juan's insistence that he does so merely highlights his incapacity, making him look ridiculous. Sganarelle uses other such references to his inability to speak. He tells himself 'vous ne savez ce que vous dites' ('You don't know what you're saying';II, ii), and warns Pierrot to say nothing to dom Juan (II, iii) - uselessly, for Pierrot insists on speaking, and both he and Sganarelle are beaten for their efforts. Their beating reflects their lack of control. He contradicts himself to Charlotte and Mathurine (II, iv), and tells them that dom Juan alone can speak about whether or not he takes advantage of women. He acknowledges his inability to challenge dom Juan: 'vous savez bien que vous me permettez les disputes, et que vous ne me défendez que les remontrances' ('You knnow quite well that you allow me to discuss things, and you only forbid reproaches'; III, i). Sganarelle can only speak if dom Juan permits it, thus dom Juan has control over how another man may speak, and can censor any critical material: thus Sganarelle's inability to criticize dom Juan means that no true discourse really occurs. And dom Juan does not allow speech out of charity: 'vous vous taisez exprès et me laissez parler par belle malice' ('you're keeping quiet on purpose and letting me talk on out of pure spite'; III, i), Sganarelle comments. In the first encounter with the statue, dom Juan irritably asks his servant, 'Dis donc, veux-tu parler?' ('Go on then, will you speak?'; III, v), but indeed Sganarelle does not want to speak: he has just seen the statue move. He insists to dom Juan: 'Allez-vous-en lui parler vous-même' ('Go and talk to him yourself'; ibid). Sganarelle only summons the courage to speak directly to dom Juan in the final act: 'je ne puis m'empêcher de parler' ('I can't help speaking out'; V,ii), but by now it is too late, and dom Juan will soon be consigned to Hell.

Referring back to the weakness of other male characters, it is worth digressing at this point to note that lack of a voice is not confined to the servant. In *Dom Juan*, Sganarelle is not alone in losing his own voice. Dom Juan prevents Monsieur Dimanche from speaking and thus requesting the money he is owed. Dom Louis also touches on the fact that male speech has no power: 'je ne veux point...parler davantage, et je vois bien que toutes mes paroles ne font rien sur ton âme' ('I don't want to say any more. I can see that my words make no difference to your heart'; IV, iv). Only dom Juan's words have any effect, and his pose of hypocrisy convinces his father of his repentance, and earns his father's forgiveness: dom Louis cries 'tout est effacé par les paroles que vous venez de me faire entendre' ('everything is cancelled out by the words I have just heard from you'; V, i). We recognize the debilitating power of dom Juan's hypocrisy when he remarks: 'l'hypocrisie...ferme la bouche à tout le monde' ('hypocrisy shuts everybody up'; V, ii). The beggar remains apparently free to assert his own voice and opinion, and refuses to forswear his faith in response to dom Juan's temptation of money. However, the beggar also remains in penury, suggesting the ineffectiveness of his prayers: his voice has no power. The loss of a voice to speak the truth also occurs in *Don Juan oder die Liebe zur Geometrie*. In Act IV Lopez cries out the truth of don Juan's faked descent to Hell, but nobody believes him. His voice has no power: he lacks the capacity to convince. The women do not listen to him (even though don Juan tells them that they should), and the legend of don Juan's damnation will be accepted by all. Lopez denounces don Juan ringingly, threatening him with the end of his career as a womanizer; but, as don Juan remarks, 'trotzdem geschieht nichts, das ist ja der Witz' (Frisch, pp.156-7).[297] Lopez's words will change nothing, they have no power. His insistence on the truth merely causes him to be banished: he loses his entire wealth in the attempt to declare the falsity of don Juan's damnation, and he will eventually hang himself (p.159). His death implies the ultimate failure of the male voice, even though that voice speaks the truth.

Death alone, perhaps, may free the male from dom Juan's tyranny: thus Sganarelle notes that the Commander's statue 'semble...qu'il s'en va parler' ('looks as if it will

---

[297] 'Just the same, nothing happens, that's what's so funny'.

say something'; III, v, 53). At the end of some don Juan plays the servant recovers his voice in order to bear witness to the fate of his master: both Catalinón and Leporello appear at the end of their respective dramas to speak of their masters' damnation. Once don Juan is dead, they can speak the truth indeed. When the king of Castile asks Catalinón: '¿Qué dices?' ('What are you saying?') he replies 'Lo que es verdad' ('The truth'; III, 1051). Tirso's don Juan has previously broken Catalinón's tooth (III, 421-2), in punishment for repeating the truth of the seducer's exploits. After don Juan's death Catalinón may speak without fear.

Given their lack of power, it is hardly surprising that the servants desire to imitate their masters, consciously or not, and acquire some of their masters' power for themselves. If we consider Sganarelle's opening speech of *Dom Juan*, about the use of tobacco, we find the servant's ambiguity immediately presented. Michel Serres takes this speech as an example of the theme of economy and exchange running throughout the play: tobacco is a symbol of commerce.[298] However, although Sganarelle indeed speaks of obligation and right thinking as inevitable outcomes of the use of tobacco, he also says: 'Ne voyez-vous pas bien, dès qu'on en prend, de quelle manière obligeante on en use *avec tout le monde, et comme on est ravi d'en donner à droit et à gauche, partout où l'on se trouve?*' (I, i: my italics).[299] The latter part of the sentence reveals a train of thought in Sganarelle's mind not too dissimilar from that of dom Juan in the following scene. Here the latter speaks of bestowing his love indiscriminately to all women as his duty: 'l'amour que j'ai pour une belle n'engage point mon âme à faire injustice aux autres; je rends...à chacune les hommages et tributs où la nature nous oblige' (I, ii).[300] Thus Sganarelle reflects, consciously or not, the philosophy of his master,

---

[298] Michel Serres, *Hermes: Literature, Science, Philosophy*, ed. by J. V. Harari and David F. Bell, (Baltimore: Johns Hopkins University Press, 1982); pp.4-5.

[299] 'Don't you see, since people started to use tobacco, the obliging way in which one shares it *with everyone, and how pleasant it is to share it out right and left, wherever one happens to be?*'

[300] 'My love for one woman cannot force my soul to be unjust to the rest; I continue to see the merit of all women, and render to each the homage and tribute exhorted by nature.'.

and when he speaks of duty and right living in his opening speech, he may subconsciously long to follow dom Juan's own notions of what duty actually is.

A similar motif occurs in *El burlador*. Catalinón reflects his master's ideas in the same ambivalent way as Sganarelle. Don Juan speaks to both Tisbea and Aminta of their icy yet fiery beauty, particularly in regard to their hands, yet Catalinón first uses the image when he meets Tisbea: 'Quiero besarte/ las manos de nieve fría' ('I want to kiss you hands, cold as snow'; I, 563-4). But servants in other don Juan plays have participated quite happily in their master's debauchery without feeling the need for reproach. Ciutti in *Don Juan Tenorio* approves of his master's career: he describes his master approvingly as 'gran pluma' ('a great writer', literally 'great pen'; line 32), and in doing so he admires not only don Juan's way with a pen but also his phallic gifts, given the symbolic equation of the pen with the phallus. He describes his master as devillish (1941), but nevertheless admires his daring: 'No he visto hombre/ de corazón más audaz' ('I've never seen a man with a braver heart'; 1954-5). Ciutti does not have to cry for his wages as Sganarelle does, for don Juan provides all he wants (20-22). Even Leporello comes to appreciate don Giovanni's career when his own turn comes to seduce Elvira on don Giovanni's behalf and disguised as his master: as the seduction progresses, he observes: 'La burla mi da gusto' ('I'm enjoying this joke!'; Mozart, p.285).

Thus while some servants warn don Juan of the consequences of his lifestyle, they may also bear him secret admiration and envy. No wonder, then, that Leporello sings:

> Notte e giorno faticar
> per chi nulla sa gradir;
> piova e vento sopportar,

mangiar male, e mal dormir.

Voglio far il gentiluomo,

e non voglio più servir... (pp.28-30).[301]

This aria, however, incorporates not only the servant's envy but also his inability to pursue his master's way of life. Leporello summarizes the servant's lament in traditional terms that have comic overtones, but his song reinforces the sense of powerlessness in comparison with don Giovanni. This song comes in the opening scene of the opera, so that the first impression we have is of a man's powerlessness. Leporello accentuates this by his remarks that seem on the surface to be mere grumbles: working night and day in all weathers, for poor bed and board in return. Nonetheless this does not detract from the fact that the servant seems merely to survive, and does not take the initiative in securing a better life that the women of *Don Giovanni*, such as Zerlina, do. The phrase 'per chi nulla sa gradir' reminds us that the male characters - certainly the servants but also the others - remain unappreciated, seen only as a means to an end. Naturally, Leporello would prefer to live as a nobleman, but, as Rank observes in his discussion of the character,[302] Leporello receives only the painful consequences of the life of his master the nobleman, and none of the pleasure, to the extent that he even gets the blame for his master's misdeeds. Ironically, his desire, expressed at the beginning of the opera, to play the part of a gentleman, brings Leporello nothing but disaster. Zerlina and Masetto catch him as he tries to escape from Elvira: and they, Elvira, Anna and Ottavio threaten him with punishment for his deceit and misdeeds (some of which have actually been committed by don Giovanni). He thus learns not to presume to be a gentleman, like his master. In this way we can appreciate that the servant, while secretly espousing the master's philosophy, cannot successfully practice it as his master can.

---

[301] 'Wearing oneself out night and day for little gratitude; putting up with wind and rain, eating and sleeping badly. I want to be a gentleman, and serve no more'.

[302] Rank, ch. 2.

Thus the servant can never fulfil his wish to be a gentleman, but instead remains only as a witness to don Juan's success and impunity - he can never himself succeed in his own ambitions. The role of the male character as spectator, referred to at the beginning of this chapter, therefore acquires a new resonance in the servant figure. Abert describes how the music of the catalogue aria reveals Leporello's increasing identification with his master, 'until in the end he adopts an air of complete triumph, as though he himself had been the hero of all these adventures'.[303] But what is also significant is that his triumph is vicarious. Leporello's catalogue of don Giovanni's conquests bears testimony, among other things, to the fact that Leporello himself spectates. He does not act, but merely records. Abert describes Leporello as: 'always a dependent, the play-thing of chance and his position. All that is real in his master is only apparent in him...his whole existence remains quite insignificant..'.[304]

Thus despite the apparent ambiguity of the servant's role in don Juan plays, the servant himself demonstrates the weakness of the male characters very effectively. The function of the male as spectator to don Juan's actions becomes particularly pronounced in the case of the servant, since the latter bears witness to all his master's deeds yet does not himself enjoy the freedom of a don Juan to make use of women and to act with apparent impunity. The constant warnings of eternal punishment indicate the envy of the bystander, too weak himself to commit the acts that don Juan does. While the servant appears more compromised than other characters, given his subordinate position, he nevertheless reveals the inadequacy of patriarchal society at all social levels.

---

[303] Abert, p.73.
[304] Abert, p.60.

The Octavio figure

The most obviously ineffectual male figure in these plays is the Octavio figure, who appears in three of the plays discussed here, those of Tirso, Mozart and Shaw (Frisch also mentions him in passing). In each play he performs much the same role, that of the idealistic lover, whose love is jeopardized by the actions of the woman he loves and of don Juan. The Octavio figure's general inability to maintain his authority over his own fiancée and his apparent inability to satisfy her, reveals a marked contrast between this weak, idealistic lover and don Juan's sexual abilities. Don Octavio in *El burlador*, for example, loves Isabela in a childish, idealized fashion, a notion that Tirso heightens by reference to a childlike attitude to play (I, 195-202). The emphasis on childhood warns us of Octavio's incapacity to act, a notion that Ripio underlines when he argues that if Octavio seriously loves Isabela, he should act at once and marry without further ado. Ripio is right, for if Octavio had acted he would have prevented the stain on his honour brought about by his procrastination and Isabela's desperation. Once the damage is done, Octavio plays at defending his honour but does not actually act effectively: his immediate response is to run away when he hears of Isabela's seduction - a childish reaction. More amusingly, the king of Castile easily manipulates Octavio into forgetting Isabela by promising a match with doña Ana; but Octavio sees this encounter rather differently: 'César con el César fui,/ pues vi, pelée y vencí' ('I was like Caesar with this Caesar; I came, I saw, I conquered': II, 86-7). Again, his stance is rather childish, suggesting an insistence on his own power that the facts do not justify. However, it also emphasizes how the male characters are vulnerable to manipulation, stressing their inability to influence events. (The irony here is that the proposed marriage will not take place, the king being as unable as Octavio to influence the course of action). Shortly after this speech Octavio encounters don Juan, and misses the opportunity to seek reparation for his honour (since he apparently does not know don Juan to be the culprit): again, a male character lacks the capacity and opportunity to act decisively. By the time he becomes aware of don Juan's guilt and asks the king for permission to challenge the womanizer, don Juan has already made his return appointment with the statue and will set out on his path to damnation. The challenge therefore comes too late: Octavio will never be able to carry out the defence of his honour. Octavio incidentally shares with the king of Naples the sense of a fortress breached: he describes Isabela as 'el castillo del honor' ('fortress of honour'), reminding us of the King's palace of the previous scene. Isabela has allowed don Juan to penetrate the castle of Octavio's honour in the same way as he penetrated the actual castle of the king.

Mozart and da Ponte's don Ottavio has become virtually notorious as the pathetic and ineffectual lover. Hoffmann in his short story *Don Juan* claims that donna Anna secretly loves don Giovanni, and does not really wish to marry the unsatisfactory Ottavio; and her actions seem at least to bear out the idea that she does not love Ottavio, since at the end of the opera she postpones her wedding for a year. Abert (1976, 66) defends Ottavio, arguing that Anna certainly loves him.[305] Even he, however, acknowledges Ottavio's inadequacy in terms that echo the general suggestion here of a masculine inability to act: 'Don Ottavio shows himself from the beginning to be impulsive but weak-minded and sanguine, full of the best intentions but lacking the strength to carry them out; he is a man who looks on and comments but never acts'[306] - the motif of spectating appears again here. Abert also points out that, while love motivates Ottavio, mere seduction motivates don Giovanni; yet love renders Ottavio totally incapable of action - Abert refers to it as paralysis - while seduction spurs don Giovanni to act.[307] Abert also argues that Mozart reflects Ottavio's nature in his arias: the music displays the sweetness and nobility of his love, but in more powerful musical passages 'the

---

[305] Abert, p.66
[306] Abert, p.67
[307] Abert, p.113.

voice remains curiously irresolute', reminding us of the character's ineffectual nature.[308] Instances of Ottavio's failure to affect the action occur throughout the opera. Despite swearing vengeance on the killer of Anna's father, Ottavio always speaks courteously to don Giovanni, even if in this he sometimes dissembles. He aims a pistol at don Giovanni but does not fire it (Mozart, p.234), a telling image suggesting his impotency in more ways than one.[309] Moreover, when he, Anna and Elvira arrive at don Giovanni's house, seeking justice, he cannot even reply to Leporello's simple query as to what they are doing there, until the women urge him to answer, another instance of the loss of the male voice. Once he knows for certain that don Giovanni holds the blame for the Comendatore's death, he acts correctly in deciding to go to the proper authorities (p.357), but this is a far cry from the oaths of vengeance he swore with Anna over her father's corpse, or indeed his desire immediately beforehand to punish Leporello, caught masquerading as his master. In his subsequent aria, 'Il mio tesoro', he sings of his plan for vengeance:

> Ditele che i suoi torti
> a vendicar io vado,
> a vendicar io vado:
> che sol di stragi e morti
> nunzio vogl'io tornar...(pp.360-1).[310]

These are apocapyptic words indicating resolution and strength of character, but since Ottavio's vengeance will be confined to reporting the matter to the authorities, they do not ring true. He vows he will not be turned back from his

---

[308] Abert, p.115.

[309] Julian Rushton observes that Ottavio is fully justified in not shooting: his immediate purpose is to defend Leporello from his master's charge of attempted rape (of Zerlina), and that in any case Ottavio could not attack don Giovanni in his own home. These are valid comments, but do not nevertheless detract from the notion of Ottavio's inadequacy. (Rushton,, p.61.)

[310] 'Tell her I will avenge her wrongs, I will be the angel of death and destruction'.

plan of vengeance, but in truth he will not himself act, but turn over responsibility for action to someone else. Otherwise, Ottavio's main thoughts lie with calming Anna in her grief, but to no avail, since Anna continues to mourn her father loudly and at the end of the play insists on a year's grace from marriage in order to continue to mourn. Ottavio cannot effectively fill the void in Anna's life left by the death of her father.

Octavius of *Man and Superman* continues this pattern of the weak lover, but Shaw turns his weakness into an ironic strength. Octavius's very inadequacy allows him to escape Ann's matrimonial plans: Ann despises his weakness, but that is what saves him. Shaw describes Octavius as the possessor of 'a slim, shapely frame...small head and regular features, the pretty little moustache, the frank clear eyes, the wholesome bloom on the youthful complexion, the well brushed glossy hair...' (Shaw, p.4). The terms Shaw uses here have a feminine ring about them at times, particularly the references to the shapely frame, the complexion and the glossy hair, as well as the adjective 'pretty' to describe the moustache. Shaw casts Tanner, however, in a more obviously masculine mould: 'a certain high chested carriage of the shoulders, a lofty pose of the head, and the Olympian majesty with which a mane, or rather a huge wisp, of hazel colored hair is thrown back from an imposing brow, suggest Jupiter...' (p.9). Tanner's character immediately comes across as rugged, imposing, essentially masculine and in distinct contrast to Octavius. The reference to carriage and to the mane of hair suggest a form of animal power in Tanner that is lacking in Octavius: while the reference to Jupiter also suggests power. We might recall at this point that Tanner/don Juan is the one destined to aim for the great, Olympian heights of Heaven, the one who will search for something beyond himself - an aim denied to women. It is also denied to Octavius, who will remain a sentimental dabbler in poetry. He shares their exclusion from heaven with the women, and this in a sense feminizes him. Shaw thus incorporates a measure of femininity into the character, and this renders him useless to women, who search for 'true men' with which to marry and reproduce. Thus Shaw suggests very strongly Octavius's emasculation, an idea that reinforces the theme of women as dangerous to men.

Octavius's idealization of women bears no resemblance to mundane female reality, as Ann and Violet all too readily demonstrate. Ann comments to him:

> ...I shall have to live up always to your idea of my divinity; and I
> dont think I could do that if we were married. But if I marry Jack,
> youll never be disillusioned...I can see exactly what will suit you.
> You must be a sentimental old bachelor for my sake (Shaw, p.151).

Ann recognizes that Octavius cannot marry if he is to retain his illusions about women; and certainly he seems to enjoy his hopelessly romantic pose. This romantic attitude that he strikes enables him, whether consciously or not, to escape the real, brutal demands of women. When Ann further comments that he will be quite happy without a wife - 'A broken heart is a very pleasant complaint for a man in London if he has a comfortable income' (p.152) - Octavius becomes 'considerably cooled' according to the stage directions. Instinctively h e realises that real women endanger his ideals. His status as the perpetual romantic bachelor will keep him safe from women. His pose is a theatrical one, a deliberately assumed role (Ann tells him he will go to the opera very often; p.152): the motif of theatricality implies the evasion of reality, reality consisting of the fundamental desires of women.[311] His single status also allows him the freedom that Tanner longs for to achieve his purpose, in Octavio's case writing poetry. Tanner remarks that Petrarch and Dante wrote excellent love poetry because '[t]hey never exposed their idolatry to the test of domestic familiarity; and it lasted them to their graves' (p.52). If Ann is to remain Octavius's muse, then he cannot marry her, as marriage

---

[311] Crompton (p.77) notes Octavius's masochistic reaction to the news of Violet's illegitimate pregnancy: Octavius relishes the theatricality of the role his sister places him in.

would destroy the illusion that gives the inspiration. He must keep his distance. We might also observe that in the Hell scene, Ottavio (Octavius's obvious counterpart in Shaw's Mozartian Hell scene) does not appear - the statue remarks that Ottavio should be 'warned' that Ana is now in Hell, to which don Juan replies that he has not seen Ottavio since Ana's arrival (p.92).

Octavius's idealism renders him rather comic. His unrealistic ideas are revealed clearly in an exchange with Straker: when he comments that 'I believe most intensely in the dignity of labor', Straker dismisses this by pointing out, 'Thats because you never done any' (p.42). In the final act, when Ottavio learns that Ann will marry Tanner, he makes the following romantic speech: 'when I am eighty, one white hair of the woman I love will make me tremble more than the thickest gold tress from the most beautiful young head' (p.151). This would sound fine indeed, were it not that we have already heard this speech before. The statue used this same speech to all the women he wooed while alive, and comments that whenever he used the speech he sincerely believed it at the time (p.122). Ann underlines this reminder when she says, in response to Octavius, 'It gives me that strange sudden sense of an echo from a former existence which always seems to me such a striking proof that we have immortal souls' (p.151). The statue's remarks thus reduce Octavius's own speech to the level of bathos. Octavius's own sincerity, and the way in which he roundly declaims the speech merely moves us to amusement. His romanticism cannot disguise from us the fact that the speech is only a part of the statue's old repertoire of seduction. Moreover, the statue's recycled speech strongly implies Octavius's unoriginality as a poet. As with the servants of other plays, he lacks his own voice.

Again, this Octavio cannot exert any influence over events. His attempts to control Violet prove useless, as he is no match for his sister. Despite his efforts to exclude her from the car excursion (p.61), she goes on the journey anyway. He vows to force Violet's supposed seducer to marry her 'or he shall answer for it to me' (p.26), but as in other plays he never carries out his threat. There is no need: Violet is already married, having the whole situation well under her control. Octavius also reveals himself to be impractical in the closing scene, as the characters gather round in an attempt to revive Ann, who has apparently fainted. He tries to come to her assistance, but does not know what to do, and becomes 'conscious of his uselessness' (p.164). Thus Octavius's ineffectuality, coupled with his retreat into romanticism and his need to remain clear of women in order to retain his ideals, reinforces the sense of emasculation that we have previously observed. Shaw effectively contrasts the inadequacy of the effeminate Octavius with the efforts of the overtly masculine Tanner to establish his own identity independent of the women; and in doing so Shaw underscores the notion of women as threatening by pointing out their capacity to emasculate. Octavius, incidentally, is the man approved by patriarchy - the patriarchal figure of Ramsden much prefers him to Tanner - suggesting again both patriarchal weakness (Ramsden approves of an emasculated character) and the fact that patriarchal interests are not those of Tanner/don Juan.

Although not immediately identifiable as an Octavio figure, the character of Roderigo in Frisch's *Don Juan oder die Liebe zur Geometrie* shares many of the same qualities as the Octavios, being a friend of don Juan whom the latter betrays, an inadequate lover and betrothed to a future victim of don Juan (Inez). As with Octavio of *El burlador* and Octavius of *Man and Superman* (and Ottavio of *Don Giovanni*, if we follow the arguments of critics such as Hoffmann), Roderigo cannot apparently satisfy women. We saw in the previous chapter Inez's frustration each night as she waits for the arrival of a man, who should be her betrothed, Roderigo. But Roderigo never appears: he does not satisfy her sexual desires. Miranda also rejects him, and compares him to don Juan, very much in the former's disfavour. Like the Octavio figure, then, Roderigo does not equal the personality of don Juan.

Roderigo does not understand his friend at all, and believes in his heroism at Cordoba, despite Juan's protests to the contrary (pp.103-4), nor can he appreciate Juan's fear of his forthcoming wedding. The discovery of Juan's treachery with Inez impels Roderigo to suicide: his choice of suicide rather than vengeance accentuates the weakness of his character. Don Juan treats his friend with some cruelty and scorn, in fact, when he tells him: 'Stürze dich nie in deine Seele, Roderigo, oder in irgendeine, sondern bleibe an der blauen Spiegelfläche...auf daß du lange lebest im Lande...' (133).[312] Juan implies by saying this that Roderigo has no depth to his personality (and that Juan himself does), and that Roderigo should continue to live life 'only on the surface', suggesting Roderigo's superficiality. Frisch introduces a strong note of irony in Juan's subsequent comment about living long; for Juan himself has revealed to Roderigo dark depths of the soul of which the latter was not aware, and in doing so drives him to suicide.

Therefore the Octavio figure proves to have no effect on the action and plays no significant part in the dialectic between don Juan and the women. The acknowledged lover, who plays the role accepted by social convention, turns out to be unsatisfactory, and the don Juan figure easily usurps his rightful place by the side of, or indeed in bed with, the fiancée. The inadequate lover exposes one of the deepest weaknesses of patriarchal society as our authors depict it, the inability to satisfy women. This may highlight a notion of women as creatures with voracious, uncontrollable sexual appetites, but it also reinforces the strong

---

[312] ' Never dive into your own soul or anyone else's, Roderigo, but stay on the blue surface...so that you live long in the land'.

impression we have of men as ineffectual. In this key sphere of their masculine nature, their sexuality, they are found wanting.

The inability of any man to set himself up as a rival to don Juan reveals itself clearly in Zorrilla's *Don Juan Tenorio*, where don Luis Mejía does indeed attempt to rival don Juan, not only in the matter of women but also in duelling and fighting. He comes very near to succeeding; and Zorrilla indicates the close similarity of the two characters in their mirrored actions and speeches at the inn. At times don Juan and don Luis use exactly the same words (e.g. 502-5 and 612-5), and their lists of misdeeds are virtual carbon copies. They even arrange to have each other arrested in the same manner and at almost the same moment. Nonetheless Mejía loses the contest with don Juan, since he could not manage to kill quite as many men and seduce quite as many women as his rival could. He cannot prevent don Juan from seducing Ana, despite guarding her home; and his eventual challenge to don Juan at the end of Part I results in his death. He does not have don Juan's power. Where Mejía fails most dismally, however, is in his capacity to receive love and salvation. There are no father figures to dispute with don Luis: no one turns up at the inn to plead with or reprimand him: nobody shows any concern for his fate. But more particularly, while don Juan achieves salvation through the love of Inés, Mejía loses Ana as a result of her seduction by don Juan. His love for Ana cannot wipe away the stain on his honour: '...yo la amaba, sí;/ mas con lo que habéis osado/ imposible la hais dejado/...para mí' (2376-9).[313] The loss of Ana will end also in the loss of salvation. When don Juan kills Mejía, the latter cries '¡Jesús!', to which don Juan replies: 'Tarde tu fe ciega/ acude al cielo' ('Your blind faith calls to Heaven too late'; 2612-3). This suggests that don Luis appeals to Heaven too late. But don Juan, who also appeals to Heaven only on the point of death, receives redemption, because he has the pure love of Inés and not the tainted love of Ana. Therefore Mejía again reflects the

---

[313] 'I loved her, yes, but after what you've dared to do it's impossible for me to marry her'.

general weakness of the male characters, which in this case leads not only to powerlessness in the sphere of sexuality, but also to the loss of salvation through pure female love.

Fear and hatred of women

Sometimes the emasculation of the male characters finds a corollary in a fear and hatred of women. We have just seen how Octavius in *Man and Superman* retreats into an unrealistic romanticism that nevertheless allows him to avoid the real demands of women: his romanticism enables him to keep the women at arm's length. The laments of Octavio, the king of Naples and Batricio concerning woman's fickleness also indicate a measure of hostility, as does Leporello's relish of his catalogue aria detailing women's general downfall and his implicit humiliation of donna Elvira as he sings of don Giovanni's exploits. The men of Zorrilla's *Don Juan Tenorio* prefer to keep all women behind closed doors: only one woman - Brígida, a nun - has any freedom of movement. We have already observed a note of hostility between don Juan and women: the male characters share in this hostility too, but on their part it is a dislike and fear that arises from their inadequacy and loss of authority, and impotence - sometimes physical as well as figurative.

In regard to *El burlador*, Conlon has detailed the dislike of the male characters for women (a dislike, according to Conlon, also shared by don Juan). He suggests that the male characters secretly fear the women, and express their fear in terms of hostility; hence, in particular, Mota's ill treatment of and malign attitude towards the prostitutes.[314] Furthermore, Batricio seems almost relieved to relinquish his claim on Aminta, yielding very easily to don Juan's claims. And Octavio seems to fear marriage, too. He muses poetically over his love for Isabela (I, 192-208), but

---

[314] Conlon, 'The *Burlador* and the *Burlados*'; see also Pendzik, pp.167-8.

he does not act upon it, so that his servant Ripio criticizes him for his 'amor impertinente' (210). The thrust of Conlon's argument is that don Juan shares with his male victims a fearful and misogynistic approach to women; and we might argue from this that as a result none of them can truly trust or love the female characters (although I do not think we can draw an equation of don Juan's and patriarchy's interests from Conlon's hypothesis). However, Conlon has also given us a detailed study of one male character's hatred and fear of women: in another essay he focuses specifically on Batricio's suspicion of Aminta, and his over-readiness to surrender her to don Juan, even though Aminta protests her loyalty to Batricio. Conlon comments:

> ...Batricio's jealousy is not so much a specific reaction to a particular sexual threat as an outpouring of a generalized anxiety. His jealousy is a pathological given of his personality, a voracious monster sleeping uneasily at the back of Batricio's mind until Don Juan awakens him.[315]

This 'generalized anxiety', Conlon goes on to remark, is in fact a fear of all women, which leads him to assume that Aminta will inevitably betray him. For Batricio, betrayal of men is an inherent part of a woman's nature, and he cannot trust any woman at all. In consequence, his certainty that Aminta will betray him, coupled with the uncertainty as to when this will actually happen, precipitates Batricio into actually offering Aminta to don Juan. However, as Conlon also notes, Batricio's attitude to women becomes merely a self-fulfilling prophecy: 'It is Batricio's lack of faith in the woman who wishes to be loyal to him - until she realizes that she has been abandoned - that brings about his sexual humiliation'.[316] Batricio thus appears caught in a vicious circle: his weakness results in his distrust

---

[315] R. Conlon, 'Batricio in *El Burlador de Sevilla*: the Pathology of Sexual Honor', in *Tirso's Don Juan: the Metamorphosis of a Theme*, ed. by Josep Sola-Solé and George E. Gingras (Washington DC: Catholic University of America Press, 1988), 86-94; p.90.
[316] Conlon, 'Batricio in *El Burlador*', p.92

of Aminta, but that in turn results in his loss of authority over her to don Juan, which heightens his sense of weakness.

In *Don Juan Tenorio*, Don Gonzalo (the living character) seems to fear his own daughter Inés, and he will kill her rather than allow her honour to be ruined by don Juan: 'primero muerta/ que esposa suya la quiero' ('I'd rather she were dead than your wife'; 181-2). This may tell us much of the severity of the honour code, but don Gonzalo also avows that honour does not concern him primarily: 'primero seré buen padre,/ buen caballero después ' ('I'll be a good father before I'll be a gentleman';185-6). On one level his comment merely expresses the paramount importance of his love for his daughter, perhaps even to an incestuous degree, but his previous remark indicates a measure of hostility, a subconscious desire to kill Inés rather than hand her over to another man. He reinforces this impression when he confronts don Juan in the inn:

> ...desde hoy
> no penséis en doña Inés.
> Porque antes que consentir
> en que se case con vos,
> el sepulcro, ¡juro a Dios!
> por mi mano la he de abrir (734-9).[317]

The repetition here of his death threat implies that Inés's death is much on don Gonzalo's mind, and indicates a subconsciously malign attitude towards her. We can observe that don Gonzalo does not at this point threaten *don Juan* with death: the innocent Inés must pay the penalty. (The threats to don Juan's own life come later, once don Juan has already taken Inés away from the convent). Indeed, don

---

[317] 'From now on think no more of doña Inés; because I swear to God that I will dig her grave with my own hand before I consent that she should be your wife'.

Gonzalo's actions do bring about the death of Inés, since his refusal to countenance don Juan results in the concluding catastrophe of the deaths of don Gonzalo and don Luis, and don Juan's flight. Inés dies as a result of these events.

We might explain the above simply in terms of the honour code that lay behind many of the Golden Age - *Don Juan Tenorio* is, after all, a *refundición* of a Golden-Age play. However, Zorrilla emphasizes in terms of imprisonment don Gonzalo's insistence that Inés remain in the cloister, indicating in the process don Gonzalo's malevolence towards his daughter. The abbess describes Inés's future in the nunnery in apparently pleasant tones that nevertheless carry a sense of aridity and death (such as in the flower image I discussed in chapter 4). Inés will lose her freedom: the abbess says 'no ansiaréis nunca las alas/ por el espacio tender'[318] (1468-9) and remarks on 'el pedazo de tierra/ que abarca nuestra estrechez,/ y el pedazo de cielo/ que por las rejas se ve' (1478-81).[319] These images strongly suggest Ines's imprisonment, trapped, with barely room to move; and Inés seems to understand the abbess in this way, listening silently with head bowed (1490-3). The abbess prefaces her speech about Ines's future with the comment: 'la voluntad decisiva/ de vuestro padre tal es' ('it's your father's absolute wish'; 1436-7). Thus don Gonzalo actively wills a life of imprisonment and misery for his daughter: we cannot perhaps be surprised that she succumbs to don Juan's charm in consequence.

Of all the authors here, however, Frisch uses fear of women to the most telling effect, not only as a matter for rather black humour but also as an indication of the disastrous state of male/female relationships. In *Don Juan oder die Liebe zur Geometrie*, don Juan fears the female characters, and longs for retreat into the abstractness of geometry. The fear experienced by don Juan, however, recurs in

---

[318] 'You will never long to stretch out your wings in the open'.
[319] 'The piece of ground that our enclosure occupies, and the piece of sky you can see through the bars'.

other characters, of which an obvious example is don Gonzalo's impotence in the harem. The scene in Act II, where don Gonzalo confesses his impotence, is comic but also reveals him in a pathetic light. He describes to Pater Diego the Moorish harem offered to him as the victor of the battle, and insists on his distaste at the thought of breaking his marriage vows. But, in response to Pater Diego's rather prurient questions (wanting to know whether the women in the harem were dressed, and what in fact don Gonzalo did), the Commander admits that in fact he did nothing (Frisch, pp.114-5). He does not possess the capacity even to be unfaithful: his impotence reflects the general sense of male sexual inadequacy in the face of the women's forceful sexual desires. His faithfulness stems not from principle but from incapacity to be anything else but faithful. Don Gonzalo's later attempts to fence with don Juan, once the latter has refused to marry Anna, also imply the former's impotence. Don Juan refuses to fight with the Commander, who remains waving his sword about uselessly - the sword, of course, being an obvious phallic symbol. Don Juan, in contrast, will kill don Gonzalo with a single stroke. Don Juan himself has witnessed don Gonzalo's impotence, and declares to the company assembled for the wedding: 'die maurischen Mädchen haben alles versucht, um ihn zu versuchen..ich habe ihn gesehen, so bleich und splitternackt, seine Hände haben gezittert, der Geist war willig, doch das Fleisch war schwach..' (p.122).[320] In response to don Juan's speech, don Gonzalo lowers his sword. Immediately before his declaration of don Gonzalo's impotence, don Juan has just described the Commander as 'marmornes Denkmal', a marble statue. This refers obviously to the statue of the don Juan legend (which this don Gonzalo will himself be unable to play - a woman must stand in for him): but the juxtaposition of the tale of the harem with the image of the stone statue, suggesting coldness and death, accentuates don Gonzalo's own impotence.

---

[320] 'The Moorish women tried everything to tempt him...I saw him, so pale and stark naked, his hands trembled, the spirit was willing but the flesh was weak...'.

Celestina summarizes men's fear of women to comic effect, in a passage debating female underwear:

> In der Unterwäsche nämlich sind sie komisch, gerade die feineren Herrn. Plötzlich entsetzt sie ein Rosa oder ein Lila, und sie sind befremdet über diesen Geschmack. Wie wenn man über Romane redet, plötzlich seufzt so ein Geck: Wir sind zwei Welten! und blickt zum Fenster hinaus. Drum sag ich euch immer, redet nicht über Romane! Plötzlich hat man die Kluft. Und mit der Unterwäsche genau so. Es gibt Männer, die vor keiner Fahne fliehen, aber ein rosa Fetzchen auf dem Teppich, und weg sind sie. Über Geschmack läßt sich nicht streiten. Keine Unterwäsche ist besser; es bestürtzt, aber es befremdet nie (pp.33-126).[321]

This passage highlights again the ability of women to emasculate men in the sexual sphere. The underlying weakness of men who show courage in battle but flee before pink underwear indicates the false premises on which this patriarchy is based: masculine gestures of military courage hide deep-rooted fears about women. The remark 'Wir sind zwei Welten!' should remind us of the inflexible opposition between men and women that has by now become rooted in the don Juan tradition, and which troubles Frisch's don Juan so much: men and women are indeed worlds apart. Ironically, Celestina bases her brothel business on this very fear of women. She tells Miranda that men do not come to the brothel in order to find love:

---

[321] 'They really are funny about underwear, even the better ones. Pink or purple suddenly frightens them, and they're taken aback by such taste. Like when you talk about books, some fancy chap will suddenly sigh: we're in different worlds! and stare out of the window. That's why I always say to you: don't talk about books! A great gap suddenly opens up. And the same with underwear. Some men will never desert their flag, but a pink scrap on the carpet and they run away. There's no accounting for taste. It's better to do without underwear: it's startling, but it's never off-putting'.

Wozu denn, meinst du, kommen die Herren zu uns? Damit du dich verliebst, damit du sie unterscheidest? Ich sag's euch Tag für Tag: Mädchen gibt's auch draußen...Hier, mein Schätzchen, erholt sich der Mann von seinen falschen Gefühlen...Ich verkaufe keine Mädchen, die innen herum von einem andern träumen. Das, mein Schätzchen, haben unsre Kunden auch zuhaus! (p.110).[322]

Men fear female sentiment, and they come to the brothel to retreat from the emotional demands that women make. It would be bad for business if a prostitute herself were to make similar emotional demands, to distinguish and select one man from among the others ('damit du sie unterscheidest') and in consequence demand love of them. The men prefer the lack of emotion involved in the commercial transaction of prostitution, where no sentiment is required or offered.

The characters discussed above exemplify a negative attitude towards women which of course plays an inherent part in patriarchy, but we must take their hostility in conjunction with their powerlessness: the two qualities are closely connected. Batricio cannot control Aminta and does not trust her: his distrust leads directly to his surrender to don Juan, even though Aminta at this point still protests her love for her husband. Don Gonzalo of *Don Juan Tenorio* cannot prevent Inés from falling in love with don Juan, or don Juan from taking Inés out of the convent where don Gonzalo has placed her. His insistence on her imprisonment in the convent indicates his fear of losing control over her, and the surrender of his authority over her to another man (which is why he will kill her rather than let don Juan have her). Frisch's don Gonzalo reveals his fear of women and his own inadequacy in the same phenomenon, his sexual impotence, an impotence mirrored in his lack of skill with a sword that will lead to his death.

---

[322] 'Why, then, do you think the gentlemen come to us? So that you fall in love, single one out from the others? I tell you all, day in, day out: there are women outside as well...Here, my dear, a

Don Juan to some extent shares in the negative attitude towards women, but he nevertheless sees them as objects of his power: he can use them to form his own identity as a seducer, or, as in the later plays, he can rise above them to greater, more transcendent spheres. The other men cannot do this. They do not act to challenge the women, but merely resent them in a passive fashion.

***

The above examples should serve to demonstrate the idea that the male characters represent a passive patriarchy that does not act but spectates. They play no part in the dialectic of identity between don Juan and the women. The marks of their weakness stand out plainly - the inability to protect their own homes and women, the inability to exercise authority that is rightfully theirs, the inability to speak for themselves, the impotence, timorousness and fear that turns at times to dislike of their female counterparts. The treatment of women changes through the course of don Juan's development, so that the women of the earlier works act subversively to survive and to accommodate themselves within a patriarchal society; while those of later plays grow to threaten that same patriarchy. The authors' treatment of the men, however, remains quite constant. Masculine powerlessness and fear of women pervade the plays.

The relations between don Juan and the women lie outside masculine control, which doubtless contributes to the resentment felt by some male characters. If the sphere of don Juan and the women lies outside patriarchal authority, then the male characters will perhaps inevitably lose any force they might otherwise have had. It is possible in consequence to read the plays in part as a warning against allowing women too much freedom, and as a call for men to reassert their authority over

---

man can escape from his false sentiments...I don't sell women who, within themselves, dream of someone else. That, my dear, our customers have at home!'.

women. But we can read the plays in another way, too, and argue that a weak patriarchal environment prevents women from living well and freely, so that some women look in desperation beyond patriarchy to a subversive force - don Juan - that allows them room for manoeuvre.

But if masculine weakness remains constant, why does the malign attitude to women increase? We could conceivably conclude that patriarchy remains constantly threatened by female power, even though the form in which that threat occurs, changes. But what occurs alongside the change of authorial approach towards women is, as I have argued, a change in the male individual rather than in masculine society as a whole. The other male characters are ineffectual to a similar degree in all six plays, regardless of the era in which each play was written. Don Juan's attitude to women, however, changes over time: he begins by using the women to give himself identity as a seducer, continues by looking beyond women in order to find salvation, and ends by attempting to evade women in order to establish an identity separate from them. By the time of Frisch, don Juan seeks actively to lose himself, to acquire anonymity. And anonymity, Frisch tells us, is a trait specific to patriarchy. Thus Miranda says:

> Don Roderigo...und alle die andern, die sich nur durch Namen unterscheiden, mich wundert oft, daß sie sich selber nicht verwechseln. Einer wie der andere! (Frisch, p.102).[323]

And as Celestina remarks to Lopez: 'Wir verlangen keine Personalien, hier genügt's, mein Herr, wenn Sie im voraus bezahlen' (p.127).[324] Thus personal details do not matter, the men are all alike and anonymous: as Miranda says, it becomes hard to tell them apart. When don Juan seeks anonymity, he seeks in a sense to return to the patriarchal fold and live a simple, passive life free from the

---

[323] 'Don Roderigo...and all the others that you can only tell apart by name, I'm often surprised you don't get yourselves muddled up. One just like the others!'

feminine sphere. This strongly suggests the crisis experienced in the male individual at this stage, which seems to require retreat into the patriarchal fold.

It would be rash to say that masculine weakness and feminine subversion and power are not closely connected: but the change in approach to women coincides with a change in the male *individual*, the protagonist, and not in masculinity as a whole. Patriarchy cannot offer don Juan identity as can the women - we remember the inadequacy of male heritage in *El burlador*, as outlined by ter Horst,[325] or the rejection of Zorrilla's don Juan by don Diego and don Gonzalo. Women offer don Juan a sense of identity. But as time goes by, that offer becomes too dangerous, and eventually don Juan seeks refuge in the anonymity that patriarchy offers. The male characters therefore bring out in greater relief the dialectic between women and don Juan, and accentuate the increasing danger of women to the male individual. Our examination of patriarchal society in don Juan plays acts as a control that serves to demonstrate not only the increased hostility towards the female characters, but also that this occurs in conjunction with a growing awareness of the male as individual, and as therefore vulnerable.

---

[324] 'We don't ask for personal details here, sir, it's enough if you pay in advance'.
[325] Ronert ter Horst, 'Epic Descent', pp.258-9.

Chapter 7: Punishment

Our review of the development of female and male characters in don Juan plays of different literary eras should by now have served to demonstrate the following: that don Juan derives, or attempts to derive, his own identity from his involvement with women; that as authorial treatment of women develops over the centuries don Juan perceives women to be more overtly threatening so that later don Juans derive identity from opposing the designs of women; and that all this takes place against a background of a consistently weak patriarchy. We have not yet touched, however, on one key area of the don Juan genre, the fantastic ending which usually focuses on a moving and talking statue, which comes to life in order to bring some form of damnation upon don Juan. In all six plays a statue appears on stage at some point. For Tirso, Molière, Mozart and Zorrilla, the statue - or statues, in the case of Zorrilla - provides the denouement of the action. While the don Juan of popular conception is remembered principally as a womanizer, Jean Rousset has emphasized the primacy of the statue, placing it in importance before don Juan's adventures with women. I believe this emphasis to be misplaced, since the women, rather than the statue, provide don Juan with an opportunity to establish individuality; nonetheless, Rousset reminds us of the vital role the statue plays in the don Juan phenomenon.[326] Pérez de Ayala claims that the supernatural elements have had the most pulling power for audiences: 'Estos sucesos sobrenaturales de la leyenda...son los que, sobre todo, enardecen la imaginación del público y le arrastran a presenciar la escandalosa vida y muerte ejemplar de *Don Juan Tenorio*...'.[327] The statue, however, does not appear solely, or even primarily, to provide the audience with a supernatural thrill. In earlier plays it represents punishment, divine judgement for sins committed. Discussion

---

[326] Jean Rousset, *Le Mythe de Don Juan*. (Paris: A. Colin, 1978), pp.8-9.

[327] 'The legend's supernatural events are what, more than anything, catches the imagination of the audience and draws them to witness the scandalous life and exemplary death of don Juan'; Pérez de Ayala p.460

of the role of the statue, and the idea of punishment that it represents, should be able to give us further insight into thematic issues developed through the course of action in each play; for I would argue that the theme of punishment reflects the development of the negative treatment of female characters that I have traced hitherto.

In the works of Tirso, Molière and Mozart don Juan receives punishment, eternal damnation, as a direct result of the dissolute life he has led: in each case the statue of the Commander comes to drag him off to Hell. In these plays, don Juan's ultimate adversary is not any of his female victims, but the figure of the statue (while don Juan attempts to derive his identity from the women, he does not oppose them in the fashion he will do in Shaw and Frisch). The import of the statue as adversary occurs clearly in *Don Giovanni*, which Mozart frames with the Comendatore's theme which begins the overture and heralds the denouement. But it is also apparent from the forgotten half of Tirso's title, which tells us of the forthcoming struggle between *El burlador de Sevilla* and his opponent the *convidado de piedra*. Don Juan must in these earlier plays receive punishment - many characters in each play warn the protagonist of his possible doom - and each dramatist casts the form of punishment in conventional Christian terms. The statue brings condemnation on don Juan because of his career as a seducer. Although don Juan has also killed,[328] betrayed the trust of his friends and disobeyed kings, his crimes against all characters arise, directly or otherwise, from his life as a womanizer. Don Juan's involvement with women thus eventually brings about his punishment, and the statue rectifies the wrongs of this seductive career by bringing damnation. Harold G. Jones perceives the statue as standing in place of the wronged women, an idea indicated by the use of the

---

[328] Don Juan does not necessarily murder but kills in self-defence. This applies to Tirso, Mozart and possibly Zorrilla. In Frisch's play, don Juan kills don Gonzalo by accident. Molière does not explain how dom Juan came to kill the Commander: this may have been murder, but dom Juan has been pardoned for the killing.

symbol of the hand - both don Juan and the statue ask their victim to take them by the hand.[329]

In the earlier plays, the consequence of punishment is to restore a communal equilibrium that allows the men to continue with some illusion of power and the women to achieve their objectives. Don Juan disturbs the intricate negotiation between the male and the female characters as they attempt to survive and gain some measure of power over their own lives; don Juan's removal means that the process of negotiation can continue. However, the twentieth-century plays conflate the notion of punishment with the fear of women, so that women themselves become don Juan's damnation. The women do not need the agency of a statue to inflict punishment, since they themselves become a form of punishment. The statue's role thus diminishes to a comic one in *Man and Superman* and *Don Juan oder die Liebe zur Geometrie*. The statue, unlike the women, is no longer to be feared. Thus even the matter of punishment demonstrates the suggestion that women appear in a more malign light as we approach and enter the twentieth century. For later authors no longer give the same emphasis to supernatural punishment: instead, the women themselves form don Juan's punishment and damnation. In the plays of both Shaw and Frisch, the don Juan figure is condemned to domesticity. This phenomenon occurs in parallel with the rise and subsequent problematization of male individualism, so that changes in the manner of punishment are to be found in the nineteenth-century work of Zorrilla, and become more pronounced in Shaw and Frisch. As the protagonist feels his individuality more under threat, so he locates that threat

---

329 Harold G. Jones, 'A "New" Source of Tirso's *El burlador de Sevilla*', in *Tirso's Don Juan: the Metamorphosis of a Theme*, ed. by Josep Sola-Solé and George E. Gingras, (Washington DC: Catholic University of America Press, 1988), 32-44; p.42. The 'alternative' version of *El burlador, Tan largo me lo fiáis*, contains lines that accentuate this point. The statue tells don Juan that by his damnation 'tienes que pagar/las doncellas que burlaste' (III, xix); which means that the statue pursues don Juan on behalf of all the women concerned and not only for Ana. In this way the statue again represents all women.

among women, and so they themselves in turn become the punishment for daring to assert his individual nature.

The need for punishment

Before we consider this phenomenon, however, we should dispense with a difficulty that has arisen recently in discussing don Juan plays. Why must there be eternal punishment at all? The notion of punishment in these plays seems to have caused great difficulties among commentators, not all of whom feel happy to accept what appears to be the outmoded idea of damnation for past sins. To them, divine retribution for don Juan's misdemeanours can seem very harsh. *El burlador* comes in particularly for severe criticism on this point: Conrad's 'monkish propaganda' is a typical - and unfair - response. [330] Much of the critical disparagement of Tirso's apparent didacticism may perhaps arise from a lack of awareness of the conventions of the *comedia*: Tirso's dispatch of don Juan to Hell for sexual misdemeanours may seem drastic to us in this century but may well in fact be in keeping with the literary demands of the time, given religious norms and the demands of the honour codes of the *comedia*. But Tirso in any case was not alone among don Juan authors in insisting on his protagonist's damnation: Molière does the same, and so do Mozart and da Ponte, to the particular discomfort of commentators. How could *Mozart*, in the spirit of the Enlightenment, resort to a vengeful God? Some don Juan authors could not in fact accept the idea of divine retribution: as far back as 1736 the playwright Carlo Goldoni dispenses with the statue for the more 'natural' dispatch of don Juan by a

---

330 Peter Conrad, p.82. Defenders of Tirso include Presberg, who takes *El burlador* in conjunction with Tirso's play *El condenado por desconfiado*, to argue that Tirso has in mind an elaboration of why some attitudes were damnable, and to conclude that the despair of Paulo in *El condenado* proved more unpalatable to Tirso than don Juan's presumption (Presberg, p.224). Don Juan in fact receives many warnings concerning his misconduct, from Catalinón in particular, and thus deserves his fate since he never wishes to reform, according to Presberg (p.228).

thunderbolt.[331] Increasingly writers would abandon the statue for other means of death. But significantly, Mozart and da Ponte keep the traditional ending even though Goldoni's play with its 'naturalistic' ending was a principal source for their opera. Till argues that divine judgement was too useful a concept to be dispensed with during the social upheaval of the later years of Mozart's life, and describes how Enlightenment thinkers were able to balance the notions of damnation and forgiveness.[332] Sganarelle puts the case for judgement succinctly: in what is otherwise one of his worst attempts at reasoning, he nevertheless defines to dom Juan the need for divine judgement: 'qui n'a point de loi vit en bête brute; et par conséquent, vous serez damné à tous les diables' ('those who have no law live like dumb animals, and so you will be damned to all Hell'; V, ii). Law - and therefore judgement - arises from the fact that humanity lives a higher form of existence that incorporates notions of morality. To live without some form of ethical structure is to live like an animal. It follows then, from Sganarelle's argument, that if dom Juan wishes to live at this higher, 'human' level, then he will inevitably incur judgement. And, regardless of what we may feel about Christian morality, this is the code of living that Molière applies in *Dom Juan*.

However distasteful to modern critics the idea might be, the notion of punishment appears inherent to the don Juan story as a whole. As George E. Gingras puts it: 'endemic to the Don Juan action is a strong moralistic strain that causes certain articulations of the theme to veer sharply towards the didactic'.[333] In literary and dramatic convention don Juan's career invites punishment: he cannot be seen to 'get away with it'. We might dismiss this as convention, but it also echoes a deep-seated need within us to ensure that transgressors do not go unpunished. The

---

[331] Smeed, p.128.

[332] Till, 219-226.

[333] George E. Gingras, 'Some Observations on the Generic Status of the Don Juan Theme from Tirso de Molina to Mozart', in *Tirso's Don Juan: the Metamorphosis of a Theme*, ed. by Josep Sola-Solé and George E. Gingras, (Washington DC: Catholic University of America Press, 1988), 106-126; p.117.

232

notion of punishment lies within the area of struggle between the individual and the community within which he or she is situated. If one acts in a social context, this must imply other members of society who can, if they wish, observe and judge one's actions. Moreover, while don Juan's freedom to act for pleasure may attract us - we may not want him punished because we ourselves do not want to be damned for our own pleasures - to wish his freedom from punishment is to privilege his desires above the concerns of others. This is the familiar conflict between liberty and duty. Given that punishment arises as a consequence of living in a social context, we can reinterpret its role in the relation between society and the individual. In chapter 2 I quoted the concept described by Weeks that the attempt to define oneself as individual automatically implies other people against whom one can define oneself: individuality ceases to have meaning if there are no others.[334] Judgement and punishment are consequences of the social balancing act between the desire for the liberty of the individual and the need for social order - respect for the concerns of others. This brings us to a principal end of the use of punishment by all six authors: punishment is aimed specifically at the male individual. Few if any of the other characters appear particularly virtuous, while others seem clearly corrupt (Mota and Mejía, for example); yet the dramatists reserve judgement and consequent punishment for the male individual, the protagonist.

Some critics have attempted to get round the issue of judgement by dispensing with the exercise of specifically *divine* power. Williams suggests that Mozart and da Ponte's statue symbolizes a more 'neutral' transcendent realm. He describes the Comendatore thus:

> He is indeed *super*natural, but only in the sense of a realm of
> cause and effects which lie beyond the natural, not one that

---

[334] Weeks, *Against Nature*, p.85.

brings a new order of guilt and judgement. Giovanni's lofty refusal to repent when the statue demands that he should is not an ultimate offence to the cosmic order, but rather a splendidly attractive and grand refusal to be intimidated.[335]

However, Williams's attempt here to elude the problematical concepts of judgement and damnation does not succeed, because he does not explain why, if there is no divine judgement, the statue should feel the need to call on don Giovanni to repent. Williams also argues that the reference to Prosperina and Pluto in the finale immediately following don Giovanni's descent to Hell indicates da Ponte's rejection of a Christian conception of Hell; but this does not prove his case either. The references to classical mythology still imply an underworld and still suggest judgement - the classical gods are no more benevolent than a Christian God. More evidence against Williams's assertions comes in the very title of the opera, the full title being *Il dissoluto punito ossia Il Don Giovanni*. While this title may assure the audience in advance of the appropriate 'happy' ending, we may also observe the title's emphasis on the idea of punishment, which goes a little way to contradicting suggestions that Mozart and da Ponte would shun any measure of didacticism. *Don Giovanni*'s collaborators took up the habit of earlier dramatists to emphasize the supernatural/judgemental element of the don Juan story or to the notion of debts paid or wrongs righted, in the titles of don Juan works.[336]

Nino Pirotta tries to disconnect the link between judgement and don Juan's career of seduction: 'I do not think that Mozart and da Ponte, of all eighteenth-century

---

[335] Williams, p.88.

[336] Such titles include Zamora's *No hay deuda que no se pague y convidado de piedra* (1744); Dorimon and Villiers' plays which both have the title *Le Festin de pierre ou le fils criminel* (both 1659); and Rosimond's *Le Nouveau festin de pierre ou l'athée foudroyé* (1669). The full title of Tirso's play is *El burlador de Sevilla y convidado de piedra*: the statue is given due emphasis right from the start.

people, were just the prudish ones to think that eroticism and libertinage were such capital sins. Only Don Giovanni's egotism, his wicked obdurate pride, his utter contempt for the feelings and lives of other beings could justify the majesty and anguish of supernatural intervention and punishment'.[337] But what is libertinage if not egotism, and utter contempt for the feelings and lives of others? Don Juan's egotism manifests itself precisely in his pursuit of seduction, through which he hopes to derive his identity by taking it from the women he seduces, as we have already seen. At bottom don Juan is judged for what he has done to women, from which all his other actions spring.[338]

When we come to deal with the theme of punishment that runs through don Juan's history, we may surely accept that Tirso, Molière and Mozart saw a need to reinforce the idea of judgement, without necessarily committing ourselves to such a belief, as some commentators seem to fear. Audiences surely experience no such dilemma when watching these works on the stage. Frisch may well be right to say, in his epilogue to the play, that a twentieth-century audience would not accept at face value the supernatural of earlier times:

> Das Absolute - daß er es als Steinernen Gast auftreten läßt, wird
> man von einem heutigen Stückschreiber kaum erwarten. Was
> sollen wir mit dieser vogelscheuchenhaftschauerlichen
> Erscheinung? Aber sie gehört nun einmal zu Don Juan...und mit
> Parodie allein ist dieser Hypothek nicht zu lösen...Welcher von
> unseren Zuschauern glaubt, daß die Toten, die man beschimpft,

---

[337] Nino Pirotta, 'The Traditions of Don Juan Plays and Comic Operas', *Proceedings of the Royal Musical Association* 107 (1981), 60-70; p.61.

[338] Till (p. 224) takes an alternative line to Williams and Pirotta, arguing that in fact the Comendatore does not bring don Giovanni judgement but a final call to repentance, since in inviting him to supper he is asking him to share the celestial food he mentions earlier in the scene, implying that don Giovanni should join him in Heaven. When don Giovanni refuses to repent, however, the statue exits, and only then is don Giovanni engulfed in the flames of Hell.

tatsächlich erscheinen und sich an unsere Tafeln setzen? (Frisch, p.174).[339]

But contemporary audiences watch *Don Giovanni* without a qualm, and apparently accept the statue's presence on stage even though they may not take it literally. And while parody is, of course an effective way of deconstructing a convention, it is also a way of coming to terms with the apparently unacceptable - death and judgement.

Affirmation of the community and suppression of the individual

One reason, perhaps, why contemporary critics feel such nervousness in the face of the idea of divine punishment arises in part from the fact that we criticize these works with twentieth-century hindsight, from a standpoint of threatened, possibly decadent, individualism much as Shaw and particularly Frisch viewed it. Tirso, Molière and Mozart emphasize *social* coherence, and elevate the needs of the community above those of the individual: at this point the individual has not yet acquired the elevated status of the Romantic era. Although the don Juans of each work highlight the contradictions and weaknesses of the society in which they live - the inadequate patriarchal society we considered in the previous chapter - each of the three works ends with the emphasis on the restoration of social harmony. As Sganarelle observes:

Voilà par sa mort un chacun satisfait: Ciel offensé, lois violées, filles séduits, familles deshonorées, parents outragés, femmes

---

[339] 'One would hardly expect a contemporary playwright to present the Absolute as a stone guest. What should we do with this horrific scarecrow of an apparition? But it now belongs to don Juan...and parody alone cannot remove this handicap...What member of the audience believes that the much abused dead really appear and sit down at our tables?'

mises à mal, maris poussés à bout, tout le monde est content. Il n'y
a que moi seul de malheureux (V, v).[340]

Sganarelle's lament (for his unpaid wages) disguises in part the balance that
Molière posits between the demands of society and those of the individual. In
Dom Juan society gains and the individual loses out, be he dom Juan or
Sganarelle. Sganarelle's speech emphasizes the restoration of institutions ('Ciel',
'lois') and social groups ('filles' and 'familles'; 'femmes' and 'maris'): it implies a
social symmetry which the solitary individual can only disturb. The endings of *El
burlador* and *Don Giovanni* reinforce this idea in another way. At the end of each
drama, the other characters gather together to pronounce a posthumous judgement
upon don Juan: 'Questo è il fin di chi fa mal' ('such is the end of those who do
evil') repeat the characters of *Don Giovanni*, again and again (Mozart, p.473ff).
While such an action obviously coincides with the conventional dictates of
theatrical endings, it also indicates the collective condemnation of society - in
these cases, the don Juan 'community', the other characters - over one individual,
don Juan himself.

The works of Tirso and Mozart stress the pairing off of different characters at the
conclusion, highlighting the problematic nature of the individual in the society of
these eras. If a character is not paired off in matrimony, he or she must have some
other person or group who can exercise control: no character can possess
individual independence with impunity. Thus donna Elvira retires to a convent,
and Leporello must look for a new master. Tisbea's fate seems uncertain: Tirso
does not confirm whether or not she will marry Anfriso, and this might be a fitting
penalty for her previous independent attitude, scorning love and marriage - she
becomes cast out from her own society of the fishermen. Furthermore, Tirso

---

[340] 'So everyone and everything's satisfied by his death: wrathful Heaven, broken laws, seduced
women, dishonoured families, outraged relatives, women gone to the bad, husbands at the end of
their tether, all are now satisfied. I'm the only one unhappy.'

specifically grounds the social institution of marriage on the death of the individual (don Juan), when the king of Castile ties together the play's loose ends:

> Y agora es bien que se casen
> todos, pues la causa es muerta,
> vida de tantos desastres (III, 1058-1060).[341]

Don Juan, while he lives, causes all the difficulties and trials faced by the other characters: once he is dead, they can marry. In this context, therefore, don Juan's solitary position is significant. As a lone figure he opposes the very basis of the society within which he lives: his solitary nature in itself implies his amorality. The independent individual follows a path that can lead only to death, and once the threat of the individual has passed, people can continue with marriage.

Tirso underscores the equation of individuality with death by distorting the traditional image of taking the hand in marriage. The frequent references to the hand in *El burlador* (as well as the duet 'Là ci darem la mano' in *Don Giovanni*), which don Juan uses in his seduction of different (usually peasant) women, reflect the final handclasp of don Juan and the statue at the end of both the play and the opera. Compare don Juan's seductive technique in *El burlador*:

> Quiero besarte
> las manos de nieve fría (I, 563-4)[342]

> Buenos ojos, blancas manos,
> en ellos me abraso y quemo (II, 743-4)[343]

---

[341] 'So everyone should now get married, since he who caused these disasters while he was alive, is now dead'.

[342] 'I want to kiss your hands as cold as snow'.

[343] 'Your beautiful eyes and white hands burn me and set me ablaze'.

Juro a esta mano, señora,

infierno de nieve fría (III, 273-4)[344]

with the request of the statue:

Don Gonzalo:　　　　Dame esa mano;

　　　　no temas, la mano dame.

Don Juan:...¡Que me abraso! ¡No me abrases

　　　　con tu fuego! (III, 946-9).[345]

Tirso makes a strong link between the hands of Tisbea and Aminta - cold, like the stony hand of the statue, yet suggesting the fires of hell - and the hand of the statue itself, offered in order to drag don Juan to Hell. The statue's request that don Juan take his hand suggests union, a ghastly form of marriage in which the individual, rejecting the common ties of marriages, becomes instead wedded to death. Jan White Albrecht takes up this point: 'La derrota de Don Juan es inevitable, y su ignorancia, debilidad y desatino han sido revelados al espectador durante todo el drama. Los símbolos e imágenes - la mano, el hielo y el fuego - son en sí irónicos porque las mismas imágenes que pueden considerarse sensuales, placenteras, funcionan al final como imágenes de castigo'.[346] Significantly, the statue of *El burlador* carries don Juan to Hell on his wedding night.

---

[344] 'Lady, I swear by your hand, ice-cold as hell'.

[345] '*Don Gonzalo:* Give me your hand, do not be afraid, give me your hand. *Don Juan*: I'm burning up! Do not scorch me with your fire!'.

[346] 'Don Juan's defeat is inevitable, and his ignorance, weakness and folly have been made clear to the spectator throughout the whole play. The symbols and images – the hand, the ice and the fire – are themselves ironic since these same images which can be thought of as sensual and pleasant, act in the end as images of punishment'. Jane White Albrecht, 'Formas y funciones de ironía en cinco obras de Tirso de Molina', *Neophilologus* 72 (1988), 546-555; p.548.

What do the female characters have to do with don Juan's damnation? At first sight, they share no involvement. However, as we saw earlier, the statue represents the women when it brings don Juan to judgement: the patriarchy that should in theory defend female honour proves in fact a feeble device for protecting the women and enabling them to survive. Batricio positively abandons Aminta to don Juan rather than encourage her to stay true to her promises; the king of Naples judges Isabela unheard; Octavio runs away; dom Carlos and dom Alonse are too busy fighting amongst themselves to defend the honour of their sister done Elvire (III, iv); Ottavio proves ineffective. The constant cries of the characters for divine justice in the earlier plays shows a justifiable distrust in the operations of human (male) justice, reinforcing a sense of patriarchal inadequacy. The statue, however, restores a social order that allows women to survive and paves the way for the realization of their aims.

We can draw further appreciation by considering the statue's own derivation. The statue was once don Gonzalo, the Commander, and particularly the father of doña Ana/donna Anna. Commentators such as Gay have understood don Juan in terms of Freud's primal father killed by his sons, returning to haunt the sons and prevent them from enjoying their father's women.[347] The don Juan theme lends itself easily, perhaps too easily, to such an interpretation; but at any rate such an interpretation neglects the fact that in *El burlador* and *Don Giovanni* the statue was once the father of a *daughter*, not a son. Don Gonzalo comes to die, and therefore to return as a statue, because he attempts to defend his daughter's honour. This point further enhances Jones's contention that the statue represents the women. Don Gonzalo's defence of his daughter proves ineffectual while he is alive, but extremely effective once dead. His metamorphosis into a statue removes him from the sphere of weak masculine society into the sphere of the dialectic

---

[347] Gay, pp.76-7.

between don Juan and the women, a more potent sphere that lies totally outside conventional patriarchy. In this sphere he is able to exact the appropriate penalty in recompense for his daughter's threatened honour.

The restoration that occurs at the end of each play encompasses the restoration to each woman of the identity of which don Juan tried to deprive her. Don Juan attempted to create his own identity by rendering each woman equal and undifferentiated, but the endings return them to their social position and their earlier lover. Williams claims that the characters in *Don Giovanni* do not return to 'normal' after the protagonist's death, that their lives will now have lost a little of the vitality that don Giovanni bestowed on them;[348] and this is perhaps true. Nevertheless this stance neglects the fact that the endings do restore each character to their rightful partner (except in the case of the Elviras and perhaps Tisbea). *El burlador* demonstrates this point strongly: the death of don Juan enables Isabela, Ana and Aminta to achieve the marriages they hoped for and worked towards. Previously, Isabela despaired of Octavio's commitment, Ana was reduced to defying her father, and Aminta was abandoned by Batricio. With don Juan's death, they can all now marry the man they love.

The only caveat we might apply to this idea is that of the 'hysterical' women, Tisbea, Elvire and Elvira, who remain free but do not succeed in obtaining the man they desire, don Juan himself. Tisbea's fate remains obscure, and we do not know whether she marries Anfriso. Elvire and Elvira, however, consign themselves to a convent (where the former, at least, lived before dom Juan came on the scene). The resolution of their fates may seem either positive or negative, depending on one's point of view: they remain free of male control but nevertheless obtain the protection of the convent;[349] yet they do not share in the

---

[348] Williams, p.90.

[349] We should not necessarily perceive the retreat to a convent in a negative light. Anderson and Zinsser (198-211) indicate that life in a convent could mean comparative freedom and power for

sense of the 'happy ending', for they have lost the man they truly care for. Nevertheless, as I suggested in chapter 3, they directly challenge dom Juan/don Giovanni in a way that no other women do, and in a way that makes the whole question of judgement hard to ignore. Their cry for restitution and their refusal to be silenced points to the inadequacy of patriarchal law and the need for some sort of intervention, outside the system of male authority, that will call don Juan to account for his actions. Indeed, the statue brings to a conclusion the process that Elvire and Elvira begin, the concerted efforts of women to oppose don Juan's attempt to deprive them of identity.

Zorrilla's pantheon

When Zorrilla wrote *Don Juan Tenorio*, he was not content with one statue, but a whole pantheon - though the effigy of don Gonzalo attends the supper in don Juan's rooms much as in other plays. At the beginning of Part II, the scene reveals all the major characters (apart from the protagonist) in stone form: don Juan's father don Diego commissioned the pantheon in honour of all don Juan's victims. The site of the cemetery was once that of don Diego's home: he has disinherited don Juan, and used the land the latter would have inherited, to found his pantheon for his son's victims. The son is to lose out while the 'community' of victims benefit, and in this way the individual receives punishment. The individual does not belong here, and in consequence the sculptor cannot include don Juan among the statues: 'Yo quise poner también/ la estatua del matador/ entre sus víctimas, pero/ no pude a manos haber/ su retrato...' (2762-6).[350] The individual goes unrecognized, and nobody knows what he looks like, so he is therefore excluded. Indeed, don Diego has specifically banned don Juan from entering the pantheon (2800-1).

---

women.
[350] 'I also wanted to put a statue of the murderer among his victims, but I could not find a likeness of him'.

But despite the prohibition don Juan does in fact enter, an indication that later he will enter Heaven similarly, despite everyone's forecasts to the contrary and attempts to bar him from Heaven (specifically those of don Gonzalo). This implies, again, the elevation of the male individual over society as a whole. Zorrilla also suggests the prospect of individual salvation in don Juan's greeting to the statues: 'Ya estoy aquí, amigos míos' ('Here I am, my friends'; 2838), and in the sculptor's surrender of the keys to him (2892). The individual wrests control of the graveyard away from the community of statues, so that even in death his victims become testimony of don Juan's life: they point away from themselves and towards him:

> *Avellaneda*: ¿Este sitio conocéis?
> *Don Juan*: ¿No es un panteón?
> *Centellas*: ¿Y sabéis
>   a quién pertenece?
> *Don Juan*: A mí;
>   Mirad a mi alrededor,
>   y no veréis más que amigos
>   de mi niñez, o testigos
>   de mi audacia y mi valor (3135-3141).[351]

Don Juan claims ownership over the pantheon, because its occupants all pay tribute to his life. His actions have brought them all together in one place. In this way he reclaims his inheritance, and regains his power as an individual against society. He does this in the pantheon, the same site where Inés will save him and reclaim him for Heaven. We might perceive a similar image in the house don Juan has bought in Seville: the original owner, a young man, ruined himself for a

---

[351] '*Avellaneda*: Do you know this place? *Don Juan*: Isn't it a pantheon? *Centellas*: And do you know who it belongs to? *Don Juan*: To me. Look around me and you will see nothing but the friends of my childhood, or witnesses to my daring and bravery'.

woman and went to the devil, dying suddenly (3252-3263). The young man clearly foreshadows don Juan himself, and don's Juan possession of the young man's house suggests his reclamation of his own inheritance. Don Juan is beginning to exert control over what people popularly perceive to be his fate, damnation.

Zorrilla has not dispensed with the notion of punishment, but he simultaneously stresses don Juan's need for repentance and salvation. Don Juan recognizes that he must reap what he has sown, and that his life merits damnation. Zorrilla highlights this point when he has don Juan repeat the same verses to describe his career (3729-3735) in the pantheon as he does in the inn (502-508). By repeating the description of his career verbatim, don Juan acknowledges that the notoriety in which he has gloried, earns him the wrath of God. But don Juan alone of the characters in *Don Juan Tenorio* receives the offer of redemption (don Gonzalo and don Luis do not have time to repent when they die). This reinforces the developing emphasis on the individual over society: one character, the hero, gains salvation while the rest remain confined to the graveyard.

The fact that don Juan's statue does not appear in the pantheon thus acquires a new significance. Don Juan does not belong in the pantheon because he belongs in Heaven alongside Inés. In a sense, salvation means to be free of the imprisonment of stone. Don Juan's statue does not exist, and Inés's statue dissolves once don Juan arrives at the cemetery - her dependence on his arrival in order to be free implying that her power over and eventual freedom from death (which I discuss below) is still subject to the male individual. She describes her existence in the pantheon of statues as purgatory in a mortuary of marble (2995-6). Thus stone statues do not so much herald divine punishment as encompass it. In this context George P. Mansour has picked up a telling detail from the final scene of *Don Juan Tenorio*, which recalls the hand motif of *El burlador*. I observed earlier that the statue offering a hand indicates a union with death and thus condemnation. Mansour comments on the significance of the repentant don Juan of Zorrilla removing his hand from the clasp of the stone statue and speaking of his conversion. This implies a break with the past and a new (eternal) life.[352]

We saw earlier how the positioning of the different statues of the pantheon reveals Inés's exalted position: she stands in the centre, while don Gonzalo and don Luis kneel either side of her. Her power over the pantheon becomes more apparent at the end of the play, when she dismisses all the statues (who have gathered with don Gonzalo around the dying don Juan) back to their places, and commands the dirges and tolling bells to stop. Inés is also the first to warn don Juan of his imminent death.

Even d eath c annot d estroy Inés's v irtue and b eauty, w hich further s uggests h er power:

¡Ah! Mal la muerte podría
deshacer con torpe mano
el semblante soberano
que un ángel envidiaría (2855-9).[353]

Inés, standing at the centre of the pantheon, thus reigns over it and has power over the death it encompasses. Virtue in this way overcomes even death, and endures beyond the grave. In statue form, Inés can truly be worshipped as an icon, and don Juan does in fact do this (2924-2974). As an object of worship, the statue of Inés now becomes a religious figure representing the possibility of don Juan's salvation rather than his damnation. Hence don Juan recognizes the possibility that Inés can

---

[352] George P. Mansour, 'Parallelism in *Don Juan Tenorio*', *Hispania* 61 (1978), 245-253; p.250.
[353] ' Ah! Even t he dull hand o f d eath c ould not d estroy h er q ueenly c ountenance t hat an angel would envy'.

redeem him even though she is dead, much as he thought she could do while she was alive: 'aún hoy mismo en ti también/ mi esperanza se asegura,/ que oigo una voz que murmura/ en derredor de don Juan/ palabras con que su afán/ *se calma en tu sepultura*' (2958-2963).[354] *Don Juan Tenorio* demonstrates the changing attitude towards punishment, and the new, active participation of women in the punitive process. Here the woman's function appears positive (though, as I indicated in my earlier discussion of Zorrilla, the elevated attitude towards women and salvation hides a certain malignancy): don Juan receives judgement, but Inés obtains his repentance and salvation. Inés's power vanquishes even her father's traditional power to consign don Juan to Hell. A man, don Gonzalo, pronounces judgement over don Juan, but a woman offers him eternal salvation. Women therefore begin to acquire more power to decide, or to act decisively, in order to settle questions of punishment - but only to the benefit of the man. The woman's power over death, symbolized by the pantheon, serves to save not herself but the male individual. Thus the individual don Juan - the owner of the pantheon - merits salvation, while others such as Mejía repent too late. The two thematic strands develop in tandem: don Juan alone of the characters (in contrast specifically to his rival Mejía) embarks on a search for salvation, which only Inés can grant him.

Twentieth-century notions of punishment

Naturally enough, given the general shift away from ideas grounded in Christianity and religion in general, more modern don Juan works moved away from the older idea of damnation, rejecting Christian ideas of eternal judgement. The statue does appear in the plays of both Shaw and Frisch, but these authors dispense with any element of the supernatural, to make the statue an element of comedy and parody. Since both authors aim to challenge conventional thinking

---

[354] 'Even now my hope rests on you, and I hear a voice that whispers around don Juan words that from within your tomb calm his desire'

through a critical scrutiny (and in Frisch's case, dismantling) of the don Juan genre, the statue inevitably receives much ironic and comic attention. Nonetheless, these authors do not dispense with the need for punishment *per se*. The abandonment of God as a significant social (and literary) force has not eliminated the need for some sort of control that will eventually restrain the protagonist. Neither Shaw nor Frisch allow don Juan to continue on his chosen path (of social reformation or geometry), but curtail his career. The notable change is that they do this by means of the female characters. Shaw refers directly to the fact that women increasingly replace the statue as the instrument of vengeance:

> Even the more abstract parts of the Don Juan play are dilapidated past use: for instance, Don Juan's supernatural antagonist hurled those who refuse to repent into lakes of burning brimstone, there to be tormented by devils with horns and tails. Of that antagonist, and of that conception of repentance, how much is left that could be used in a play by me dedicated to you [Arthur Bingham Walkley, to whom Shaw addressed his preface]? On the other hand, those forces of middle class public opinion which hardly existed for a Spanish nobleman in the days of the first Don Juan, are now triumphant everywhere. Civilized society is one huge bourgeoisie...The women...are become equally dangerous: the sex is aggressive, powerful: when women are wronged they do not group themselves pathetically to sing 'Protegga il giusto cielo': they grasp formidable legal and social weapons, and retaliate (Shaw, p.xiii).

Shaw's hostility towards the women, which comes across very clearly in this passage, leads him to overlook the fact that men, rather than women, have constructed the laws which uphold bourgeois society. Women in Shaw's day (if not now) were not in a good position to formulate law and convention. Thus if women use bourgeois laws to defend themselves, they are making use of a tool that men have created. Nevertheless, Shaw makes his point clearly here: the old-fashioned form of damnation has become outmoded, because women themselves now assume that role. Tools of judgement and restraint that men created, are now taken up by women, who turn masculine notions of punishment to their own ends. Hence Shaw also demonstrates his fear of women, who have encroached even on to the masculine territory of judging and awarding punishment: he refers to them as 'aggressive, powerful', and within the body of the play will go on to equate them with 'the forces of middle class opinion' that now triumph everywhere. We may remember that in *El burlador* the statue represents the women calling for justice: now Shaw reverses the roles. Women are the avengers who pursue don Juan and take him to a new sort of Hell. By conflating women with notions of punishment and damnation Shaw underscores, as does Frisch, the negative sense of women as a threat to the male individual.

Shaw particularly stresses the link between women and punishment in the Hell scene. Women feel at home in Hell because they are themselves, for men, a sort of Hell. The opening dialogue between Ana and don Juan reveals this quickly and clearly. Ana, newly arrived in Hell as an old woman, is horrified to discover that she herself is damned; but when she confesses to don Juan that she feels no pain, he replies that she obviously belongs with the damned: '...hell, Señora, is a place for the wicked. The wicked are quite comfortable in it: it was made for them. You tell me you feel no pain. I conclude you are one of those for whom Hell exists' (Shaw, p.86). This speech immediately tells us that Ana herself is 'wicked', and that her rightful place is in Hell. The wickedness of women lies in their espousal of bourgeois values, as Shaw mentioned in his preface, quoted above ('Civilized society is one huge bourgeoisie'):

> Hell is the home of honor, duty, justice, and the rest of the seven
> deadly virtues. All the wickedness on earth is done in their name:
> where else but in hell should they have their reward? (p.87).

Women's propriety and adherence to convention, so much in evidence in the main action of *Man and Superman*, is the embodiment of Hell: as Stockholder perceives it, Hell is a drawing-room on a grand scale.[355] If all the evil in the world is done in the name of the virtues which women like Ana (or her counterpart Ann) so much prize, it therefore follows that women espouse evil. These speeches express very strongly the sense of woman as Hell, and we cannot in consequence fail to interpret Tanner's eventual capitulation and marriage as a form of damnation. But if we had any doubt, don Juan says it plainly: 'wherever ladies are is Hell' (p.87). And even in Hell the woman plays out her role of feigning to be the object of pursuit while herself pursuing the hapless male:

> *Ana*:...Don Juan Tenorio! Monster! You who slew my father! even here
> you pursue me.
> *Don Juan*: I protest I do not pursue you. Allow me to withdraw [*going*].
> *Ana* [*seizing his arm*]: You shall not leave me alone in this dreadful place
> (p. 89).

Ana's grasp of don Juan's arm obviously suggests her capture of him, and her contradictory speeches, wishing to be both left alone and protected by don Juan, imply the veneer of bourgeois values with which she barely conceals her true intentions. Her insistence that don Juan keep her company in Hell further underlines the sense of women as themselves bringing Hell. This contrasts with the attitude of the Devil, a male character (he resembles Mendoza), who positively encourages don Juan to go to Heaven.

---

[355] Stockholder, p.49.

The sense of women as Hell, as a form of punishment, recurs in the main action of the play. Most men accept this without apparent concern. Malone senior encourages Violet to grind Hector down with domesticity: 'Dont be discurridged: domestic pressure may be slow; but it's sure. Youll wear him down. Promise me you will' (p. 148). But while most of the male characters seem unaware of the penalty of marriage, Tanner, the individual, realizes all too well what is in store for him as a husband. At the play's conclusion, he summarizes the living hell of marriage - women's ultimate aim:

> I solemnly say that I am not a happy man. Ann looks happy; but she is only triumphant, successful, victorious. That is not happiness, but the price for which the strong sell their happiness. What we have both done this afternoon is to renounce happiness, renounce freedom, renounce tranquility, above all, renounce the romantic possibilities of an unknown future, for the cares of a household and a family (pp. 165-6).

In this manner Tanner receives the punishment for daring to try to live as a free man and strive for higher things, by being condemned to marriage. Don Juan himself does not feel comfortable in Hell, thus separating himself from the women (who do feel comfortable there) and placing himself in opposition to them. He exercises his option of leaving the Hell of sentiment and conventional virtue for a Heaven of striving and achievement. He can do this, however, only because he is dead. Tanner lives, and must undergo the living Hell of marriage. This idea foreshadows one which Frisch makes more explicit: the choice between death or capitulation. For Shaw, only death releases don Juan from the damnation of matrimony, to ascend to Heaven and seek higher things.

Shaw's statue, meanwhile, rather than avenge the wrongs don Juan has committed against him, embraces a philosophy of Hell reminiscent of earlier don Juans. The statue and don Juan in fact swap places in Heaven and Hell, thus turning the traditional don Juan story on its head. The statue is delighted to accept the pleasures of Hell, and leave the worthiness of Heaven to the once licentious don Juan. In many ways the two characters exchange their roles, to the extent that don Juan even warns the statue in Mozartian tones that 'your laughter will finish in hideous boredom before morning' (p.101). The statue replies with laughter, echoing other don Juans of previous works. He also joins the devil in a duet from *Don Giovanni*, singing lines usually sung by don Juan himself: 'Vivan le femmine!/Viva il buon vino! Sostegno e gloria/D'umanità' ('Long live women! Long live good wine! The sustenance and glory of humanity'; p. 95). In short, the statue celebrates the principles of Hell, abandoning a Heaven of work and stark reality (as don Juan perceives it: p. 100). But despite the reversal of roles between don Juan and the statue, the absolutes of Heaven and Hell are still under debate: the opposites of freedom and constraint recur, even though their exponents have changed places. Now Hell has become the place where women are, while Heaven becomes the place where men can pursue greater goals unhindered by domestic demands. Moreover, this distinction between Heaven and Hell is only perceived by the individual, the protagonist don Juan/John Tanner, while the rest of male society remains ignorant of the danger. For his awareness Tanner receives the punishment of marriage while other characters such as Octavius manage to escape, or, like Hector Malone, remain ignorant of their true position. In this manner Shaw links the punishment of marriage specifically to the attempt of one man to pursue his quest for great philosophical and socio-political truths.

In *Don Juan oder die Liebe zur Geometrie* don Juan stages his own descent to Hell, and the part of the statue is played by the local madame. Yet the witnesses to the event believe the fake completely, and this despite don Juan's refrain of 'nichts al Theater' throughout the scene and the attempts of Lopez to alert the women to the truth. And subsequently all Spain believes that don Juan has gone to Hell, despite the protests of Celestina in the subsequent intermezzo that she played the part of the statue and bitterly regrets it. Frisch thus accentuates the falsity of don Juan's staged damnation - despite the threats of vengeance from don Gonzalo, don Juan lives on untouched. Frisch simultaneously reveals, however, that don Juan has after all gone to a sort of Hell along the lines that Shaw envisages, a caged domesticity in thrall to Miranda - which his geometry can do nothing to alleviate: 'ich bin ja ihr Gefangener...ich kann ja nicht aus diesem Schloß heraus' (Frisch, p.163).[356] That the Bishop of Cordoba sees the castle as a sort of paradise only heightens the irony of don Juan's hellish existence. Miranda shows her power over him by making him wait for meals, and when she herself leaves the castle Juan misses her (p.163-4), demonstrating the hold she has over him. Her final punishment of don Juan comes when she announces her expectation of a child, which, as don Juan says earlier (p.165), gives the final twist of the noose around his neck.

Celestina implicitly equates the notion of Hell with the prospect of life with Miranda, the Duchess of Ronda:

> Tausend ist das mindeste, was ich dafür [acting as the statue] haben muß. Nämlich wenn ich Sie an die Herzogin von Ronda verkaufe, dann bekomm ich auch meine tausend Pesos und blank auf den Tisch (p.143).[357]

Celestina sells both her services as a statue and don Juan's 'services' to Miranda, for the same price, a thousand pesos. By selling at the same price, she equates the two things, the descent to Hell (in which she will act the part of the statue) and life with Miranda in Ronda. Of the two options, don Juan himself prefers the option of faking his own damnation: he refuses to listen to Celestina's offer of the

---

[356] 'I'm her prisoner now...I can't go out of this castle any more'.

[357] 'I won't do it for less than a thousand. After all, if I sell you to the Duchess of Ronda, then I'll

castle of Ronda as a preferable haven from his difficulties. Better damnation than marriage, he believes, and reiterates his refusal to marry, both to Celestina (p.143) and to Miranda herself: 'eher fahre ich in die Hölle als in die Ehe' - 'I would rather go to Hell than get married' (p.144). This, indeed, is the reason for staging his descent to Hell, to escape the constant demands of women. A significant detail is that he intends to leave the scene of his damnation as a monk, thus to be free of female society (p.150).

Don Juan states explicitly the power of women to make him afraid: he has more fear of them than any threat of death or Christian damnation:

> Kein Bann der Kirche...und keine Klinge der Welt haben mich je
> zum Zittern gebracht; aber sie, eine Frau, die mich liebt, sie bringt
> mich jeden Tag dazu (p.164).[358]

Don Juan suggests, in effect, that a woman is the most fearful thing he can imagine, and this in turn indicates that women have indeed replaced the statue as symbols of damnation. The motif of damnation reappears in the closing scene as don Juan and Miranda eat supper together. We recall the traditional ending when the statue drags don Juan to Hell from the supper table. Miranda's presence at the table, replacing the statue, suggests that women have taken over the role of inflicting eternal punishment. Frisch stresses the change from punishment by statue to punishment by woman in his 'Nachträgliches', where he argues that for his fate don Juan can only ever choose between death or surrender, that is, between the statue and the woman: 'Als Parasit in der Schöpfung (Don Juan ist immer kinderlos) bleibt ihm früher oder später keine andere Wahl: Tod oder Kapitulation' (p.171).[359] We may remember Celestina's equation, above, of selling

---

get my thousand pesos, and cash down'.
[358] 'No excommunication...and no sword in the world has made me tremble; but she, a woman who loves me, makes me tremble every day'.
[359] 'As a parasite in creation (don Juan is always childless), sooner or later he is left with no other

don Juan a descent to Hell and selling him to Miranda. The reference here to don Juan as a parasite reminds us of his generic individuality opposed to society, as does the reference to childlessness - don Juan's line will not carry on after him, and thus he has no social continuity. The Bishop reinforces the link between don Juan's individuality and his damnation by means of a woman. In discussing with don Juan and Miranda the 'new' play by Tirso de Molina, the Bishop argues that as a whole society cannot know the truth about don Juan, and so audiences see the traditional descent to Hell that Tirso depicted. Audiences must not realize that 'Die Ehe.. das ist die wahre Hölle!' 'marriage...that is the real Hell!' (p.166):[360] only don Juan may know this. Thus the perception of Hell, embodied in a woman, occurs at an individual and not a social level, much as it does in *Man and Superman*.

As for the statue, it reappears in comic guise, but also underlines the idea of woman as a form of punishment. Celestina plays the part of Frisch's statue: thus a woman - and a procuress at that, a provider of other women - acts out the part of vengeance, taking over the bestowal of punishment from don Gonzalo, who himself has not returned in statue form to drag don Juan off to Hell, despite the message engraved on the statue, 'der Himmel zerschmettere den Frevler', 'may Heaven crush the evil man' (p.147). Although don Juan treats his descent to Hell strictly as a fake, 'nichts als Theater', he indeed goes to a sort of Hell since, in order to be free of his own reputation he must remain hidden at the castle of Ronda, in thrall to Miranda. Celestina aids his descent to both the faked and the true Hell.

***

---

choice: death or capitulation'.
[360] In 1953, when *Don Juan oder die Liebe zur Geometrie* was first published and performed, Frisch separated from his first wife.

Tracing the development of don Juan's damnation through our six plays should serve to demonstrate again the way in which authors increasingly regard the female characters in a hostile light, and understand this hostility in relation to an increasingly troubled sense of male individuality. Tirso, Molière and Mozart privilege the needs of society over the rights of the individual, so that the statue condemns the individual for his challenge to society, and specifically for his challenge to the women's ability to survive in and subvert the patriarchy in which they live. We may not care for the terms of Christian judgement with which these authors cast don Juan into Hell, but Jones' observation that the statue represents the claims of women for justice seems valid.[361] Whatever don Juan's crimes, they arise from his pursuit of women in order to derive his identity from them. The earlier plays, then, appear to favour the claims of women to survive in society rather than individual freedom.

Romanticism, however, saw increasing privilege given to the rights of the individual, specifically the *male* individual. Inés, the idealized female figure, clearly possesses power over death, a sign of the growing influence the female characters have, which the protagonists will perceive more and more as a threat to their individual masculinity. In *Don Juan Tenorio* female power seems inherently good and benign (although we can perceive a latent hostility to women elsewhere, as I argued earlier). Even here, however, Inés's control over death remains subordinate to the needs of don Juan, enabling him to come into his earthly and divine inheritance, allowing the individual to be redeemed. Zorrilla privileges the redemptive need of the individual over the demands of society, the community of statues, so that all the statues - and even Inés - will point to the glorious quest for salvation of don Juan.

---

[361] Jones, p.42.

In *Man and Superman* and *Don Juan oder die Liebe zur Geometrie*, the function of women changes again. Already more closely involved in the punitive process by the time of Zorrilla, women become themselves the form of punishment. The protagonist sees himself more and more as under threat, as the pursued, and actively flees the company of women, preferring abstract studies of philosophy and geometry. The development of women as punishment occurs alongside the protagonist's growing sense of doubt over his own individual nature. As we saw in chapter 2, the don Juans of Shaw and Frisch attempt to separate their own identities from the female sphere, so that Tanner/don Juan seeks to pursue revolutionary goals in a 'heavenly' sphere that excludes women; and Frisch's don Juan seeks actively to *lose* his identity and thus escape the sexual demands of women and retreat into abstract study. The confusion over identity of Frisch's protagonist in particular should indicate to us the growing insecurity of the male individual (a growth not reflected in the patriarchal society around him, which has always been weak). The attempts of these twentieth-century don Juans to assert their male individuality fail, and the punishment for failure is a descent into the female sphere of domesticity.

Some critics have perceived the statue as a Freudian father figure, and indeed the conflict between don Juan and the statue over women very neatly coincides with the Freudian concept of the primal father. Using such a model to frame our discussion of don Juan, however, neglects the various functions of the female characters, treating them as passive, unable to survive, subvert or threaten. Such a treatment of the female characters is not inevitable. Otto Rank sees the woman, rather than the man, as the avenger, in this way bestowing some measure of positive action to women in the matter of damnation. What I have presented here should serve to demonstrate that women do feature in the question of punishment, but it should also be obvious that their role becomes more malign as we approach the present day and as the protagonists suffer more and more from the angst of the individual male.

Chapter 8: Conclusion and coda: a reappraisal of Tirso de Molina

In bringing this discussion of the don Juan genre to an end, I should first point out that whatever my conclusions are, I do not affirm that they apply to every single don Juan work. While I would claim that my proposal of increased hostility towards women, in conjunction with the elevation and subsequent decadence of masculine individualism, is valid, I have drawn my arguments from six works; yet there are hundreds of don Juan plays, operas, poems, novels, and so on, not all of which would necessarily fit in with my proposed development of malevolence towards women. Nevertheless, I have selected six major works from the genre, as well as briefly considered the impact of two important studies of don Juan (by Kierkegaard and Hoffmann), and I believe that their combined resonance would have its echoes elsewhere in the genre. In this concluding chapter, I will suggest what the interplay of the different don Juans with their female 'victims' might tell us about male/female relationships in general: but I would qualify my comments by saying that they must inevitably be tentative. To draw out a complex picture of male/female relations from a body of literature would be a vast undertaking, and I am hardly contemplating that here. I do, however, feel that this review of donjuanian women suggests a parallel shift in men's perception of their own individual natures and in their attitudes to women. I intend now to look back over our progress towards an understanding of the male/female dialectic in the don Juan canon, and will close with a coda, arguing for a fresh appraisal of Tirso de Molina in the light of what we have learned.

I began my argument by suggesting that don Juan cannot understand his identity except in relation to women. In the earlier plays his character centres around his life as a seducer, a career for which a succession of women are essential. A seducer cannot seduce without victims. Don Juan does not necessarily require success in his endeavours: while dom Juan and don Giovanni fail for the most part in their campaigns to seduce Charlotte, Mathurine and Zerlina, they nevertheless possess the reputation of incorrigible womanizers. Molière's protagonist spends more time in debate with Sganarelle than in pursuit of women, but his immoral philosophies nevertheless are closely related to his seductive career. The entire action of the play, and the philosophical debates that arise from it, stem from dom Juan's original seduction of, and subsequent flight from, done Elvire. These early don Juans correspond on the whole to the popular archetype of don Juan the womanizer that has developed over time. Later authors steered their don Juans away from this straightforward path of seduction, but they did not - could not - dispense with the need for women. With the Romantic era, don Juan became not only a protagonist but a hero, pursuing a quest for his own salvation. The concern for personal redemption reflects don Juan's desire to establish his own identity, but again he requires a woman to do this. The woman will ensure his forgiveness and salvation: her purity will counterbalance don Juan's own sinful life. Zorrilla's play exemplifies this tendency. Twentieth-century don Juans attempted to establish themselves in opposition to the women, who nonetheless remained essential to show don Juan's personality in greater relief. Frisch's don Juan even goes as far as to repudiate the traditional reputation as a seducer which the women try to foist upon him. They wish to give him an identity, but he opposes them by aiming to submerge his own individuality in abstract study. He asserts himself, against the women, ironically by *not* asserting himself, by wishing instead to lose his identity. He can be truly himself by neglecting his own self in favour of geometry.

Regardless of the approach don Juan takes to form his own identity in these six plays, he intends that the consequence for women remains a loss of identity, a retreat into an undifferentiated female mass. Thus noblewomen and peasants alike become the victims of his indiscriminate pursuit, for his refusal to discriminate implies that he cannot or will not distinguish between them. The pure woman of the Romantic era, who nevertheless submits to the control of don Juan, herself must lose her own identity, surrender it in order to redeem the identity of the male. Inés is not a woman, with a life of her own, but Woman, an idealized concept of passive femininity which serves to define the male. Later don Juans also perceive women as all the same, but by now they believe these women to threaten their own individual identity. Their opposition to women assumes that women are alike and act in the same way. Shaw's women threaten men with domesticity, while Frisch's threaten them with sexuality. No woman differs from the rest. Miranda argues that she is different from other women, in making no claims upon don Juan but loving him for himself; but in the end she differs from the other women only in that she succeeds in capturing don Juan and imprisoning him in a beautiful Hell of domestic life. This point reinforces the idea that the individual must be male, since the women seem to be all alike.

However, I went on to observe that to begin with, the female characters resist don Juan's attempt to deprive them of their own individuality. In the works by Tirso, Molière and Mozart, the women manage on the whole to maintain their position in society and their prospects, despite any susceptibility to don Juan's seductive techniques. These women do not challenge the society around them in any way, but nevertheless survive in it and subvert it. Most of the women end the play secure in the knowledge that they can, if they wish, marry the prospective partners to whom they were linked before don Juan emerged on the scene. They subvert male control and male desires - even those of don Juan - and thus achieve their objectives of marriage. The exceptions, the hysterical women, appear to remain alone and cast out, but their very hysteria has enabled them to stay free of male power, including that of don Juan. While we would go too far to argue that perhaps Tirso, and certainly Molière and Mozart, assumed some sort of proto-feminism, we can nevertheless appreciate their reasonably benign treatment of their female characters. They do not envisage a female sphere greater than that of love and marriage, in keeping with the eras within which they lived, but they do grant the women a good measure of effective action within that sphere. Ultimately, don Juan's efforts do not change the destinies of the majority of these women, who continue to 'subvert and survive'.

The treatment of women in the Romantic works appears less benign; and at first sight more confused. The voyeurism of Kierkegaard and Hoffmann initially seems to contradict the idealization of Zorrilla's characterization of Inés. While Kierkegaard and Hoffmann understand women - donna Elvira and donna Anna respectively - as sexual objects for the enjoyment of don Juan (and vicariously, Kierkegaard and Hoffmann themselves), Zorrilla gives to Inés the virtually divine role of redemption and power over the grave (or, more literally, power over a graveyard). Yet the contradiction is more apparent than real. Fundamentally, all three authors require that the women become subject to don Juan: these women are there primarily to serve his overall purpose, whether this be sexual or spiritual. In any case, as I observed in my discussion of Zorrilla, don Juan's idealized approach towards Inés masks a desire to control Inés sexually; and her response of awakening sexual desire echoes those sexual desires Kierkegaard and Hoffmann believe Elvira and Anna to possess. Furthermore, Zorrilla's insistence that Inés die and risk her own soul in order to save that of don Juan, indicates a notion of women's expendability. Women are subject to men to the extent that they must even sacrifice themselves for a male individual of rather dubious worth. When we contrast these Romantic treatments of women with those of Tirso, Molière and Mozart, we can immediately comprehend a marked move towards malignancy in the Romantic works. The earlier female characters show no such subjection to men, but determine their own futures for themselves. They accommodate themselves to a male-dominated society, but they do not surrender to it. Inés shows no such power of self-determination, particularly since don Juan will decide her fate as well as his own through his decision whether or not to repent.

The women in the twentieth-century plays show the strength of the earlier female characters, but their strength has become negative. Rather than surviving and coming to terms with the society in which they live, these women wish actively to control it. Shaw and Frisch discard the idealization of the Romantic woman, and stress women as dangerous and terrifying. Shaw reduces women to a virtually bestial level with his animal imagery. Ann Whitefield devours John Tanner's individual identity, bringing him down to the level of an inseminating machine. For her, his pretensions to philosophy and social reform do not matter, since all that concerns her is his capacity to father children. Thus the male individual capitulates before the woman, and will only find respite after death, in the Heaven envisaged by don Juan in Shaw's Hell scene. As Frisch puts it in *Don Juan oder die Liebe zur Geometrie*, 'Tod oder Kapitulation' (Frisch, p. 171). Frisch himself does not see women as quite so manipulative and menacing as Shaw does but, like Shaw, his protagonist understands women as creatures from which to flee. Frisch reverts to the overtones of female sexuality that the Romantics incorporated into their own studies of don Juan; but Frisch's don Juan fears rather than desires female sexuality. He manifests his hostility towards women through his fear of them. As with Shaw, a woman eventually thwarts don Juan's desire to follow more rarefied pursuits. As Tanner wishes to promote his social philosophy, so Frisch's don Juan longs to study geometry in peace - geometry itself removing him from the level of human relationships to a more abstract plane where women cannot interfere. But like Tanner, he ends his play with the imprisonment of domesticity and impending fatherhood.

The changes that occur in the attitudes towards women of the protagonists, do not affect patriarchal society as a whole, which remains relatively unchanged and ineffectual. The male characters of the later plays succumb to female manipulation without a struggle. Male characters - apart from the protagonist - spectate. Fathers and kings cannot control their sons or subjects, the servant has lost his voice except to bear witness to his master's actions, the timid lover cannot compete with don Juan's essential masculinity (to the extent that Shaw renders his Octavius rather effeminate). The particular point I wanted to make here was that men in general remain uniformly inadequate in all six plays, so that the growing sense of hostility towards women seems not to correspond directly with a growing sense of masculine powerlessness in general. In the don Juan genre, the men have *always* been powerless. I would suggest that this reinforces the link between the women and the male *individual*, don Juan: the increasing hostility towards women seems to relate closely to the protagonist's increasing awareness of the precarious nature of his individuality. The protagonist, the central male individual, rather than patriarchy as a whole, perceives the female threat.

Finally, I argued that the endings of all six plays serve to underline the more and more perilous dialectic between women and the male individual. We should not dismiss the sense of punishment that recurs in each play merely from an idea of its obsolescence, since the notion of an individual acting in opposition to society implies that society will in consequence take measures to stop him. The earlier three plays use the device of the statue to represent the female characters, and to drag don Juan to Hell in retribution for a life that aimed to harm women. Thus the women vicariously take their revenge. We find a change of attitude with *Don Juan Tenorio*, where Zorrilla appears to give Inés power over death and Hell itself, but only in order that don Juan can reassert his own individuality, reclaiming both his soul and his inheritance. Ultimately her divine powers serve to benefit him rather than her. Shaw and Frisch reduce the statue to a comic role, and replace it with the women themselves as instruments of punishment. Women damn don Juan through domesticity. Again, we can observe the increasingly overt hostility in the more recent treatments of don Juan's punishment. The concept of punishment for the individual, and the growing malevolence towards women converge, until they become one and the same thing.

In this manner the six authors I have discussed here together reveal through these different components of the don Juan genre - the female and male characters, and the theme of punishment - attitudes of greater and greater hostility towards women concurrent with the elevation and subsequent problematizing of the male individual. That the modern era, which our six plays encompass, has seen the rise of the individual to a privileged social position, has become a commonplace thought. In general the rise of the individual - always understood as male until comparatively recently - has come about through a variety of social factors, including economic and political. Nonetheless, the privileging of the male individual must in consequence affect his relations with others and specifically with women. The six plays demonstrate what this might mean in practice. Tirso de Molina lived in what was arguably a pre-modern era during the Counter-Reformation in Spain. His plays reflect a greater emphasis, typical of the *comedia*, on the community and general social harmony. *El burlador de Sevilla* incorporates this general attitude in order to indicate the need for individuals to accommodate themselves to, and perhaps subvert, the dominant society while simultaneously realizing their aims. Tirso's women do this admirably. When the *male* individual attempts to defy rather than subvert the prevailing social order, he is damned. But by the time we arrive at the Romantic era of Zorrilla, things have changed. The individual reaches his most elevated point, to the extent that he is redeemed while the rest of society remains trapped for eternity in the pantheon. Even the salvation of the pure, ideal woman is subject to his own salvation. We have already seen the consequences of this notion for women. By the end of the nineteenth century and into the twentieth two social processes had got under way: women's concerted demand for equality and an increased sense of troubled masculinity. One process may not necessarily have caused the other, but the intricate connection between the two should be obvious.

Although I have given greater emphasis to the elaboration of female malignancy, therefore, we should not divorce this from the troubled notion of male individuality experienced with greater force by the later don Juans. Since I argue that hostility to women and male individual angst grow together, I must naturally conclude that we cannot separate the two in order to study and understand them. But furthermore, I believe that the unchanging depiction of patriarchy in the six plays underlines our need to get away from a simple dualistic interpretation of male/female relationships in the don Juan genre, since while there has been a marked shift in relations between the women and the protagonist, there has been no similar change in the portrait of masculinity as a whole. The other male characters continue to spectate passively - suggesting a patriarchy more historically insecure than has been popularly imagined - but their presence also implies a more complex set of relationships between men and women than dualism allows. For the male individual of these plays changes, but male society as a whole does not. The nature of donjuanian patriarchy therefore indicates that different parts of the male-female equation shift at different times, and are not essential givens. This is one reason why I prefer an approach of literary history to study the don Juan phenomenon. The psychoanalytic approach that has become customary in donjuanian studies, is valuable - I draw on Otto Rank, for instance - but psychoanalysis carries the possible danger of neglecting history and changes to society as a whole over long periods of time. It is not the best approach for dealing with the incessant negotiations over time undertaken by men and women in the course of their coexistence.

The historical approach undertaken here readily reveals the shifting nature of gender relations, demonstrating a gradual alteration from a dialectic of accommodation to a more confrontational stance between men and women. This approach also reflects the significance of gender relations in the determination of individual identity: we can perceive that male individuality, far from being an unproblematic given, must be worked out in the context of sexual and social relations, in this case relations with women. Thus not only female but also male identity must be negotiated. We can remind ourselves here of the arguments of Weeks, who takes issue with the idea that the sexual natures of men and women remain fixed and beyond social change:

> ...we cannot afford to question...oppressive social regulation, political prejudice and the like - and ignore what lies at the heart of all these things, the shaping and reshaping, in a complex and prolonged history, of the sexual categories we inhabit and the identities we bear.[362]

And he also comments: 'Sexual activities...are always contextual and relational. They do not have a fixed or absolute meaning beyond time and place...'.[363] Weeks is primarily discussing homosexuality, his particular historical concern. Yet his principle holds good not only for specific spheres of sexual activity, but for all activities that entail gender differentiation - for I do not think, and I believe Weeks would not argue either, that sexuality remains divorced from other spheres that determine how we define 'man' and 'woman'. Rather, these spheres overlap and affect each other. Literature reflects or sometimes prefigures these shifts in sexual and gender relations. With the don Juan figure, a locus for the dialectic of male/female relations, we have seen clearly enough such shifts, as the male individual reconceives his own position in society and adjusts his relations with women in the light of his new understanding. These shifts demonstrate, incidentally, the precariousness of undertaking to define don Juan as a myth, as I

---

[362] Weeks, *Against Nature*, 86-87.
[363] Weeks, *Against Nature*, 4-5.

argued in chapter 1: myth implies some sort of unchanging essence and, as Weeks points out, this cannot be done in terms of the history of sexual, and in consequence gender, relations.

Another commentator, Giddens, observes the changes in love relationships that have resulted in a masculine alienation from love:

> Passionate love was originally one among other passions, the interpretation of which tended to be influenced by religion. Most emotional dispositions can be passions, but in modern society passion is narrowed down to the sexual realm and once there becomes more muted in its expression.[364]

The muted passion that Giddens points out can be found in *Man and Superman* and *Don Juan oder die Liebe zur Geometrie*. The retreat of the twentieth-century don Juans into political philosophy and geometry indicates the alienation from love relations that Giddens traces. With the rise of the individual, the interlocking social activities of passion - sexual and marital relationships - and religious belief became separated. Interestingly, from our point of view, Giddens here makes a direct connection between the passion of earlier times and religion. Sexual passion cannot be seen in the earlier plays apart from the entire social context which includes concepts of religion and, in consequence, punishment and damnation. For our purposes, this implies in turn that the link between a career of seduction and of eternal damnation may perhaps be more natural than some critics would like to think. Giddens's arguments here, however, also underscore the point that male as well as female identity must be negotiated: men must, as does Zorrilla's don Juan, work out their own 'salvation'. Their inability to do so gives rise to the increasing male angst we have traced in the six plays here. Giddens also points to the consequences of male alienation in love relationships - a loss of commitment and a growth in violence towards women. Regrettably, we can find traces of this shift in the later plays in a desire for control and domination (Zorrilla), and then outright hostility and an attempt to abdicate from gender relations altogether (Shaw and Frisch).

Weeks and Giddens thus argue against an essentialist approach to concepts of gender, and this agrees with our discoveries here. Those who would see don Juan as myth assert his unchanging nature in doing so; but the six plays studied here suggest that on the contrary don Juan and his women change in time, and reaffirm the contentions of Weeks and Giddens that sexual identity, and gender identity, are not essentialist notions but changing entities with implications for both men and women.

So far, I have touched briefly on how our study of the historical phenomenon of don Juan may provide a few clues to changes in gender relations. But new understandings of historical shifts in gender relations may in turn illuminate our appreciation of literature, impelling us to reinterpret them in the light of new perspectives. Of course, this process is a continual one in reading, viewing and critique of literature. The final point I would like to make is the need to embark on a reappraisal of the originator of don Juan in the context of historical changes in male/female relations. The Hispanic school has already begun to re-evaluate Tirso and other Golden-Age dramatists in terms of gender relations. There is now a need to reassess his position within the don Juan canon in the context of these changes.

---

[364] Giddens, *Transformation of Intimacy*, p.201.

Coda: Tirso de Molina and the characterization of women

If we can trace an increased sense of malevolence towards women through the history of these plays, we can also review this history in reverse, and look back to Tirso's positive portrayal of women. In the opening chapter I tentatively suggested a model of family relationships as a mechanism for studying the don Juan phenomenon, a way of overcoming certain difficulties that arise in studying the figure. One of the advantages of this model is that we can look backwards as well as forwards, entering don Juan's literary history at any point we feel appropriate. We have here looked at don Juan principally in a 'forward'-looking manner, moving more or less chronologically from the seventeenth to the twentieth century. When we reverse the process, we should see that the portrayal of women becomes less obviously malignant the further back we go, until we arrive at Tirso's positive characterization of four very different women. I would not, of course, say that life was necessarily better for women generally in the seventeenth century than it has been for women in the twentieth. Nor would I go so far as to say that Tirso was an early feminist, but it seems very clear that he perceived women in a benign and vibrant light, which is not what we would popularly assume of a seventeenth-century monk.

We may remember the comments of McKendrick which I mentioned in chapter 3; McKendrick highlights the subtle and tolerant approach Tirso takes towards his female characters. Her view is supported by Smith, who refers to Tirso's 'female characters, more prominent and perhaps more sympathetically portrayed than in other [Golden-Age] dramatists'.[365] Our consideration of *El burlador* bears this out. Isabela, Tisbea, Aminta and even Ana are three-dimensional characters, who take positive steps to defend their own futures and maintain control over events. Tisbea's case reveals some ambiguity: we do not know whether she remains free

---

[365] McKendrick, *Women and Society*, p.330; Smith, p.144.

or whether she marries Anfriso. Nevertheless, in her opening soliloquy Tirso grants her a relish of her solitude and her sensual appreciation of nature. Tisbea may be punished for her independence, but there is no doubt that she enjoys her freedom from male control. Isabela and Ana both succeed in securing the men they love as prospective husbands, despite the efforts to the contrary of don Juan. Aminta remains stubbornly loyal to Batricio for as long as she can, and only surrenders to don Juan in the belief that Batricio has abandoned her. All four women have faults; Isabela schemes, Tisbea is proud, Ana deceives her father, and Aminta wishes to rise beyond her station in life. Yet Tirso mixes in all four a measure of good and bad qualities, making them more truly rounded than, to go to the opposite extreme, Inés in *Don Juan Tenorio*.

Nonetheless, outside of Hispanic studies, Tirso's contribution to the don Juan canon as a whole has been neglected or disparaged by many commentators. Kierkegaard does not deal with *El burlador* at all, while Shaw dismisses the play as a one of 'monkish morals'. Conrad (1990, 82) echoes this sentiment, describing the play as 'monkish propaganda', a sweeping judgement.[366] One of the worst criticisms of *El burlador* comes from Georges Gendarme de Bévotte, who praises *Dom Juan* specifically at the expense of Tirso's play which, he believes, caters precisely for a credulous, superstitious Spanish nation.[367] So much of this disparagement seems to centre on Tirso's status as a monk. Not only should this make us wonder what critics such as these would do were it to be conclusively proved that Tirso did *not* in fact write *El burlador*, but it should raise some measure of concern in us that they can argue that Tirso, merely because he was a monk, must be narrow-minded and overly moralistic.[368] Such poor critique

---

[366] Conrad, p.82.

[367] Georges Gendarme de Bévotte, *La Légende de don Juan: son évolution dans la littérature des origines au romantisme*, (Geneva: Slatkine Reprints, 1993).

[368] Gerald Wade counters such an idea in his discussion of Tirso's own personality: he argues that Tirso was in fact a *bon vivant*. Gerald E. Wade, 'Tirso de Molina: Priest-Playwright', *Bulletin of the Comediantes*, 38 (1986), 117-135.

neglects the artistry of this supposedly bigoted monk in creating such a lively protagonist which would attract other authors, composers and artists for centuries to come. The advantage that Hispanists have over other schools of commentary is that they are better able as a rule to see Tirso in the context of the *comedia*, and appreciate that his treatment of issues and characters in his plays was perhaps more unusually enlightened than, but certainly of a piece with, the attitudes of other Golden-Age dramatists.

Our study of the depiction of women in the don Juan genre helps to draw this point out more strongly. Tirso's approach to female characterization in *El burlador* does not in fact match the disparagement of the play as 'monkish'. Ironically, of all the authors we have considered here, Shaw and Frisch show perhaps the most monkish stance by regarding women as temptresses and pursuers, to be shunned at all costs. In the plays of Shaw and Frisch, but not in that of Tirso, men must preserve themselves for higher goals than mere sexual pleasure. Inevitably, perhaps, Frisch's don Juan dreams of escaping women and disguising himself as a monk. Given his portrayal of women, however, Tirso does not automatically fit the stereotyped image of a monk of inflexible religious attitudes, to which critics such as Conrad and Gendarme de Bévotte are resorting. Thus tracing the development of don Juan and the female characters in reverse immediately elicits the point that notions of prudery and narrow thinking occur in the place where we would not expect them and perhaps prefer not to expect them - in two twentieth-century works.

Tirso's female characters reveal to us, apart from anything else, the shifting nature of literary judgement as well as gender relations. The women of *El burlador* have not always been regarded in a favourable light. In particular they have come in for specific disparagement, from Weinstein,[369] and from Gendarme de Bévotte:

> ...on peut s'étonner que dans une fable toute remplie d'aventures d'amour, les caractères de femmes soient aussi ternes et leur action aussi insignifiante. Dans la plupart des conceptions postérieures, au contraire, la femme aura un rôle vraiment actif, et son influence s'exercera d'une façon plus ou moins efficace sur la vie du héros.[370]

Much of the critical distaste for Tirso's women seems to be a hangover from Romantic ideas of women as inspirers and noble characters. Gendarme de Bévotte looks to the female characters to fulfil the function of an Inés, to redeem the protagonist. He claims here that women's activity is in fact a form of passivity, for the women act by influencing. He reflects the viewpoint of Ortega y Gasset (that Mandrell criticizes):[371] Ortega y Gasset argues that woman's only proper function is simply to be a woman. In other words, woman's only appropriate act is to be female. Now, this hardly applies to the women of *El burlador*. Only Isabela seems to inspire anybody, and that is only Octavio, who praises her merely in terms of childish desire. For the most part, the play deals with the contrast of fine words and dubious actions, and of a feeble society in which women make shift as best they can.

Tirso does not, in fact, privilege one sex over another. The women move in a limited sphere but are for the most part successful in their aims. No man, on the other hand, succeeds in his aim. Don Juan himself may successfully seduce the victims he selects, but he does not manage to derive his identity from them by

---

[369] Weinstein, p.33.

[370] 'We might be surprised that in a tale full of amorous adventures the women are so tender and their actions so insignificant. In most of the later intepretations, on the other hand, the woman would have a truly active role, and her influence would act in a more or less effective manner on the life of the hero'. Gendarme de Bévotte, p.86.

[371] Mandrell, 241ff.

robbing them of theirs: the women keep their own individuality very much intact. In any case, don Juan does not succeed in postponing divine retribution or eluding divine judgement as he h as eluded e arthly penalties. The other male c haracters also fail in their aims: to bring don Juan to earthly justice, to marry women off to the m an who i s n ot o f t heir c hoice, t o c ontrol t heir kingdoms o r t heir so ns, t o punish the women for their supposed transgressions. Tirso thus achieves a sense of balance, though one could not really call it harmony, in the community of characters of *El burlador*. The sex that is apparently weaker and more confined nonetheless proves more powerful and effective. Women's aims are more limited, but they are more likely to achieve their aims. Tirso deliberately posits an ironical balance of power in which men and women live in a wary coexistence. Compare this with the outright opposition between men and women in Shaw and Frisch, where men perceive women as potential conquerors, and must either die or surrender. Tirso's notion of coexistence is hardly a pleasant one where it apparently allows don Juan to get away with seduction and deprivation of a woman's honour and thus character. Indeed, the world of *El burlador* is no utopia if men such as Octavio are able to cry 'La mujer más constante/ es, en efeto, mujer' ('the most constant woman is still a woman, after all';I, 357-8). Yet the women trade insults with the men ('¡Mal haya la mujer que en hombres fía!': 'Woe to the woman who trusts in men!' III, 394 and 408), and manage to survive don Juan's attempts on their honour. At the end of the play, their honour is restored to them, and don Juan's seductive career has proved to be no more than a passing hitch in their plans to obtain the men they desire (though again, Tisbea's position is exceptional).

Thus the creator of the don Juan figure hypothesizes, not the simple conflict between male desire and female social position that figures in later versions of the story, but a more intricate interrelation of the personal goals of each of the male and female characters. We have established that don Juan cannot be understood except as existing in some sort of relation to women. But in the case of *El burlador* we cannot appreciate any of the characters except in relation to the other characters and what they are trying to achieve throughout the course of the play. The women succeed, but we need to be aware of the failure of the male characters, including don Juan, in order to perceive the women's success. Therefore the women cannot be understood as separate from the men: we must place them in the context of the dialectic between men and women in *El burlador*, in order to understand what the women achieve. Of the other authors, however, only Mozart and da Ponte have possibly taken up the complex structure of gender relations that Tirso has posited, into their own don Juan work. Most authors settle instead for a simplistic male/female dichotomy that Tirso did not envisage. To re-examine Tirso's contribution to the don Juan genre, therefore, might be to recover this sense of complex gender structures that has been to a great extent lost in subsequent versions. Such a recovery of gender structures might in turn affect our understanding of the resonance of a major literary figure, and how this reflects and influences surrounding literature and culture.

Let us go back, finally, to Anderson and Zinsser's claim that modern history has proved on the whole the worse for women, as I quoted in my introduction. The question arising from this claim is: why have things historically got worse for women? The concurrent shift in perception both of the male individual and of women in general cannot in itself answer such a big question. However, it can go some way to enlarging our understanding of why things indeed got noticeably worse for women after the Renaissance and as the modern age progressed. I have argued that these shifts are apparent within the don Juan phenomenon as it is played out over literary history. Don Juan, in all his different historical incarnations, needs to be reinterpreted in the light of our new appreciation of male/female relations, including the oppression of women and their subjection to male desires and objectives. Some commentators have already embarked on such a re-evaluation: Mandrell, for instance, looks at the way in which economic theories of exchange and notions of woman as muse have subordinated women to men.[372] But as yet, the notion of change that I have discussed has not yet been taken up into don Juan studies as a whole, and in consequence the more positive appreciation of Tirso has not yet begun to influence what *donjuanistas* have to say about him. Tirso was the originator of a literary figure that has inspired artistic creativity for nearly four centuries: yet while many writers derived from don Juan a negative perception of women, Tirso himself did not. If we now grant Tirso a more positive understanding of women, this should in turn influence our own understanding of don Juan's literary development. And an awareness of Tirso's benignness to women may also help us to see the historical shifts in gender relations, and take us one, small, step further to understanding why these happened. If literature gives us clues to humanity's social, economic and political development and its underlying causes and effects, then those who look to understand gender relations within literature cannot afford to neglect don Juan, or Tirso's interpretation of him.

---

[372] Mandrell, ch.4.

Bibliography

Abert, Hermann, *Mozart's Don Giovanni*, trans. by Peter Gellhorn, (London: Eulenberg, 1976).

Adams, Elsie, 'Feminism and Female Stereotypes in Shaw', *Shaw Review* 17 (1974), 17-22.

Albrecht, Jane White, 'Formas y funciones de ironía en cinco obras de Tirso de Molina', *Neophilologus* 72 (1988), 546-555.

Anderson, Bonnie S. and Judith P. Zinsser, *A History of Their Own: Women in Europe from Prehistory to the Present*, Vol. 1., (London: Penguin, 1988)

Apostolidès, Jean-Marie, 'Molière and the Sociology of Exchange', *Critical Inquiry* 14 (1988), 477-492.

Arias, Judith H., 'Doubles in Hell: *El burlador de Sevilla y convidado de piedra*', *Hispanic Review*, 58/3 (1990), 361-377.

Baker, Felicity, 'The Radical Poetry of *Don Giovanni*', in *Cross-references: Modern French Theory and the Practice of Criticism*, ed. by D. Kelley and I. Llasera, (London: Society for French Studies 1986).

Benabu, Isaac, 'Reading the Opening of a Play: Tirso's *El burlador de Sevilla*', *Bulletin of the Comediantes* 47(1995), 191-200.

Butler, Judith, *Gender Trouble: Feminism and the Subversion of Identity*, (New York: Routledge, 1990)

Butler, Michael, 'Die Flucht in die Abstraktion: zu Max Frischs *Don Juan oder die liebe zur Geometrie*', in *Frischs 'Don Juan oder die Liebe zur Geometrie'*, ed. by Walter Schmitz, (Frankfurt: Suhrkamp, 1985)

_____, *The Plays of Max Frisch*, (London: Macmillan, 1985)

Carpenter, Charles A., 'Sex Play Shaw's Way: *Man and Superman*', *Shaw Review* 18 (1975), 70-74.

Conlon, Raymond, 'Batricio in *El Burlador de Sevilla*: the Pathology of Sexual Honor', in *Tirso's Don Juan: the Metamorphosis of a Theme*, ed. by Josep Sola-

Solé and George E. Gingras, (Washington DC: Catholic University of America Press, 1988), 86-94.

_____, 'The *Burlador* and the *Burlados*: a Sinister Connection', *Bulletin of the Comediantes* 42 (1990), 5-23.

Conrad, Peter, 'The Libertine's Progress', in *The Don Giovanni Book: Myths of Seduction and Betrayal*, ed. by Jonathan Miller, (London: Faber, 1990), 81-92.

Crompton, Louis, *Shaw the Dramatist: a Study of the Intellectual Background of the Major Plays*, (London: Allen and Unwin, 1971)

Davies, Ann, 'Inés and Brígida: Sexual Presence and Absence in Zorrilla's *Don Juan Tenorio*', *Bulletin of Hispanic Studies*, LXXVI/3 (July 1999), 327-336.

_____, 'Hysteria: female desire versus male rationality in early don Juan works' in *Selected Interdisciplinary Essays on the Representation of the Don Juan Archetype in Myth and Culture*, eds. by Andrew Ginger, John Hobbs and Huw Lewis (Lewiston: Edwin Mellen Press, 2000), 269-289.

_____, ''Don Juan and Foucauldian Sexual Discourse: Changing Attitudes to Female Sexuality', in *Morality and Justice: the Challenge of European Theatre* eds. by Edward Batley and David Bradby (Amsterdam: Rodopi, 2001), 159-170.

Dent, Edward J., *Mozart's Operas: a Critical Study*, 2nd edn, (London: Oxford University Press, 1947)

Dijkstra, Bram, *The Idols of Perversity* (New York: Oxford University Press, 1986)

Donington, Robert, 'Don Giovanni Goes to Hell', *Musical Times* 122 (July 1981), 448-451.

Dupuy, J-P., 'Quasi-objet et échange symbolique: de l'Alidor de Corneille au Dom Juan de Molière', *MLN* 104 (1989), 757-786.

Evans, P. W., 'The Roots of Desire in *El burlador de Sevilla*', *Forum for Modern Language Studies* 22/3 (1986), 232-247.

Feal, Carlos, *En nombre de Don Juan: estructura de un mito literario*, (Amsterdam: John Benjamins, 1984)

Feal Deibe, Carlos, '*El Burlador* de Tirso y la mujer', *Symposium* 29 (1975), 300-313.

Felman, Shoshana, *The Literary Speech Act: Don Juan with J. L. Austin, or Seduction in Two Languages*, trans. by Catherine Porter, (Ithaca: Cornell University Press, 1983)

Foucault, Michel, *The History of Sexuality: an Introduction*, trans. by Robert Hurley (Harmondsworth: Penguin, 1990).

Frisch, Max, *Gesammelte Werke in zeitlicher Folge*, III, 95-175, ed. by Hans Mayer, (Frankfurt: Suhrkamp, 1976)

_____, *Don Juan oder die Liebe zur Geometrie*, ed. by D. G. and S. M. Matthews, (London: Methuen, 1979)

Gay, Peter, 'The Father's Revenge', in *The Don Giovanni Book: Myths of Seduction and Betrayal*, ed. by Jonathan Miller, (London: Faber, 1990), 70-80.

Gendarme de Bévotte, Georges, *La Légende de don Juan: son évolution dans la littérature des origines au romantisme*, (Geneva: Slatkine Reprints, 1993)

Giddens, Anthony, *Modernity and Self-Identity: Self and Society in the Late Modern Age*, (Cambridge: Polity Press, 1991)

_____, *The Transformation of Intimacy: Sexuality, Love and Eroticism in Modern Societies*, (Cambridge: Polity Press, 1992)

Gingras, George E., 'Some Observations on the Generic Status of the Don Juan Theme from Tirso de Molina to Mozart', in *Tirso's Don Juan: the Metamorphosis of a Theme*, ed. by Josep Sola-Solé and George E. Gingras, (Washington DC: Catholic University of America Press, 1988), 106-126.

Haslett, Moyra, *Byron's* Don Juan *and the Don Juan Legend*, (Oxford: Clarendon Press, 1997)

Heartz, D., 'Che mi sembra di morir: Donna Elvira and the Sextet', *Musical Times* 122 (1981), 448-451.

Henning, Cosmo, 'Thematic Metamorphoses in *Don Giovanni*', *Music Review* 30 (1969), 22-26.

Herwitz, D., 'The Cook, his Wife, the Philosopher and the Librettist', *Musical Quarterly* 78 (1994), 48-76.

Hesse, Everett W., 'Tirso's Don Juan and the Opposing Self', *Bulletin of the Comediantes* 33 (1981), 3-7.

_____, *La mujer como víctima en la comedia y otros ensayos,* (Barcelona: Puvill, n.d.)

Hodges, Sheila, *Lorenzo Da Ponte: the Life and Times of Mozart's Librettist,* (London: Granada, 1985)

Hoffmann, E. T. A., 'Don Juan: eine fabelhafte Begenbenheit, die sich mit einem reisenden Enthusiasten zugetragen', *Fantasie- und Nachtstücke,* (Munich: Winkler, 1960), 67-78.

Jones, Harold G., 'A "New" Source of Tirso's *El burlador de Sevilla*', in *Tirso's Don Juan: the Metamorphosis of a Theme,* ed. by Josep Sola-Solé and George E. Gingras, (Washington DC: Catholic University of America Press, 1988), 32-44.

Kierkegaard, Søren, *Either/Or: a Fragment of Life,* trans. by Alastair Hannay, (Harmondsworth: Penguin, 1990)

Kofman, Sarah and Jean-Yves Masson, *Don Juan, ou le refus de la dette,* (Paris: Galilée, 1991)

Kristeva, Julia, *Histoires d'amour,* ([n.p.]: Denoël, 1983)

Leary, Daniel J., 'Don Juan, Freud and Shaw in Hell: a Freudian Reading of *Man and Superman*', *Shaw Review* 22 (1979), 58-78.

Lipking, Lawrence, 'Donna Abandonata', in *The Don Giovanni Book: Myths of Seduction and Betrayal,* ed. by Jonathan Miller, (London: Faber, 1990), 36-47.

Lundelius, Ruth, 'Tirso's View of Women in *El burlador de Sevilla*', *Bulletin of the Comediantes* 27 (1975), 5-14.

Mandrell, James, *Don Juan and the Point of Honor: Seduction, Patriarchal Society, and Literary Tradition,* (University Park: Pennsylvania State University Press, 1992)

Mansour, George P., 'Parallelism in *Don Juan Tenorio*', *Hispania* 61 (1978), 245-253.

McKendrick, Melveena, *Woman and Society in the Spanish Drama of the Golden Age,* (London: Cambridge University Press, 1974)

_____, 'Women Against Wedlock: the Reluctant Brides of Golden Age Drama', in *Women in Hispanic Literature: Icons and Fallen Idols,* ed. by Beth Miller, (Berkeley: University of California Press, 1983), 115-146.

Mills, Carl Henry, 'Shaw's Superman: a Re-examination', *Shaw Review* 13 (1970), 48-58.

_____, 'Shaw's Debt to Lester Ward in *Man and Superman*', *Shaw Review* 14, 2-13 (1971).

Molière, [J.-B. P. de.], 'Dom Juan, ou le festin de pierre', *Œuvres complètes*, ed. by Georges Couton, vol. II, (Paris: Gallimard., 1971)

Monleón, José B., 'Vampiros y donjuanes (sobre la figura del seductor en el siglo XIX)', *Revista Hispánica Moderna* 48 (1995), 19-30.

Mozart, Wolfgang Amadeus, *Il dissoluto punito ossia il don Giovanni*, Neue Ausgabe sämtlicher Werke Serie II, Bühnenwerke Werkgruppe 5, Band 17, (Basle: Bärenreiter Kassel, 1968)

Müller-Salget, Klaus, 'Diegos Aster: imagologische Anmerkungen zu Max Frischs *Don Juan oder die Liebe zur Geometrie*', *Arcadia* 22 (1987), 66-69.

Parakilas, J., 'The Afterlife of *Don Giovanni*: Turning Production History into Criticism', *Journal of Musicology* 8 (1990), 251-265.

Parr, James A., 'On the Authorship, Text, and Transmission of *El burlador de Sevilla y convidad de piedra*', in *Tirso de Molina: His Originality Then and Now* ed. by Henry W. Sullivan and Raúl A. Galoppe, Ottawa Hispanic Studies 20, (Ottawa: Dovehouse, 1996), 206-220.

Pendzik, Susana,'Female Presence in Tirso's *El burlador de Sevilla*', *Bulletin of the Comediantes* 47 (1995), 165-181.

Pérez de Ayala, Ramón, *Tigre Juan y El curandero de su honra*, ed. by Andrés Amorós, (Madrid: Castalia, 1980)

Pérez Firmat, Gustavo, *Literature and Liminality: Festive Readings in the Hispanic Tradition*, (Durham: Duke University Press, 1986)

Pirotta, Nino, 'The Traditions of Don Juan Plays and Comic Operas', *Proceedings of the Royal Musical Association* 107 (1981), 60-70.

Presberg, Charles D., '*El condenado por presumido*: the Rhetoric of Death and Damnation in *El burlador de Sevilla y convidado de piedra*', *Bulletin of the Comediantes* 47 (1995), 223-243.

Pym, Richard J. 'The Subject in Spain's Seventeenth-Century *comedia*', *Bulletin of Hispanic Studies*, LXXV/3 (1998), 273-292.

Rank, Otto, *The Don Juan Legend*, trans. by David G. Winter (Princeton: Princeton University Press, 1975)

Rogers, Daniel, *Tirso de Molina: 'El burlador de Sevilla'*, Critical Guides to Spanish Texts 19, (London: Grant and Cutler, 1977)

Romero, Héctor R., 'Consideraciones teológicas sobre la muerte de Don Juan en la obra de Zorrilla', *Hispanófila* 54 (1975), 9-16.

Rousset, Jean, *Le Mythe de Don Juan*, (Paris: A. Colin, 1978)

Ruano de la Haza, J. M., 'Doña Ana's Seduction in *El burlador de Sevilla*: Further Evidence Against', *Bulletin of the Comediantes* 32 (1980), 131-133.

Ruiz Ramón, Francisco, 'Don Juan y la sociedad del burlador de Sevilla: la crítica social', in *Estudios sobre teatro español y clásico contemporáneo*, (Madrid: Fundación Juan March y Cátedra, 1978) 71-95.

Ruppert, Peter, 'Max Frisch's Don Juan: the Seduction of Geometry', *Monatshefte* 67 (1975), 236-248.

Rushton, Julian, *W. A. Mozart: 'Don Giovanni'*, (Cambridge: Cambridge University Press, 1981)

Schlossmann, B., 'Disappearing Acts: Style, Seduction, and Performance in *Dom Juan'*, *MLN* 106 (1991), 1030-1047.

Serres, Michel, *Hermes: Literature, Science, Philosophy*, ed. by J. V. Harari and David F. Bell, (Baltimore: Johns Hopkins University Press, 1982)

Shaw, Bernard, *Man and Superman: a Comedy and a Philosophy*, (London: Constable, 1931)

Showalter, Elaine, *Hystories: Hysterical Epidemics and Modern Culture* (London: Picador, 1998).

_____, *Sexual Anarchy: Gender and Culture and the* fin-de-siècle,(London: Virago, 1992)

Singer, Armand E., 'Don Juan's Women in *El burlador de Sevilla'*, *Bulletin of the Comediantes* 33 (1981), 67-71.

Smeed, J. W., *Don Juan: Variations on a Theme*, (London: Routledge, 1990)

Smith, Paul Julian, *Writing in the Margin: Spanish Literature of the Golden Age*, (Oxford: Clarendon Press, 1988)

Soufas, C. Christopher, 'The Sublime, the Beautiful and the Imagination in Zorrilla's *Don Juan Tenorio*'. *MLN* 110 (1995), 302-319.

Steptoe, Andrew, *The Mozart-Da Ponte Operas: the Cultural and Musical Background to 'Le nozze di Figaro', 'Don Giovanni' and 'Così fan tutte'*, (Oxford: Clarendon Press, 1990)

Stiefel, Richard, 'Mozart's Seductions', *Current Musicology* 36 (1983), 151-163.

Stockholder, Fred. E., 'Shaw's Drawing-Room Hell: a Reading of *Man and Superman*', *Shaw Review* 11 (1968), 42-51.

Stoll, Anita K. and Dawn L. Smith, *The Perception of Women in Spanish Theater of the Golden Age*, (London and Toronto: Associated University Presses, 1991)

Sullivan, Henry W., *Tirso de Molina and the Drama of the Counter Reformation*, (Amsterdam: Rodop, 1976)

ter Horst, Robert, 'Ritual Time Regained in Zorrilla's *Don Juan Tenorio*', *Romanic Review* 70 (1979), 80-93.

_____, 'Epic Descent: the Filiations of Don Juan', *MLN* 111 (1996), 255-274.

Till, Nicholas, *Mozart and the Enlightenment: Truth, Virtue and Beauty in Mozart's Operas,* (London: Faber, 1992)

Tirso de Molina, 'Tan largo me lo fiáis', *Obras dramáticas completas*, ed. by Blanca de los Ríos, vol.II., (Madrid: Aguilar, 1952)

_____, *The Trickster of Seville and the Stone Guest (El burlador de Sevilla y el convidado de piedra)*, ed. by Gwynne Edwards, (Warminster: Aris and Phillips, 1986)
_____, attrib., *El burlador de Sevilla*, ed. by Alfredo Rodríguez López Vázquez, 6th edn, (Madrid: Cátedra, 1994)

Turco, Alfred, *Shaw's Moral Vision: the Self and Salvation*, (Ithaca: Cornell University Press, 1976)

Vázquez, Luis, '*El burlador de Sevilla*: claramente de Tirso, y no de Claramonte (breve anotación crítica)', *Bulletin of the Comediantes* 47 (1995), 183-190.

Wade, Gerald E., 'The Character of Don Juan of *El burlador de Sevilla*: a Psychoanalytical Study', *Bulletin of the Comediantes* 31 (1979), 33-42.

_____, 'Tirso de Molina: Priest-Playwright', *Bulletin of the Comediantes*, 38 (1986), 117-135.

Walsh, John K., 'Tisbea's "Fire": the Imagery of Tirso's *El burlador de Sevilla*, Vélez de Guevara's *La serrana de la Vera*, and Lope's *La mejor enamorada la Magdalena*', in *Tirso's Don Juan: the Metamorphosis of a Theme*, ed. by Josep M. Sola-Solé and George E. Gingras, (Washington DC: Catholic University of America Press, 1988), 74-85.

Wardropper, Bruce W., '*El burlador de Sevilla*: a Tragedy of Errors', *Philological Quarterly* 36 (1957), 61-71.

_____, 'El tema central de *El burlador de Sevilla*', *Segismundo* 17/18 (1973), 9-16.

Warner, Marina, 'Valmont - or the Marquise Unmasked', in *The Don Giovanni Book: Myths of Seduction and Betrayal*, ed. by Jonathan Miller, (London: Faber, 1990), 93-107.

Watson, Barbara Bellow, 'The New Woman and the New Comedy', *Shaw Review* 17 (1974), 2-16.

Weeks, Jeffrey, *Sex, Politics and Society: the Regulation of Sexuality Since 1800*, (London: Longman, 1981)

_____, *Sexuality and its Discontents: Meanings, Myths and Modern Sexualities*, (London: Routledge and Kegan Paul, 1985)

_____, *Against Nature: Essays on History, Sexuality and Identity*, (London: Rivers Oram Press, 1991)

Weinstein, Leo, *The Metamorphoses of Don Juan*, (Standford, CA: Stanford University Press, 1959)

Werner, Johannes, 'Ein trauriger Held: Vorgeschichte und thematische Einheit von Max Frischs *Don Juan oder die Liebe zur Geometrie*', in *Frischs 'Don Juan oder die Liebe zur Geometrie'*, ed. by Walter Schmitz, (Frankfurt: Suhrkamp, 1985)

Whitton, David, *Molière: 'Don Juan'*, (Cambridge: Cambridge University Press, 1995)

Williams, Bernard, 'Don Giovanni as an Idea', in *W. A. Mozart: 'Don Giovanni'*, by Julian Rushton, (Cambridge: Cambridge University Press, 1981), 81-91.

Wittgenstein, Ludwig, *Philosophical Investigations*, trans. by G. E. M. Anscombe, (Oxford: Basil Blackwell, 1975)

Zorrilla, José, *Don Juan Tenorio*, ed. by David T. Gies, (Madrid: Castalia, 1994)

Index

Abert, Hermann, 99, 109n, 131n, 206, 208
Adams, Elsie, 155
Alas, Leopoldo, 8
Albrecht, Jan White, 238
Anderson, Bonnie S., 14, 77, 240n, 273
Apostolidès, Jean-Marie, 53, 155
Arias, Judith H., 24n
Azorín [José Martínez Ruiz], 7

Bassi, Luigi, 47n
Benabu, Isaac, 42n, 89
Bertati, Giovanni, 5
Butler, Judith, 9n
Butler, Michael, 67, 68-70, 71
Byron [Lord George Gordon], 6, 22

Calderón, Pedro de, 80
Camus, Albert, 8
Carpenter, Charles, 161
Conlon, R., 85n, 87, 216-217
Connell, R. W., 11
Conrad, Peter, 4n, 230, 269, 270
Corneille, Thomas, 5
Crompton, Louis, 164, 211n

da Ponte, Lorenzo, see Mozart, Wolfgang Amadeus
Davies, Ann, 77n, 100n, 145n
Dent, Edward J., 79, 92, 131n
Djikstra, Bram, 14
Donington, Robert, 47n
Dorimon, N., 5, 233n
Dracula, 44
Dumas, Alexandre, 7
Dupuy, J.-P., 51n

Edwards, Gwynne, 4n
Evans, P. W., 24n, 45n, 101-102

Feal, Carlos, 57, 85n, 138-139, 188-189
Felman, Shoshana, 27, 51n
Foucault, Michel, 2-3, 8, 15, 18, 19
Frisch, Max, 8, 17, 21, 24, 25, 28, 32, 36, 37n, 38, 39, 40, 48n, 61, 66-75, 84, 108, 120, 121, 129, 133, 148, 151, 152, 170-185, 190-192, 194, 196, 200, 202, 207, 213-214, 219-222, 224, 228, 229, 234-235, 245, 247, 249, 250-253, 255, 258, 259, 261, 262, 267, 270-272

Gay, Peter, 44n, 91, 239n
Gendarme de Bévotte, Georges, 269, 270
Giddens, Anthony, 10n, 10-11, 12, 14, 17-18, 37, 266-267
Gingras, George E., 231
Goldoni, Carlo, 5, 230-231

Haslett, Moyra, 6n
Heartz, D., 109
Henning, Cosmo, 109
Herwitz, D. W., 81, 124-125, 126
Hesse, Everett W., 79-80
Hodges, Sheila, 47n
Hoffmann, E. T. A., 5-6, 26, 32, 91n, 93, 123-124, 127, 129-134, 139, 149, 170, 176, 188, 209, 213, 257, 260

Jones, Harold G., 228-229, 239, 254

Kierkegaard, Søren, 6, 24, 26, 28, 32, 38-39, 51, 110, 123-129, 130, 131, 133-134, 139, 149, 170, 176, 188, 257, 260, 269
Kofman, Sarah, 43n, 52n
Kristeva, Julia, 8, 31n, 48

Leary, David, 156, 165-166
Lipking, Lawrence, 109-110, 113,
    126
Lope de Vega, 78-80
Lundelius, Ruth, 85n

Mandrell, James, 2n, 20, 23, 27, 31n,
    39n, 53n, 86, 135, 156, 176,
    188, 271, 274
Mansour, George P., 243
Maraña, don Juan de, 7
Marañon, Gregorio, 1, 39n
Masson, Jean-Yves, 43, 52n
Matthews, D. G., 75, 171
Matthews, S. M., 75, 171
McKendrick, Melveena, 78-81, 82,
    101n, 268
Mérimée, Prosper, 7
Micale, Mark, 105-106
Mills, Carl Henry, 64, 65, 167n
Molière [Jean-Baptiste Pocquelin], 4,
    5, 6, 25, 26, 32, 36, 40, 45,
    49, 50-54, 66, 77, 78, 81-82,
    84-87, 93, 94-96, 100, 113-
    120, 127, 128, 132, 135n,
    149, 165, 169, 184, 195, 197,
    200, 202, 227, 228, 230, 231,
    234, 235-236, 239, 240-241,
    254, 258-259, 260
Monleón, José , 45, 139, 142-144
Mozart, Wolfgang Amadeus, 4, 5, 6,
    23, 25, 26, 28, 30, 32, 37, 38-
    39, 40, 45-50, 60, 66, 77, 78,
    81-82, 84-87, 89, 91-101,
    107-113, 117-120, 122, 124-
    134, 149, 156, 165, 169, 184,
    189, 196, 200, 204-206, 207,
    208-210, 212, 213, 216, 227,
    228, 230-231, 232, 233, 234,
    235, 236-237, 250, 254, 259-
    260, 273
Müller-Salget, Klaus, 174

Nietzsche, Friedrich, 7, 63, 64, 168

Ortega y Gasset, José, 7-8, 39n, 271

Parakilas, J., 78n, 113, 131n
Parr, James A., 4n
Pendzik, Susana, 83, 94, 106, 216n
Pérez de Ayala, Ramón, 7, 30, 143,
    227
Pérez Firmat, Gustavo, 27n
Pérez Galdós, Benito, 8
Pirotta, Nino, 233
Presberg, Charles, 42-43, 230n
Pym, Richard J., 19n

Rank, Otto, 1, 8, 44n, 92n, 139n,
    156, 196, 205, 255, 264
Rodríguez López Vázquez, Alfredo,
    4n
Rogers, Daniel, 4n, 101n
Rojas, Fernando de, 179
Romero, Héctor, 60n
Rosimond, C. la Rose de, 233n
Rousset, Jean, 227
Ruano de la Haza, J. M., 90n, 93n
Ruiz Ramón, Francisco, 24n, 89-90
Ruppert, Peter, 71
Rushton, Julian, 49, 93, 209n

Schlossman, Beryl, 4n, 87-88
Serres, Michel , 52n, 203
Shadwell, Thomas, 5
Shaw, George Bernard, 8, 17, 23, 24,
    25, 27, 32, 37, 39, 40, 48n,
    61-66, 71, 84, 108,119, 120,
    121, 129, 131, 133, 148, 151,
    152-170, 172, 173, 174, 175,
    181, 182, 183, 184-185, 190,
    194, 197, 207, 210-213, 216,
    228, 229, 235, 245-250, 251,
    255, 259, 261, 262, 267, 269,
    270, 272
Showalter, Elaine, 14
Singer, Armand, 85n

Smeed, J. W., 5-6, 8, 21n, 30, 31, 49n, 231n
Smith, Dawn L., 78n
Smith, Paul Julian, 268
Soufas, C. Christopher, 56n
Steptoe, Andrew, 46, 108-109
Stiefel, Richard, 98
Stockholder, Fred E., 169, 248
Sullivan, Henry W., 4n, 18, 35

ter Horst, Robert, 43, 55-56, 83-84, 225
Till, Nicholas, 49-50, 231, 234n
Tirso de Molina, 3-4, 6, 7, 8, 14, 18, 21, 23, 26, 30, 32, 35, 37, 38, 39, 40, 41-45, 47n, 49, 50, 52, 61, 66, 68-69, 74, 76n, 77, 78, 79, 81, 82, 84-91, 94, 99, 101-107, 117-120, 123, 127, 128, 132, 134, 135, 144, 148, 149, 165, 169, 184, 189, 190, 192-193, 194, 195, 198-199, 203, 204, 207-208, 213, 216-218, 225, 227, 228, 230, 234, 235, 236-238, 240, 243, 247-249, 254, 257, 259, 260, 267, 268-274
Torrente Ballester, Gonzalo, 7
Turco, Alfred, 64

Unamuno, Miguel de, 7

Valle-Inclán, Ramón del, 7

Vázquez, Luis, 4n
Villiers [Claude Deschamps], 5, 229n

Wade, Gerald, 9n, 44n, 269n
Walsh, John K., 118
Wardropper, Bruce W., 23n, 189n, 192n
Warner, Marina, 139n
Watson, Barbara Bellow, 152-153, 158,170
Weeks, Jeffrey, 9n, 11, 16-17, 18-19, 35-36, 41, 232, 265-267
Weinstein, Leo, 135, 271
Werner, Johannes, 71n
Whitton, David, 78n
Williams, Bernard, 46, 82, 83, 232-233, 234n, 240
Wittgenstein, Ludwig, 22n

Zamora, Antonio de, 7, 233n
Zinsser, Judith P., 14, 77, 240n, 273
Zorrilla, José, 7, 21, 23, 25, 27-28, 30, 32, 36, 37n, 40, 45, 48n, 55-61, 76, 77n, 85, 99, 120, 123, 125, 130, 133-149, 151, 152, 155, 167, 168, 170, 176, 182, 183-184, 190, 194, 196, 204, 215-216, 219, 222, 225, 227, 228n, 229, 241-245, 254, 255, 258, 260, 262, 263, 266, 267

SPANISH STUDIES

1. Gerardo Piña Rosales, **La obra narrativa de Segundo Serrano Poncela: Crónica del Desarraigo**

2. **A Bilingual Edition of Fray Luis de León's** *La perfecta casada*: **The Role of Married Women in Sixteenth-Century Spain**, edited and translated with introduction and notes by John A. Jones and Javier San José Lera

3. John Gilmour, **Manuel Fraga Iribarne and the Rebirth of Spanish Conservatism 1939-1990**

4. Vanessa Knights, **The Search for Identity in the Narrative of Rosa Montero**

5. **Personal Memories of the Days of the Spanish Civil War, in Catalan and English: Lluís Puig Casas**, introduced, edited and annotated by Idoya Puig

6. Carmen Gleadow, **History of Trial by Jury in the Spanish Legal System**

7. Diane M. Almeida, **The** *Esperpento* **Tradition in the Works of Ramón del Valle-Inclán and Luis Buñuel**

8. Sarah Leggott, **History and Autobiography in Contemporary Spanish Women's Testimonial Writings**

9. Kevin Krogh, **The Landscape Poetry of Antonio Machado: A Dialogical Study of** *Campos de Castilla*

10. Francisco Loubayssin de Lamarca, **Engaños Deste Siglo y historia sucedida en nuestros tiempos 1615**, edición, introducción y notas de Elisa Rosales Juega

11. Susana Bayó Belenguer, **Theory, Genre, and Memory in the** *Carvalho* **Series of Manuel Vázquez Montalbán**

12. Mariá Jesús González del Valle, **Una comparación de tres traducciones al inglés de** *La familia de Pascual Duarte,* **de Camilo José Cela / A Comparison of Three English Translations of Camilo Jose Cela's** *La familia de Pascual Duarte*

13. Enrique J. Porrúa (ed.), **The Diary of Antonio de Tova on the Malaspina Expedition (1789-1794)**

14. Francisco Xavier Clavijero, **Historia de la Antigua o Baja California / History of Ancient and Lower California (1789): A New Translation from the Spanish Text, with a Review and Annotations**, translated and edited by Felix Jay

15. **Urban Communities in Early Spanish America 1493-1700**, translation of original texts by Felix Jay

16. **Three Dominican Pioneers in the New World: Antonio de Montesinos, Domingo de Betanzos, Gonzalo Lucero**, translations from original sources with introduction by Felix Jay

17. Antonio de Remesal, **Bartolomé de Las Casas (1474-1566) in the Pages of Father Antonio de Remesal**, translated and annotated by Felix Jay

18. Philip G. Johnston, **The Power of Paradox in the Work of Spanish Poet Antonio Machado (1875-1939)**

19. Daniel Breining, **Dramatic and Theatrical Censorship of Sixteenth-Century New Spain**

20. Margaret A. Rees, **The Writings of Doña Luisa de Carvajal y Mendoza, Catholic Missionary to James I's London**

21. Laurie Kaplis-Hohwald, **Translation of the Biblical Psalms in Golden Age Spain**

22. Rosabel Roig-Vila, **La articulación de las Tecnologías de la Información y la Comunicación en la Educación**

23. Rosabel Roig-Vila, **Análsis y valoración de sitios web de centros escolares**

24. Laura Delbrugge, **A Critical Edition of Andrés de Li's** *Summa de paciencia*, **1505**

25. Linda E. Lassiter, **An Etymological Vocabulary and Study of** *La Estoria de los godos*, **1243**

26. Rob Stone, **The Flamenco Tradition in the Works of Federico García Lorca and Carlos Saura: The Wounded Throat**

27. Margaret Ann Rees, **Doña María Vela y Cueto, Cistercian Mystic of Spain's Golden Age**

28. Ann Davies, **The Metamorphoses of Don Juan's Women–Early Parity to Late Modern Pathology**